This synopsis relates to the manuscript entitled "Cop O' the north" which runs to 17 chapters and approximately 100,000 words. The work encompasses the period 1975 through 1992 and in the main outlines the writers personal experiences of policing the far north of Scotland and the Orkney and Shetland islands.

These first 17 years of a 31 year career attempts to tell the writers story in a frequently amusing, occasionally hilarious, often sad and sometimes tra~i~ ~se but at all times truthful although slightly unbelievah¹~ ᵀ⁻ ll the stories that don't make it to the papers in enti~

CHAPTER 1

Outlines the writer's initial interest in joining the p ~~what unusual reasoning, the recruitment process and a li~ ~~rsonal background.

CHAPTER 2

Highlights the experiences of his first day, having illusions of the police immediately shattered, (shades of ashes to ashes) a case of mistaken identity with an arrested drunk and a somewhat unusual swearing in process kept secret for years.

CHAPTER 3

A summary of the first few months. Description of the force area. The story of Gustav the hunting Falcon. The quickest transfer in history. First fatal road traffic accident where victim dies in writer's arms and how he is affected by it. The writer meet's the love of his life. The beach incident where the writer encounters a much older but extremely attractive woman but manages to escape with his integrity intact. The first horrific experience of post mortem examinations.

CHAPTER 4

Experiences of the Scottish police college. Descriptions of the military style regime and being pushed to your limits. Physical exercise, weekend escapes to Edinburgh, good times with the Waverly station postie's and passing out.

CHAPTER 5

Back to Thurso where the writer isn't quite ready to be let loose on his own. Incidents with travelling salesmen generating considerable jealousy. Another case of mistaken identity when the writer is suspected of a crime. Castletown country dances and a near death experience. Changing from a boy into a man and a transfer to Shetland.

CHAPTER 6

Dialect difficulties and strange introductions. The oil industry and related policing incidents. Sheriff court hilarity. Two very strange suicides. Fighting with fishermen and amorous advances from older women. Irish oil workers and jewellery shop smash and grab. Leaving event gets out of hand.

CHAPTER 7

Back to Thurso. Renewing friendship with love interest. The giant crab incident. How a death message can go seriously wrong. How local knowledge can save a lot of grief. Police vehicles and outrageous budgetary restraints. Love interest get's transferred and writer is devastated. Walking the hills in search of lost shepherd.

CHAPTER 8

Transfer to Wick. Renew friendship with love interest again. Smash and grab Woolworth incident. Public street brawl and first real experience of serious police complaint. Tragic first date with love interest. Comatose drunk driver using outrageously dangerous vehicle. Fatal R.T.A. involving child being driven by drunken parent in same vehicle as previously mentioned. Getting married.

CHAPTER 9

A period with C.I.D. Losing your wardrobe and getting a new look. Foreign sudden death and language difficulties. New starts and resultant problems. The undertaker incident. Housebreaking and detecting the culprits. Attempted murder on American soil.

CHAPTER 10

Back on the beat. Sumburgh air disaster. Is it a sheep or a dead body in the river, jump in and see. Warrant arrests and an eye opener for some on how the other half lives. Trying for babies and the problems that caused.

CHAPTER 11

Shetland again. The Queen opens Sulom Voe oil terminal, the difficulties in getting there and several instances of believing that you may have breathed your last. The weekend from hell and the I.R.A. decide to flex their muscles.

CHAPTER 12

Three weeks in three days worth of clothes. The bombing enquiry, threats to our life and some stupid people doing stupid things.

CHAPTER 13

The sea cadets and me. The first baby ever born. Having managed once it seems that there is no stopping. Transfer to Orkney.

CHAPTER 14

Stewart Irvine provides much hilarity. Removal problems in reaching the islands. Birth of man child and another case of mistaken identity, who is the father? Ridiculous call outs. The story of Genghis Hen. House fires and an unbelievable suicide. Ceilidhs and wanting to die at the Orkney folk festival.

CHAPTER 15

Still in Orkney. Drug incident. Encounter with a wizard and related strange sexual activities. Proving a local legend, wild dogs and sudden death. Televised climb of the Old Man of Hoy and busting the myth. First stint in community safety dept.

For my gorgeous wife

my favourite girl

and my rock star son

I got all three right

COP OF THE NORTH

CHAPTER 1

However much you may think you know what the police service is about, take my word for it, unless you are or have been a part of it, YOU DON'T. You may ask on what basis I make that observation, quite simply, 31 years as a serving police officer with Northern Constabulary. Before I begin to get into that story let me tell you how I perceived the police.

A 1970s or possibly 1980s,(my memory isn't all that it was) television advert depicted two police officers walking along a High Street at regulation pace, their hands clasped behind their back having a somewhat intense discussion about whether or not a particularly attractive young lady was, or was not wearing a specific brand of hairspray.

You may find that scenario to some degree believable, but I am fairly confident that the conversation would have gone a little more like this.

"Will you look at that?"

"God yes its gorgeous."

"Look at the body on her."

"What would you like to do with that?"

"Nothing I could repeat in polite company."

Or words, to that effect.

I have clearly diluted the final sentence which in truth would have been much more graphic and sexually explicit in its nature.

From my point of view, in my naivety, it is more than probable that I would have accepted that depiction as reasonably accurate right up to a point about 10 minutes into my police career.

By this point in the narrative I hope you have now realized that these writings are intended to record my experiences of the police service and how those 31 years were so different from anything I could ever have anticipated.

Prior to going there I feel it is necessary to outline my beginnings just to let you know how I got to where I am today.

I was born on the 9th of November 1954 at the Henderson Memorial nursing home at Wick, the youngest of 8 children, 3 boys and 5 girls.

My oldest 4 siblings were old enough to be my parents as my fathers reproductive capacity had been somewhat curtailed by the onset of the second world war in which he served in the Seaforth Highlanders.

On demob, my dad more than made up for this enforced period of separation and sexual abstention by keeping my mother in a prolonged state of pregnancy. I can only assume that on my birth he considered that he had achieved perfection and felt that this would be a good point to stop.

My sisters for some reason unknown to me take particular issue with this theory and an alternative that they frequently offer contain terms such as "ugly" "evil" "disappointment" and "devastated." Those of you who have older sisters will understand just how vicious and nasty they can be, but I suppose they are sent to try us.

Anyhow, during my, what I suppose you may term my nursery years, I survived a number of plots by my doting elder sisters to dispose of me by blaming me for misdemeanours of which I was entirely innocent, and went on to Primary education at Pulteneytown Primary School.

An excellent performance in the then 8+ and 11+ ensured me a place in language classes in Wick High School. Believe it or not, I really felt that this was a waste of my time and effort as there was almost an expectation at that time, in educational circles, that these were the pupils that were most likely to go on to a university education. I knew that, in my case this was never going to happen as firstly, my parents couldn't afford to send me to further education, and secondly, my dad wanted me to get a trade. He himself had been a highly skilled Cooper who made barrels for the Herring fishing trade which was still a reasonably thriving business in Wick prior to the second war.

Obtaining an apprenticeship consequently became my focus and I left school at age 15 having obtained a place on a pre apprenticeship course at Thurso Technical College which led to an engineering apprenticeship at the now infamous Dounreay Experimental Reactor Establishment. I personally, have a lot to thank Dounreay for. It was while serving my apprenticeship here that my interest in the Police Service was kick started and certainly not for any reason you may imagine.

Can you imagine thirty five sixteen and seventeen year old boy's together, day in and day out, and what the chief topic of conversation may be? It will come as no surprise to you to be told that the answer is girls. It was 1971 and something appeared on the streets of the nearby town of Thurso in a police uniform. She was gorgeous, slim, attractive smile, somewhat aloof and clearly beyond our wildest aspirations as we collectively drooled during our tea break discussions. Quite frequently, as I stood waiting for the shift bus outside of the Bank of Scotland in Thurso (we attended Thurso Technical College for block release and day release training) she would saunter past swinging her radio, and if you were lucky we would receive the occasional "Hello boys" in what I can only describe as a somewhat teasing manner.

This only made matters worse and the testosterone would soar and lead to the inevitable wet dreams. I undoubtedly fell in love from a distance.

Living in Wick and being some 31 miles distant from my then place of employment I was obliged to catch one of the many provided shift buses which left at the ungodly hour of 6:30 am. I suppose from the point of view of most teenagers, who if I was anything to go by had a particular affinity with the warmth of their bed and a real inability to leave it prior to the striking of any PM o clock, this was a nightmare.

This was particularly the case during the winter months when I would wend my way half asleep, thoroughly wrapped in a somewhat smelly Parka to the bus stop at the Pulteneytown Distillery. It was here that I would add myself to the end of the line of my fellow travellers, all equally heavily swathed, cold and miserable and each one of us in collective thought as to whether or not we would get a decent bus that day with a heater that worked.

It was here on a particularly cold morning with soft crisp snow lying on the ground, that my mind was finally made up. Through the half haze of sleep I could hear what I immediately identified as the sound of a vehicle making slow progress towards where I stood, the crunch of its tyres as it disturbed the unbroken snow and the unmistakable sound of a heater going at full blast. It was at this point that a small white police van hove into view. The driver appeared to be reasonably alert but the same could not be said of his partner who was fully reclined in the passenger seat, sound asleep.

It was then that I thought "That's for me."

So, it would be reasonable to conclude that my inspiration to join the police was heavily influenced by sex followed by sleep. I am sure that some people must have had worse reasons for taking a job.

So it was on one Friday morning, as I was waiting for the service bus to take me to the college in Thurso, along came the regular paper boy selling the local rag, (John O Groat Journal) at vastly inflated prices. I suppose nowadays you would call that Free Enterprise or indeed the law of Supply and Demand. I however still maintain it was a plain and simple rip off.

At this stage I was approaching the end of my apprenticeship and questioning whether or not I really wanted to continue in that field. I suppose I was looking for something a bit more exciting when there in the "Situations Vacant" column, I spotted the words, "Where would you like to work? Northern Constabulary are looking for officers aged between 19 and 34 years of age, physically fit and must have at least five standard grade passes or equivalent qualification."

That was the point that I decided to bite the bullet and the very next day I went along to Wick Police Station to, in police jargon, make some enquiries.

Wick police station was at that time the oldest operational police station in the United Kingdom and in truth it was certainly showing its age. The entrance to the building, off the town's main street was less than inviting and at just short of 21 years of age, not particularly street wise and lacking in confidence I seriously considered making an about turn and forgetting about the whole idea. Having come that far I resolved to at least go in and ask. I was met by a policewoman sergeant who asked how she could help me and on telling her that I was there in response to a recruitment advert almost swept me of my feet and invited me in. Not quite the response I expected but more than positive and I left the station armed with Police application forms. The recruitment process at that time was quite lengthy but not nearly as much so as it is today. I completed and submitted the application form, was invited to sit the entrance exam, interviewed in my home environment and finally called in for an interview with the station Inspector.

The station Inspector was a very imposing English gentleman who sported a large handlebar moustache and gave off an air of considerable indifference, leaving me somewhat unsure as to whether I had been successful or not in my application.

Shortly after this interview I received a letter offering me a post as a Constable in Northern Constabulary stationed at my preferred posting of Wick.

I joined Northern Constabulary as PC 518 Robert McCrae Sutherland on 20th September 1975.

CHAPTER TWO

The First Day

It is not my intention to go through 31 years of police service on a day by day basis but I hope you will understand that the first day is particularly significant as indeed are the first weeks and months which pretty much forms not only your approach to, how you do the job, but also your understanding of the police culture.

From this point on I have taken the necessary precaution of changing names in order to protect the clearly guilty with a few exceptions of those I left in no doubt that I have every intention of landing in the shit. This is a bit of a "no win" situation as a number of ex colleagues have threatened to sue me if they are mentioned whilst an even greater number have threatened similar action if they aren't.

Police officers can be very strange people.

Anyhow, I had been instructed to attend at Wick Police station at 9 am on Monday 20th September where I was to meet with the duty sergeant who would make varying arrangements to confirm my appointment. On the day, I might add, my dad who was by now retired was still not very happy about my decision to give up my trade and join the police. Undaunted however, he was there in the morning to see me smartly dressed, shoes brushed and shining and saw me off. Butterflies in the stomach and a real feeling of trepidation accompanied me on the probably mile and a half walk to the police station. I didn't own a car or even a bicycle at that time as I quite simply couldn't afford either. I wouldn't want you to imagine that I am playing the violin here or even seeking some degree of sympathy that just happened to be the way it was.

I arrived at the station and was welcomed by Sgt Willie Forbes, then close to retirement and engaged to some degree in setting himself up as a civilian driving instructor. Willie, I learned, was a Police class one driver, instructor and examiner, a set of qualifications, back in those days as rare as hen's teeth. To obtain all three qualifications, even today, is still considered quite an achievement. Also on duty at the time was Constable Colin Gunn. I had known Colin previously when he had served an apprenticeship as an Instrument Mechanic, also at Dounreay, but a few years ahead of me. Colin had served a short period with Scottish North Eastern Counties, returned to his trade and then reapplied to join Northern Constabulary. Colin was destined to leave and return once more and eventually retire as a police sergeant and lives today in the Orkney Islands. With the exception of a female secretary the only other person on duty was the very same female police sergeant who had virtually dragged me into the police station on the day I had called to enquire about joining. In 1975 female officers were a separate department from male officers, received nine tenths of the wage and were not expected to work night shifts. They were also designated Woman PC or Woman PS and by the time I saw a female promoted to the rank of Inspector that designation had long since been dropped.

Maybe ten minutes was something of an exaggeration when I take into account the questions being put to me in respect of my family and my now colleagues satisfying themselves that they had me fairly well taped, but my first shock certainly occurred within the half hour. I most definitely do not recall what prompted this particular incident but years of experience and witnessing of other incidents not too dissimilar, lead me to the positive conclusion that the catalyst would have been minor.

There I was, standing in the front office, fielding questions from all sides, being polite and trying to appear interested when I was in fact extremely nervous and if I am being honest quite literally shitting myself, when I heard a high pitched scream.

I really didn't have a clue as to what was going on until I heard the sergeant shout, "Get the bitch" and promptly begin to pursue the female member of staff around several circuits of a rather large desk in the front office whilst she was screaming at the top of her voice. You may imagine that I was not unsurprisingly, somewhat taken aback at what I considered to be extremely strange behaviour which escalated to a point I had difficulty in believing could possibly occur amongst what I had believed to be pillars of the community. Willie Forbes called for Colin's assistance and I witnessed a first class pincer movement which succeeded in quite literally, pinioning the female victim to the top of the table, by now screaming hysterically and threatening all forms of vengeance to her two male captors. I suppose it was reasonable for me to assume that they may well have released her at this point, but then again I had absolutely no idea of the then police mentality. If I was thinking things were already bad enough, it was about to get worse when I now heard someone say "stamp the bitch." All I can say for certain was that particular statement wasn't uttered by me, and I very much doubt it was spoken by the victim. The next step in this, as I was later to learn, historic and acceptable process, was the stamping of the victims upper thigh area with the police station date stamp. Even at this early stage in my career I had enough sense to be worried about the potential appearance of a senior officer, but now, on reflection, I have no reason to believe other than they would probably have joined in. Any concerns I had surrounding the consequences of, what by today's standards, would be considered outrageous action, was very quickly alleviated when all three protagonists erupted into gales of laughter whilst threatening various forms of reprisal to each other. So, almost immediately, any pre conceived notion I may have had about how I expected police officers to behave was thoroughly shattered.

I spent the remainder of the morning acquainting myself with the operations of the front office, and reading the station log book which gave me a real insight into the myriad of incidents a police officer is expected to deal with, from drunk and incapables to breaches of the peace, road accidents, minor and serious assaults, missing persons, suicides and other forms of sudden death, to name but a few. Little wonder then, that I began to question whether I was not only suited to this form of employment but whether or not I was capable of doing the job.

None too soon it was time for lunch and since it was my first day, the sergeant who was out and about on some enquiries said he would give me a lift home and pick me up later. Needless to say I was still too excited to eat anything and before I knew it there was the police van. Seated in the back of a police vehicle, dressed in plain clothes, (I was yet to be issued with a uniform), I suppose it was not unreasonable to assume that I had been arrested and that is exactly what happened. Whilst en route to the police station and no distance from my own home, at the rear of the local distillery the sergeant spotted the inert form of a male lying face down in the mud. Being no stranger to seeing those the worse for wear I didn't make any assumption of foul play or imagine that day one was going to present me with my first murder to solve. Even I had guessed that this was no more than a simple drunk.

Leaving me seated in the van, both officers went to investigate and spent some time in bringing the offender round to some level of consciousness, before deciding that he was far too drunk to release and placed him under arrest. The prisoner wasn't quite carried to the van but offered little assistance to the officers who each held an arm around their neck and supported his back whilst the drunk barely managed to place one foot in front of the other. Observing this process from where I was seated I began to realize that I had a number of causes for concern. Firstly, I recognised the now prisoner as a local from the next street over, not much older than me, alcoholic from a teenager who had never worked a day in his life, and never did. Secondly, fairly filthy and smelly on a normal day he was now totally dishevelled, covered in wet mud and about to be placed in the rear of the police vehicle, seated next to me. I hadn't realised just how bad things were until he was bundled into the back of the van. His normal offensive odour was by now mixed with the smell of stale drink and drying urine where he had lost control of his bladder during his drunken stupor. The stink was not only offensive to me, but also these two hardened officers who had dealt with similar and much worse on numerous occasions, evidenced by both the driver and passengers windows being fully wound down to create a through draft. To make matters worse, the drunk recognized me and began to berate the two uniformed officers for having arrested someone who had never done anything wrong in his life. Added to this, for some unknown reason he decided that I required some comforting in my misfortune and commenced to grab hold and offer me some words of reassurance. No matter how much I protested he refused to let go and maintained a firm hold all the way to the police station still berating my two colleagues who found the whole incident extremely amusing at my expense. I was to find out that this minor incident was to be of small consequence to my delicate stomach which would be tested to its limits on countless occasions.

That afternoon I was handed over to another officer rapidly approaching retirement and who held the grand title of training sergeant. Tony Ryrie was a very nice fellow who quickly put me at ease and explained what would be expected of me during my two year probationary period. He also told me that he had arranged an appointment that very afternoon with a local Justice of the Peace to have me sworn in as a Police Constable.

I accompanied Tony to the harbour area and the offices of a local Agricultural Supplier and grain merchant where we were met by the salesman and Justice of the Peace, Jamesie Mowat. It is possibly necessary to point out that Wick is a small town of 8000 inhabitants and just about everybody knows everybody else, and if they don't know you they most certainly know your parents. Tony introduced me and once again I was interrogated about my background until Jamesie satisfied himself that he knew my parents, all of my uncles and aunts and huge extended family which pretty much made up the largest percentage of the town's population. It was now that we got down to the business of the day and from what I had understood I would be expected to stand to attention, raise my right hand and repeat the oath of allegiance to the Queen. That wasn't quite how it happened. Jamesie had spent so much time in general chit chat that he was by now running late for a pre arranged appointment and much to my surprise and Tony Ryrie's horror I was asked if I had read and understood the Oath, to which I replied yes and I was then instructed to sign the form. Jamesie then wished me all the best in my chosen career and quickly vanished from the building. On the way back to the police station Tony made me promise never to repeat what had happened at my swearing in ceremony and up until now I never have. So, having served 31 years in the police service I have to question if I ever really was a Police Officer.

On completing my first day of duty I returned home to a very expectant dad who was keen to learn about all I had been involved in. The best diplomatic response I could offer was that it was interesting.

Day one, although interesting and unusual, could never have prepared me for what was to come.

Chapter 3

The first few months

The first two years of a Police Officers service is spent in serving a sort of apprenticeship, learning the ropes whilst being mentored by older experienced officers, attending the Scottish Police College at Tulliallan and learning how to prepare reports and give evidence in Court. I have to say, I never agreed with the term "probation", as I felt that this was something handed down by the courts in punishment for some or other form of misdemeanour.

I had joined Northern Constabulary, the "teuchters" of the Scottish Police Service. We have been called much worse chiefly relating to unnatural acts with woolly animals and a term also bestowed on Highlanders in general. I am consequently happy to stick with the term "Teuchter" also bestowed on Highlanders in general.

Northern Constabulary Is one of eight police forces in Scotland, the best known of which are probably Strathclyde and Lothian and Borders whilst the remaining forces are made up of, in no particular order, Central Scotland, Tayside, Grampian, Fife and Dumfries and Galloway. Call me biased, but in my opinion, none of the others even come close and Northern Constabulary is not only the superior police service in Scotland, but probably in the United Kingdom. There are tens of thousands of police officers who would disagree with that statement and even a small number of members of the public, but that is my opinion and I am happy to stick with it. It may be of some help to describe the police area just to give an idea of the expanse and obvious difficulties in policing. Northern Constabulary covers three island groups, Orkney Islands, Shetland Islands and the Western Isles of Scotland plus the whole of the Highland Region ranging from John O Groats in the far North to Fort William in the South. The land mass equates to no less than one sixth of the whole United Kingdom which in turn equates to a country the size of Belgium. It is also true to say that human beings are far outnumbered by sheep and this particular statistic may impact to some degree on the other less than flattering nickname bestowed on us by other Police Services in Scotland. This huge area is policed by somewhere in the region of 700 officers of all ranks and specialism's.

Very quickly, I was kitted out and ready to start my first day of real duty which was equally eye opening. I had already decided to expect the unexpected and I wasn't to be dismayed in that thinking. The other Constable on duty that day was George Miller Douglas known throughout Caithness as the Queen Mothers Bobby.

George hailed from Dunnett which is in close proximity to the Castle of Mey, the then Queen Mothers holiday retreat. George was a big, strapping country boy who

I often thought would have been better suited to an agricultural lifestyle, dressed in bib and brace and Wellington boots, whiling away his days speaking with, and offering his own pearls of wisdom to everybody who passed his way. Here was an extremely popular officer with both his colleagues and public alike, and let me tell you, just nobody could direct traffic like him. He was also an occasional Highland Games athlete, and amiable as he was, I often thought I wouldn't like to get on his wrong side. Even in his thirties, George had an affinity with his bed akin with that of a teenager, and frequently found himself on the wrong side of the duty sergeants tongue when he would amble in late, offering some outrageous excuse as to why. It may also be of interest to know that at that time he was engaged in semi serious relationships with no less than three females, all of whom were deeply in love with him and caused him extreme difficulty in juggling dates, and making sure that each one never met, or became aware of the others existence. "Stud or what."

The sergeant on duty was Ian Mackay who hailed from the West coast and although I suspect a fluent Gaelic speaker I never heard him make use of the language, other than to offer an occasional "slangy" whilst imbibing a wee dram of the amber nectar. A very soft spoken and apparently imperturbable man, as I have found is not uncommon in the West coasters I have known and most of whom have a great respect for the healing powers of the whisky, purely, as you will understand for medicinal purposes.

Anyhow, the front office took a report relating to, of all things, a missing Falcon. "Gustav" as this hunting bird had been named by his German owners, who by the way, were childless and treated this bird as something of a surrogate baby, were frantic. I have known people to treat their pets almost as children, something of which both me and my wife are clearly guilty, since both of our horrors are now in their mid twenties, but I had never seen this practice manifest itself in a Falcon. Ian Mackay was doing his best to comfort the distraught couple while at the same time obtaining a description of the said bird. Hmmm, now what form might that description take? "It's a bird, it's got feathers, it flies and oh yes, by the way its name is Gustav." Much to my disbelief, in the midst of much weeping and wailing we received a phone call to the effect that a strange bird had been spotted flying about in the area of the harbour. George and I were immediately dispatched to maintain observations and to report back by radio to the station, keeping them updated on Gustav's movements. It didn't take long to locate our prey (pardon the pun), as Gustav was distinctly different from the hundreds of Seagulls which normally populate harbours and was the only bird in flight which was emitting a jingling noise from the bells attached to his leg. I think that's called deductive reasoning.

Having satisfied ourselves that Gustav was in fact Gustav, George then commenced to drive at what I considered to be a reasonably high speed, along the riverside road, up the Scalesburn hill, about turned and drove back at an equally frantic pace to our initial starting point. This process of racing back and forth, it seemed to me, went on for hours while we waited for the owners to obtain lures, to entice Gustav back into the arms of his waiting parents. I have to say that even to this day, I never understood the need to race endlessly back and forth along the river front as we could have kept an eye on the bird, probably more effectively from a static position.

Gustav never moved beyond a three quarter of a mile circuit, attracted, as I believe he was, to the abundance of easy pickings milling about the harbour. Eventually, Gustav's parents arrived accompanied by others of the Hunting, Shooting and Fishing fraternity and made their way down to the shoreline, where, after a few casts of the lure, Gustav was enticed back into the bosom of his loving parents. A nice footnote to this particular story resulted a few weeks later when Ian Mackay received a beautiful fountain pen engraved "with thanks from Gustav"

Anyhow, I hope, now having set at least a little of the scene, I had in my first week travelled to Force Headquarters in Inverness where I was issued with uniform and accoutrements, signed a mountain of forms, some of which removed ill affordable amounts of money from my already meagre wage and been issued with my official police notebook. Not to finish there, I was also transferred to Thurso. I don't know if this was the quickest transfer in police history but it must be in the running, especially since this transfer was in total contradiction of the promises made in the recruiting advert to which I had responded. That particular advertisement was very quickly scrubbed and consigned to the Police HR Dept bin of boo-boos.

Thurso is the larger of the two towns in Caithness although Wick has always been, and remains, the County town. Thurso grew from little more than a village of some 1500 population to, in its heyday some 15000 with the influx of workers from all over the country during the construction and initial operating phases of the Dounreay Experimental Reactor Establishment. Here, you can see a mix of the old and new town and Architectural and now considered, town planning mistakes, popular in the sixties, but now a legacy with which we have to contend. Add into the mix, a very cosmopolitan population and the main ferry link from Scrabster to the Orkney Islands and you have an interesting little town.

Anyhow, I had been transferred to Thurso, and coming from Wick, although only 21 miles away, my taking up residence here would equate in today's terms to the status of an unwelcome refugee. Wick and Thurso and the underlying, but today, pretty much unspoken rivalries is reflected across Scotland, such as Glasgow and Edinburgh and even Stromness and Kirkwall in the Orkney Islands. I do not claim for one second that this is a bad thing, as I believe this makes for healthy competition and motivates communities to go one step better than its neighbour. Given that I didn't own any form of transport I attended at Wick police station, dressed in full uniform, as this was a normal duty day and carrying a large suitcase. The haste with which I and my belongings were bundled into a police vehicle to be transported to Thurso, left me with a feeling of being somewhat unwanted. I was to be no stranger to that particular feeling over the years to come. The vehicle in which I was travelling, was met at the recognised mid way point between the two towns by another police vehicle from Thurso. Both drivers barely acknowledged the others presence and any communication carried out between them, appeared to me, to consist of little more than a series of grunts which I was unable to interpret. On transferring my belongings and seating myself in the passenger seat, I immediately became one of them "A, Thurso Bobby," and I might add, over the years, was frequently referred to by local youngsters as "Robbie the Bobby." It would be wrong to give you the impression that I wasn't frequently referred to by much less flattering names, but that just goes with the territory. Shortly after, I arrived at Thurso police station where I was greeted by the (yes you've guessed it) fast approaching retirement, Sergeant Duncan Cormack. It seemed to me that almost all of the supervisory ranks I had been meeting were due to retire and I very much hoped that this was as a result of their attaining pensionable service, rather than my joining being the final straw to break the camels back. O.K. maybe I was young and just a little bit paranoid, but, as my dad often said, "Just because you're paranoid it doesn't mean people aren't talking about you." The station was an old Victorian building which looked more like a townhouse than a police station, an effect probably added to by the fact that one half of its frontage was in fact a family home for a serving Sergeant. Once inside however, there was no mistaking where you were, a reasonably busy front office kitted out with, what I can only describe as antiquated, but functional telephone and radio equipment. This was a real contrast to what I had seen in Wick, but then again Wick was the divisional headquarters. Locker rooms, Muster room, C.I.D. office, Dark room, interview room, cell block and most ominously a mortuary left any visitor in no doubt that this was exactly what it purported to be on the sign outside.

"Thurso Police Station!"

Duncan Cormack was, even by the day's standards, a very tall man, of military bearing, with very distinct views on how a police officer was expected to conduct him or herself, and I have to say, the closest to the image I had formed of a policeman.

Duncan, and, may I say, I never referred to him directly as Duncan until after his retiral, and even to this day, I frequently refer to him as Sarge, escorted me to the upstairs Muster room, where I was introduced to the outgoing and incoming shifts.

My immediate impression was that they were a jovial bunch of individuals who clearly liked a laugh, and once again it was to be at my expense. One of the officers on duty, Bill Hargreaves, you could only describe as a Del Boy Trotter type with the distinct difference of rather than having a Cockney accent, spoke in broad Inverness, piped up with, " PC Snow, doesn't he look like Snowie off Z Cars." So Snowie I was and Snowie I remained throughout all of my service. Even my retiral notice as announced in the official Force Information Bulletin bore the name Snowie and as a Strathclyde colleague once said to me, "You're Snowie, you're infamous in your force," my reply was, " I prefer to use the term Well Known."

Sergeant Cormack had made arrangements for me to go into accommodation in Castle Street in Thurso, little more than a hundred or so yards from the station. The proximity of my digs to the police station was to prove a real boon, particularly on the day shift, when I was wont to snatch every possible additional minute of sleep before leaving the warmth and comfort of my bed. The lady of the house was an elderly widow by the name of Cathy Shanlon, who made a living by taking in boarders and casual Bed and Breakfast clients. During the period that I lived there, Mrs Shanlon had three full time boarders to whom she provided, Bed, Breakfast, Evening meal and Supper, did washing, ironing, made up and changed the beds, kept the place immaculately clean and tidy and took in, as I have already said, casual bed and breakfast clients. You may ask what is so marvellous about that, nothing I suppose, except Cathy only had one arm. She provided me with full board for the princely sum of £2 per night and didn't charge for my rest days when I would go home to Wick. I suppose she could have used my room for bed and breakfast clients when I wasn't there but she never did.

If up to this point, assuming you have continued to read this far, you have considered what I have written to be at least mildly amusing, let me warn you that I am now about to tell it like it is and you can't write about the Police without including considerable tragedy, so throughout the remainder of this read expect humour, expect tragedy and just occasionally the humour that can unexpectedly, accompany tragedy.

I had only been in Thurso a few days, familiarising myself with the office and its workings, meeting new people and being taken for the occasional walk, or to give it its technical term, Foot patrol of the town centre when we received a report of a serious road accident on the Scrabster Brae leading to the Orkney Ferry Terminal.

If memory serves me correctly, I was directed to accompany PC Charlie Simpson to the locus of the incident directly followed by Sgt Harry Garriock. Seated in a police vehicle, for the first time displaying blue lights and sounding two tone horns, my feeling was that of excitement but mixed with trepidation at what I may encounter, and a worry that I would be able to cope with, at this point, the unknown.

On arrival at the scene of the incident, I was met with, what at least appeared to me to be, a scene of total carnage. The two way carriageway was totally blocked across its width by a large removal lorry which had been making its way towards the Ferry Terminal and a small saloon car which had been travelling up the brae, and was now badly crushed against the road retaining wall. Obviously, in this type of situation, numerous vehicles had already backed up on either side of the accident and a small crowd of onlookers begun to gather. My next most immediate memory was the three young girls, all of whom were from the local secondary school, crying, and in some instances, I suppose understandably, screaming and covered in blood. The scene was such that my only thought was that they were all going to die. This was to be my first real lesson "Worry about the quiet ones." The driver, an elderly man, whose name and occupation I still remember but will not put down here, was trapped in the car and had clearly suffered fairly severe crush injuries and whose only concern, even under these circumstances, was for the safety of the girls, seemed very calm. At this point, I was already mentally wrecked and carrying out the directions given to me by my colleagues, almost as an automaton as I knew that it was only with activity that I was able to deal with what I was witness to. The local retained fire unit was very quickly in attendance as was the only, at that time, locally based ambulance which was also a part time service and operated from a garage base. The three girls were quickly removed from the scene and transported to hospital while the fire unit worked frantically to free the driver from the car using hacksaws and wrecking bars. They were not then equipped with the hydraulic jaws and other rescue equipment which can nowadays so quickly release a trapped driver. The driver was released and we laid him as gently as possible on the cars rear seat which we had placed on the roadway, and making use of my scant knowledge of first aid I covered him with a blanket from the rear of the police vehicle which we carried for just such purpose. There was still much to be done and I was given the task of looking after the casualty while waiting for the only other ambulance which had been dispatched from Dounreay, some ten miles away. As I knelt on the road, I suppose I knew enough to support his head, and with my other hand I held his shoulder and offered him some words of reassurance. I remember saying to him "You will be O.K. the ambulance will be here soon." This, I know, fine old gentleman, then turned his head slightly towards me and said, "I don't feel too good son" and then he died in my arms. I will never forget that first real tragedy in which I played a small part and to this day I can still hear him say "I don't feel too good son" and then drift away peacefully, without any complaint. From statements we obtained from the lorry driver, the evidence of eye witnesses and some time later, the passengers in the vehicle, who all made a full recovery, what we saw ourselves on the day, enabled us to verify the major factor which contributed to the cause of the accident. A fierce sun beating down the brae had quite literally blinded the driver, who reached over to find a pair of sunglasses, and in so doing caused the car to drift over directly into the path of the oncoming lorry.

Dare I admit that night in the privacy of my bedroom, I did cry and lost my appetite for a number of days as I struggled to deal with what had occurred? As I wrote this particular piece, I cried again.

A few days later, I was to receive a surprise that would lift me out of my depression, and although I should have guessed, I didn't. I was sitting alone in the upstairs Muster room, reading reports prepared by various officers and bringing myself up to date with reported crimes which had so far gone undetected, as you were expected to do, when I heard the front door open and close, accompanied by the sound of a girl's cheerful singing as she negotiated the stairway. It was then; she of the "hello boys" appeared through the Muster room door and on noticing me, immediately stopped, broke into the most wonderful smile and said "Hello, you're new." She sat down directly opposite to me, introduced herself as Joyce Inrig and asked me my name. She couldn't have known how long I had already been in love with her and I was not about to declare undying devotion at that point as I felt that this would be far too soon in this fledgling relationship. We spoke for quite a while, during which time I discovered that I knew her father, a local Lobster and Crab fisherman and she in turn had been in the same class in school as my youngest sister. The more we spoke, the more my heart raced and the more I was convinced she had to be mine. This is beginning to sound more like a Mills and Boon romance than a factual study of policing the Highlands; therefore I shall leave this particular subject and move on, although I will return to Joyce.

It wasn't terribly long after I arrived at Thurso that we were joined by none other than George Miller Douglas on transfer from Wick. George seemed to be used for the purposes of manning up, and it didn't much seem to matter to him, which station he operated from as his home at Dunnett was pretty much mid way between both. This next incident I am about to relate, really had little if in fact, anything to do with George, other than he offered a theory which was considered plausible and I was one of three officers instructed to act on it.

It was another day shift in Thurso and when I came on duty I learned that the previous night a very serious incident had occurred in the nearby village of Castletown. A tinker family, well known to the local Constabulary had been celebrating their weekly cash windfall, as provided by the welfare state, by consuming copious quantities of cheap wine, initially in good spirits. The initial feeling of goodwill to all men had clearly begun to sour as the booze ran out which resulted in a violent argument between the man and woman of the house, the culmination of which saw the husband stab his wife on no less than two occasions in the head. Miraculously, the woman survived this attack, but the husband, thinking he had murdered his wife took to his heels. C.I.D. and uniformed officers had spent all night in the village, gathering evidence and attempting to locate the would-be murderer.

George Douglas, by now booking of duty had theorised that the perpetrator, who was known to him, and every other policeman, including me, had, in a fit of remorse decided to take his own life by throwing himself into the harbour at Castletown. The powers that be considered this theory worthy of investigation and I was consequently dispatched, in the company of two other officers to search the shoreline, either side of Castletown for the remains. En route to Castletown, the first to be dropped off, Constable Mark Ronald had been tasked to walk the shoreline from Murkle into the harbour, a distance of some three miles. I was transported onward, through the village of Castletown and on to the Dunnett Bay camping and caravan site where I in turn was dropped off with the instruction to walk the shoreline into the harbour, again approximately three miles. Mark Ronald had clearly drawn the short straw as he was obliged to walk over shingle and large boulders, punctuated by patches of slippery seaweed and rock pools whilst I had been sent to a well known beauty spot frequented by tourists and locals alike. You may imagine that this was little more than a pleasant stroll across golden sands, which it indeed would have been, if it were not mid November. My remaining colleague, Constable Stuart Williamson had returned to Castletown to meet up with the village bobby there Constable Derek Oag, and assist him with the ongoing enquiry. I have to admit, I did not relish this particular duty, and the thought of discovering a dead body and having to remain in its company whilst awaiting the arrival of my colleagues, filled me with dread. To add to my discomfort, an extremely chill breeze was blowing in from the Pentland Firth and finding no difficulty in penetrating my Police issue raincoat. The caravan site and shop facility was of course, at this time of year, closed for the season, and deserted with the exception of a few static caravans permanently located there for the purposes of renting to tourists.

Having to the best of my limited ability, steeled myself against the often pitiless Caithness elements, and determined to carry out my duty, I was about to set out on my lonely trudge when, a short distance away I noticed a woman who seemed to be taking a particular interest in my presence on the beach.

Even as I began my walk I was very aware of this woman's continued scrutiny, and made a very positive effort not to catch her eye, as believe it or not, having barely turned 21 years of age, and not yet grown a moustache, I was still a very shy young man. Dunnett Sands being a fairly wide, long, flat and generally undisturbed stretch of beach, afforded me a clear view for some considerable distance and allowed me to reassure myself that I was not about to unexpectedly encounter that which I was dreading. In essence, I knew that I would be able to spot any irregular formation from some distance away, allowing me a cautious approach and the opportunity to steel myself for what I may find. Consequently, I was able to focus my attention to seaward and concentrate on the possibility that the body I was looking for was still in the process of being washed ashore. I was walking rather close to the waterline and watching the waves breaking on the shore, and being a local boy and having walked many a beach I can't believe I got caught as I was. I had forgotten about the notorious seventh wave, in general, larger than the preceding six and breaking much further inshore. I saw it coming and I thought "shit, its going to hit me" then I thought, "no its not" and as all these things seem to happen in slow motion, the terrible truth dawned on me, it was going to hit me and I wasn't fast enough to get out of its way. The wave didn't hit me with any great force but I was soaked to the top of my thighs and the water was bitterly cold. I didn't much relish the continued walk into Castletown, soaked as I was, and anticipating the serious ribbing I was going to get from my understanding and sympathetic police colleagues, and what was worse, the whole incident had been observed by the lone female watcher.

How embarrassed was I, but at least I was walking away from her and she would never know my name. So when she was telling the story to her friends and getting a laugh, the young policeman would remain anonymous and nobody would ever know it was me. Comforting myself with this thought, I was about to resume my journey when my two way radio crackled into life. This was Stewart Williamson informing me that the body had been arrested walking along the main street in Castletown and I was to return to my drop off point where I would be uplifted once a police vehicle became available. Oh well, the best laid plans of mice and men! Retracing my steps, I had already made a conscious decision to avoid any contact with my observer, find some shelter and settle down as best I could for a miserable, and god knows how long wait to be picked up. Very quickly however, it became apparent that I was not going to be successful in my planned strategy as she began to mirror my movements and come to a stop at the only point where I could make a dignified exit from the beach. As alternatives go, the only other option left to me was to scale a sand dune and negotiate a couple of fences which I felt may well indicate to this woman that I was making a positive effort to avoid her, and that off course would have been rude. At this juncture, it should be made clear that I have never been comfortable in the company of women, especially attractive women, and I frequently find myself becoming extremely nervous if they give even the slightest indication that they may be attracted to me. My wife can vouch for this statement and could confidently state to any of her friends: "Robert could never have an affair, he is incapable of it." I often wonder how I ever managed to marry and have a family. I suspect a psychiatrist may suggest that this is a legacy of having five older sisters, and if that is indeed the case, let me assure you I have taken considerable measures of revenge over the years, to which they can vouch.

Anyhow, the nearer I got to this woman, the more embarrassed I became and to add insult to injury as I approached, she said "excuse me officer, but I couldn't help but notice that you got wet." I blurted out a reply, something to the effect that it wasn't too bad, I would be fine and my colleagues would be returning soon to pick me up. (Lie, I was soaked to the arse) Maybe I was trying to scare her off and find some polite method of telling her to leave me alone, as standing in front of me was an extremely attractive, older woman who I would have placed somewhere between her mid thirties and early forties.

The term, I believe attributed to such a vision encountered by a much younger man today is MILF, not that I have the slightest clue what that might mean. It may be argued that I suffer from a degree of low self esteem; I never considered myself much of a catch for any woman, never mind an attractive one but add to this the animal instincts of any young rutting male and you have a recipe for total frustration. So there I was all wet and cold, totally unsure of myself, unable to deal with this encounter and being invited back to her caravan where I would be able to get dried off. All of my instincts were screaming at me to refuse this invitation which may well have amounted to little more than a warming cup of tea and an opportunity to shelter whilst at the same time my imagination was already working overtime and conjuring up erotic visions potentially yet to come. Believe me when I say I did refuse, not once but twice and she wasn't taking no for an answer quite forcefully insisting that I return with her to her caravan. This forceful attitude being displayed by my, by now, protagonist was the catalyst for a rethinking of my previous erotic imaginings, updating them from a gentle seduction to a potential violation of my innocence. (Whichever way it was likely to go sounded pretty good to me) Having been quite comprehensively beaten into submission I obediently followed her to the said caravan, whilst at the same time mentally preparing myself to fulfil the role of an older woman's plaything.   On entering the caravan I was instructed to take a seat while she busied herself putting on the kettle, so at least here was the promised, warming cup of tea and I had clearly been allowing my imagination to run wild, or had I? Having semi settled down and become slightly less uncomfortable with the circumstance of being alone with an attractive married woman, she, quite naturally removed her scarf and overcoat revealing a very trim figure which was garbed in a fashion which left very little to the imagination. It was now she suggested that I should remove my raincoat and hat, and not having any reasonable or plausible reason why I should refuse, I felt obliged to comply as it would be impolite not to do so.

If I consider this incident logically, after all I was wet, (possibly behind the ears) then it was not unreasonable for her to have me remove my shoes and my tunic, which I also did. By now I am down to my shirt and trousers, suffering panic attacks and seriously shitting myself. I know I have used the term "shitting myself" several times, and will probably use it many more, but allow me to reassure you, I never actually followed through, although there would be a few occasions I would be touching cloth. Every suggestion up to this point had been reasonable, but the next one, I was by now anticipating would undoubtedly place me in some considerable quandary. Pondering my situation, I began to ask myself, "Would it be unreasonable for her to suggest that I should remove my shirt," the answer to which had to be "yes" as my shirt was bone dry, while on the other hand a suggestion that I may remove my trousers could be viewed as reasonable, as they were soaking wet. Total panic, shitting myself, climbing the walls, sheer terror, none of these phrases could adequately describe how I felt at that moment and it seemed to me that it was through the force of my own will that my saving grace in the form of a police van appeared through the entrance to the caravan park. Wasting not a moment, I shoved my feet into my unlaced boots, grabbed my tunic, raincoat and hat which I bundled unceremoniously under my arm, made hasty thankyou's and quite literally sprinted from the caravan as fast as my legs could carry me, with her calling "Why don't you invite your friend in too." I raced to the police vehicle, jumped in and suggested to my colleague that we should leave immediately but not before noting the huge cheesy grin on his face, enquiring, "Just what have you been up to young fellow?" Even with the short time I had been a police officer it had been easy to anticipate the ribbing coming my way as I was thoroughly interrogated about the whole incident, forced to endure countless retellings of the story, as embellished by my colleagues and worst of all, berated for being such a wimp. It's true, Policemen can be so insensitive.

Insensitivity is something that a police officer can occasionally be accused of, but I honestly believe that is indeed not the case; the nature of the job can be such that this perceived insensitivity, certainly for me, and many more I would be happy to speak for is really a mask to hide their true feelings. We must be seen to be impartial and mask our emotions; otherwise we would never be able to get the job done. It takes quite some time, not to harden yourself, but to develop a style if you will, which allows you to cope with difficult situations and tragedy while hopefully giving off an air of professionalism and calm. I still hadn't made it to my first training stage at the Scottish Police College when I was instructed to accompany Constable Alfie Mackay to Raigmore Hospital in Inverness, where we were to deposit two bodies for Post Mortem examination. I have up until now; made no secret of my then inability to deal with any form of death and this particular task was to test me to my limits. Alfie and I loaded up the police Cortina estate car and set off on the then three hour plus drive to Inverness, throughout the whole of which, I was extremely uncomfortable with the close proximity of the two deceased. I will not go into any detail of that journey, other than to say that Alfie was happy to converse in generalisations, whilst my own responses were somewhat limited as I was preoccupied with procedures at journeys end. I strongly suspect that Alfie had detected my misgivings. On arrival at Raigmore, then and still today, the largest hospital in the Highlands, we went directly to the rear door of the mortuary where we parked at what I can only describe as a loading bay and rang the doorbell. We were greeted by the, guess what, even the Mortuary Attendant was fast approaching retirement; I really was beginning to wonder if it had something to do with me. He appeared to me to be a rather jovial fellow, which struck me as slightly strange given the nature of his job, but I might say I have long since re evaluated that opinion and now I think, why shouldn't he be a jovial fellow.

"What have you got for us today boys ?" was how we were greeted, in what I imagine was his best business like manner, and on being made aware of our load, tutted and tssked while expounding on the unfairness of life and in particular, death. On unloading the vehicle we were ushered through double doors into a large, open, very sterile hospital hallway off which I noted a number of doors which for me could have led anywhere and I was none to keen to investigate. As we walked towards yet another set of double doors the mortuary attendant informed us that it had been a particularly busy week and the pathologists were having real difficulty keeping up with the demands for Post Mortem examinations, which came in from all over the Highlands, and on entering through the double doors I saw for myself exactly what he meant.

I had been in small hospital mortuaries and I had been in our own police mortuaries, but nothing I had previously seen was able to prepare me for what I was to encounter here. It seemed to me that there was bodies everywhere, no matter in what direction I averted my eyes I saw a corpse either awaiting examination, or post examination and to make matters worse, I could do absolutely nothing about it. I couldn't run out of the door, which is exactly what I wanted to do, neither could I display any indication of being concerned by the situation so I just had to deal with it as best I could. I don't think I did very well in hiding my emotions as I suspect my face must have said it all when Alfie asked me if I was all right, to which I replied, in as monotone a voice as I could muster "I'm fine" (another lie to save face). To their credit, neither Alfie nor the attendant pressed me on this issue which they could easily have turned to my disadvantage and had a good laugh, once again at my expense.

Accuse me of being a bit of a girl if you wish, and up to this point you might be quite justified in thinking just that, but let me tell you it was going to get much worse before it got better. As I stood there, surrounded by bodies and frantically searching for an inoffensive point on which to settle my gaze, my peripheral vision was drawn to an internal set of double doors, the top half of which was glazed and from where I had detected some movement. I know that my brain must have exaggerated the situation, but through the doors I saw what was obviously the

Pathologist, and it seemed to me that he was delving into an open body and to make matters worse he appeared to be covered in blood. Any horror film I had ever watched just couldn't hold a candle to what I now found myself right in the middle of and I couldn't get out of that place quick enough. It did strike me that Alfie was taking some considerable time dealing with paperwork and I couldn't fail to notice that he and the attendant were engaged in considerable discussion which, up until now, I had been unable to take any particular heed of. It seemed that their was some dubiety surrounding the exact Christian name of one of our deceased and this would have to be clarified prior to our identifying the bodies to the Pathologist, and off course would have to be correct on the death certificate issued by him. Alfie asked where he may obtain the use of a telephone and was directed to another room outside in the hallway. I had decided that under no circumstance, was I about to be left alone with all these bodies and where Alfie went, I was going too.

Tucked in at Alfies back, looking neither right nor left, I can only imagine that to any casual observer we must have looked a little bit like a two man bobsleigh team, but I wasn't really caring and I wasn't about to let Alfie get away from me. I cannot describe the relief I felt on leaving that room, but neither can I describe the equally strong emotion of knowing that I would have to go back. On entering the identified room it was only then that I realised that my situation had gone from bad to much, much worse. I was now in the Pathology viewing area and little more than an arms length away from me, separated by no more than a two foot high sterile barrier was the Pathologist, working on an already opened body and next to him, another attendant in the process of opening a skull with an air powered saw. Let me tell you, between what I had already seen in the reception area, the sight of the Pathologist working at the first table and the high pitched whine of the air powered saw cutting into bone, as far as I was concerned this was the stuff nightmares are made of, and to this day I wonder I didn't collapse on the spot. We moved into a changing room where the phone was located and throughout the full conversation all I could think about was having to go back out the same way as we had come in. On the return trip you couldn't have put a cigarette paper between me and Alfie, which must have been causing him some concern as he was a happily married man with three kids. Everything sorted, we very quickly now carried out the formal identification and headed for Police Headquarters, for, of all things, "lunch."

I had strangely lost my appetite, which is extremely unusual for me as my lifelong thinking has been, "if it's eatable, eat it." Alfie continued to ask me if I was alright and I continued to lie through my teeth, making alternative, plausible, I felt excuses for not eating, like "I'm not hungry" which he responded to with a look that said "Oh yeah, whatever you say." All too soon it was time to return to the mortuary to pick up the bodies for the return trip home. By now there was little activity and the plethora of bodies apparent on my arrival had either been removed by undertakers or police officers engaged on the same duty as ourselves. Under these circumstances my presence in the mortuary was much less trying until I learned that the attendant had to store a few bodies in the chilled compartments before he could deal with us, but suggested we could get away much quicker if we could see our way to giving him a hand. As the compartment doors were opened all I could see was racks of dead bodies, some of which had to be taken out and transferred to other compartments and the vacant spaces filled by other bodies. That job couldn't be finished soon enough for me and I was never so happy to be loaded up and on my way home.

When I reflect on this particular, not very nice story, I cannot help but think of the old adage "It's an ill wind that blows no good," as for me, this experience showed me that I could cope with death, and I might add, in most of its forms.

CHAPTER 4

SCOTTISH POLICE COLLEGE

The Scottish Police College at Tulliallan in Fife is the central training school for all police officers in Scotland. Training in most police disciplines is carried out at this location, including basic and advanced courses, all driver training, initial and senior detective training, community safety, architectural liaison and Forensics, to mention just the tip of the iceberg. In this respect, I believe the Scottish Police College is unique in the United Kingdom as the forty plus forces in England and Wales have a number of training schools which officers attend. It would however be fair to acknowledge that there are only eight police forces in Scotland which clearly makes this scenario more workable.

Quite recently, I myself made the remark that I was visiting the college to bathe in its ambience, as the campus can today, easily compete with and occasionally surpass some of the best five star hotels. May I assure you that this was not the case in the mid seventies?

What I did know prior to attending was that the college was a very disciplined regime and I had heard numerous horror stories from my many colleagues who had passed that way before me, which did nothing to endear me to the place. There was off course one exception to the rule and that was my, by now, good pal Joyce. She told me that she had enjoyed her time at the college and she had made lots of friends when she was there, and I shouldn't pay any attention to the rest of the boys as they were only trying to wind me up. Well, they were succeeding. One evening Joyce and I were out on foot patrol when we met Jimmy Johnson, a local bobby who had been promoted to Sergeant when he had been selected to serve a term as instructor at Tulliallan. Jimmy came back to the station for a cup of tea and spent some time reassuring me that I wouldn't have any problem as long as I kept my nose clean which I had every intention of doing. Being introduced to Jimmy that night was to stand me in extremely good stead on my very first day at College.

As I didn't own a car and being expected to arrive on the Monday I was obliged to travel by train on the Saturday as far as Inverness where I had a number of hours wait before I could continue my journey as far as Edinburgh. On arriving in Edinburgh I was met by my very good friend Sonny Anderson and spent a little time with him and his wife Jean and their family before travelling by bus to Tulliallan on the Monday morning. Jean had very kindly invited me to stay with them each weekend as it was impossible for me to travel home and I was more than delighted to accept her invitation. It also meant that I had freshly washed and ironed white shirts every week, for which I remain eternally grateful.

On the approach to the village of Kincardine via the famous Kincardine Bridge I could barely make out the turrets of Tulliallan Castle, one time headquarters of the Polish forces during World War two, and was unable to form any immediate impression of what I was likely to be in for. My very limited and undoubtedly exaggerated or at least I thought it had to be, pieces of information gleaned from my good friends! Could only lead me to the conclusion that I was going to hate every minute of my time there. On disembarking the bus and uplifting my two very large, very heavy suitcases, I began to make my way to the rear gatehouse entry to the Castle, stopping several times to rest my aching arms as I felt with every step they were likely to be wrenched from their sockets. After what seemed like an eternity of torture I arrived at the main entrance to the building and was directed to an area known as the middle landing where I joined on to the end of a line of equally heavily laden recent recruits. I had, I thought, made some effort to arrive appropriately attired and was garbed in heavily checked, green flared trousers, brown lace up platform shoes, brightly patterned open necked shirt and to complete the ensemble a cream three quarter length jacket with white fur collar and cuffs. Please remember this was the seventies, I was a teuchter from the hills and I was only about five years out in fashion sense. This having been said, and as hard as it may be to believe there was some far worse looking sights than me in that queue, or at least that's how I prefer to remember it.

As I stood waiting for whatever was going to happen next I entered into idle conversation with later arrivals and swapped information relating to what force I was with, how much service I had and where I was stationed. The final piece of information almost inevitably met with the response "Where's that?" and "How long did it take to get here?" It may also be necessary at this point to make you aware that the Caithness, in particular, Wick accent is not dissimilar to that of Northern Ireland and over the years I have frequently been mistaken to be Irish and was christened that very day as Mick, and was frequently referred to as such by my fellow students throughout my time at Tulliallan. As I stood in line I was more than aware of considerable bustle and toing and froing of uniformed personnel, some of whom were I guessed instructors and considerably more I supposed, students. I could only guess at who may be what as I was somewhat confused at the presence of numbers in plain clothes, frequent shouts of "course" and people leaping to attention everywhere I looked. This strange behaviour seemed to be constant and to some considerable degree unsettling causing me to question my presence at this institution. As I stood in line leaning against a window with my hands in my pockets I saw a known face approaching from along the corridor. It was Jimmy Johnston making what appeared to be discreet hand signals to me and as he got to where I stood, quietly said, "For god's sake take your hands out of your pocket's, they will crucify you here for that." I immediately complied and mumbled my thanks to Jimmy who continued to walk in the direction of a number of tables at the far end of the corridor at which point my attention was grabbed by a mountain lion type roar and the sight of three sergeant instructors, including Jimmy, descending on an unsuspecting recruit and tearing him to pieces. As I, and everybody else looked on this poor recruit was screamed at, called lots of unpleasant names and questioned as to why he thought he could ever make a police officer. My own feeling at the time was that I was glad that I wasn't in his shoes as I was quite comprehensively terrified as a mere onlooker. And what was his crime? He had his hands in his pockets!

It was a long first day, and I have every reason to believe it was meant to be a long day as we were rushed from pillar to post, issued with bed clothing, ill fitting sports attire, lectured on what was expected of us and walking around in never ending circles in order to make up our lecture notes which had been laid out page by page in a large hall. I also had my first experience of college food. With regard to taste and culinary excellence I would have to say neither was present on that first or any other day throughout my incarceration. We were eventually released about nine pm to a supper of tea and sandwiches before making our way to designated dormitories to make up our beds and meet with those we would be living in close proximity with for the next eight weeks. The dormitories were in fact old classrooms into which they had thrown ten beds, ten wardrobes and the odd hard backed chair to serve as a home comfort. Let me assure you this place was nowhere like home and I was already missing my mum and my good pal Joyce. I had already concluded I was most definitely not in Kansas.

It was now I was to meet the three guys who maintained my sanity throughout those eight weeks and I like to think I helped maintain theirs. Alan McGowan was the same age as me and possessed the same sort of sense of humour whilst at the same time having a serious side for a young fellow with an intense interest in the game of chess. Alan spent hours poring over chess books and practising game strategies, all of which was beyond me and just about everyone else on the course including the instructors. He was also extremely athletic and built as you would expect an athlete to be built and could run like a greyhound. Alan Dawson was on the other hand somewhat different, not a serious bone in his body and looked for a laugh anywhere he could get it. Again roughly the same age Alan was to perpetually get himself into some kind of bother with the instructors and more frequently found himself on the dreaded extra duties than anyone else I can think of. Andy Jones was the last of the trio and again very different from the other two. He was a late starter in the police service already in his early thirties, married with a family and probably the most sensible head of the group. All three were Strathclyde officers with their routes in Scotland's largest city, Glasgow, and the sense of humour to go with it. I suppose I could liken us to the three musketeers, Athos, Portos and Aramis, the three city wide boys whilst I fulfilled the role of Dartagnan, the clueless country bumpkin. It was early morning before we all managed to retire to bed as there was so much to be done getting ourselves to some degree prepared for the days to come. And so it was I was awoken at the ungodly hour of six am by the perpetual ringing of an electronically controlled bell which I was destined to curse for eight whole weeks.

I would like to be able to say that the college sorted out the men from the boys, but more accurately what it did succeed in doing was sorting out the boys from the mummy's boys. The rate of dropout in the first week was a real eye opener whilst week two still saw a number decide that the police service was not for them. The very occasional loss following that initial period was decided on an entirely different basis, not by the individual but the police making the decision for them that they weren't suited to the post.

The college was a very disciplined environment, the running of which appeared to be based on a military style regime. This was certainly true of the two basic courses who had to be on their toes at all times and when instructed to jump was only expected to enquire as to how high. I have witnessed, on more than one occasion, in excess of one hundred uniformed officers being brought to rigid attention with that cry of "course" from some anonymous wit acknowledging the progress of a janitor or particularly attractive member of the untalented kitchen staff. Again, take my word the janitor was the most deserving.

As with most of these unknown situations when an individual is thrown into close proximity living with total strangers, there appears to be a common lemming like rush to purchase new pyjamas. I do not claim to have been any exception to this behaviour and appeared in the large communal shower and toilet block in my brand new Paisley pattern pyjamas still showing clear signs of the creases formed whilst still in the packaging. With the very odd exception I couldn't help but notice numerous clones of myself, all of whom displayed equal signs of discomfort with their mode of garb and trying to project telepathic messages to the effect that they were real men at home and slept in the nude. I suppose, in order to compensate for the insecurity of this situation their seemed to be more growling than you would expect and loads of inappropriate cursing designed to enforce individual masculinity. Needless to say, the ninety plus percentage of pyjama wearers dropped to less than ten in the first week.

The college was all about learning the fundamentals of Road Traffic Law, Crime and General Police duties mixed with the knowledge of being able to research the more obscure crimes and offences which you may infrequently encounter throughout your service. Added to this was a big emphasis on physical fitness which already by age twenty one, I wasn't. Every day saw us in the Olympic class swimming pool, not for a leisurely swim but two hours of intense swimming exercise. Non swimmers became swimmers by the end of eight weeks whilst swimmers became excellent swimmers. I became one of the latter having been brought up swimming in the local harbour, the sea and outdoor swimming pools and was one of only five in my course of one hundred and fifteen to complete the college survival swim. I was quite proud of this particular achievement until brought down to earth by my often sceptical but fully supportive dad who reminded me that my achievement was all very well but never to forget that "Shit floats." It was almost inevitable that any period of intense physical activity immediately preceded either Lunch or the evening meal and all meals were treated as a duty you must attend whether you ate or not. This practice mixed with the garbage served up under the pretence of being food serviced not only me but several others most effectively in achieving rapid weight loss.

Swimming was not the only physical activity we were expected to take part in.
The mundanity of a daily two mile run was only relieved by its extension to five miles twice a week and an expectation that you would improve your run time, or suffer the consequences. The sight of students pushed to physical extremes, throwing up in various corners was not uncommon. As stupid as I may have been, I

was clever enough to pace myself in earlier runs and consequently cut a few seconds off my time, keeping the physical training instructors as happy as they were ever likely to be. I would also have to admit that there was the occasional pleasing distraction during these periods of torture, generally taking the form of female officers. It is not my intention to be chauvinistic and the last thing I would want to do is alienate any potential female readers but I feel it is particularly important to tell it like it was. Every one of us had been issued with sports kit, the men receiving a white vest and black shorts whilst the females were issued with a leotard. In every case both male and female were issued with kit that just didn't fit, and I believe this to have been very deliberate. The consistency with which big lads and big girls were issued with shorts or leotards which they could barely fit into and vice versa, little guys and little girls being garbed in enough material to make a parachute, never ceased to amaze me.

It was also treated as a punishable misdemeanour to do the obvious thing and swap kit with an appropriate counterpart, thus sparing you any embarrassment. Suspicious or what! The phrase "it's an ill wind that doesn't blow somebody some good" very much comes to mind in this particular instance. Myself and many other male officers frequently found ourselves running behind our female counterparts, the girls off course being much better runners than us and nothing at all to do with the particularly revealing leotards they were forced to wear. This pleasant distraction was frequently cut short by the arrival of an instructor who knew exactly what was going on and urged us lads on with a good tongue lashing only to take up the position we had previously occupied.

As if swimming and running wasn't enough there was also the gymnasium and the assault course. I can only imagine that my military background as a Wick sea cadet saw me through the trials and tribulations of attending the Scottish Police College.

No matter what form of employment you may take up in life there are some things that remain constant, and that is the presence of (as put in a well known Scottish comedy sketch show), Good Guys and Wanks. The police service is no different in this respect and neither was the college. Chiefly, the Wanks took the form of instructors who wouldn't even have been loved by their mothers and went seriously out of their way to prove to the world that they were total arseholes. On the other hand their were quite a number of instructors who were seriously good guys, it just seemed that when God had dished out personalities and senses of humour a considerable number of these fellows navigated themselves into the additional arsehole queue.

Strangely enough, the instructors I didn't like during my first stage training were the same ones I didn't like during my second stage training and just in case I have come across as somewhat opinionated, these feelings were pretty much reflected by the entire course. Surely one hundred and fifteen students can't all be wrong?

I have made some brief mention of the college culinary delights and maybe unjustifiably described the food as garbage but I would like to take this opportunity for you to make up your own minds. As I have said, every meal had to be attended and as bad as it may have been the survival instinct present in us all forced you to eat.

Each designated table of ten, generally your dormitory, and change seats on pain of death, was issued ten bread rolls for which we would frequently barter a fun size cereal box and watered down milk or portion of the wonderful cooked aspect of the daily breakfast. The cooked breakfast consisted of the strangest combinations of food I had ever encountered, and I might add, only two items. For instance, heated up, catering size tins of plum tomatoes accompanied by unidentifiable overcooked baked beans were rarely surpassed by half a slice of burned fried bread topped off with the left over tomato from yesterday.

Occasional rumours relating to the appearance of sausage and egg, all be it one of each, caused some real buzzes of excitement only to have your hopes dashed with the presence of these bloody tomatoes. This was the sort of food that the college would describe as a healthy and nutritional start to an active day. Lunch was little better, always starting with a welcome, warming bowl of soup. To describe college soup as dishwater would be a compliment to the chef. Each day the soup bore a different name with no sight of the main ingredient and a flavour which was remarkably similar to a stock cube. I was always particularly frustrated at the serving counter as I would stand with my plate proffered to a potential benefactor, feeling I suppose, not unlike Oliver Twist, but not daring to ask for more in the fear that some Beadle like cook would descend and berate me for being an ungrateful child. It really was that bad. We were not allowed to complain as it was not unlikely that the slightest negative observation could, and on more than one occasion did, lead to a walkout by the kitchen staff. I won't bore you with the evening meal and beg your indulgence to take my word for it, it was shite as well.

With the very odd exception, and I believe today there are no exceptions, ninety plus percent of officers attending basic training at the college came directly from a force training/induction programme. I was one of the rare exceptions who had been working on the street and taken a role in practical policing prior to attending. As the lecturer would present his subject for either a single or double period, whether it was Breach of the Peace, Assault or Sudden Death it was common practice to seek out the limited experience of the students. I think this would be called participative learning in today's education circles. As wet behind the ears as I was, I wasn't nearly as much so as the vast majority of my fellow students and even I became sick of my hand constantly being raised and then being asked to relate a particular experience.

Maybe the role of a police officer is different in the North, I don't really know but the frequency with which I heard the expression "They do things different up there" following one of my narratives, certainly gave me cause to believe that maybe we did.

I had reached the conclusion that training at the college took account of all of the black and white issues a police officer may encounter throughout their service but did little to address the often much more important grey areas that would have a considerable effect on your decision making. This process was left to your training on the street and I have to admit, with hindsight, would have been impossible to teach at the college. It seemed to me that my fellow students were destined in due course to experience every bit as much of an eye opening to what policing was really about as I already had. Doing things differently up North didn't strike me as such a bad thing.

The disciplined regime of the college was constant from early morning right through to the respite of sleep with very little opportunity of any real relaxation in between. Others who have attended the same institution may rubbish that statement and say, but we went to the bar, or used the swimming pool. To them I would say "Your right" but remind them that they were constantly under scrutiny and every aspect of their behaviour was being noted. How often was a student informed of the time they left the bar or cautioned in respect of their alcohol intake, or indeed advised that it had been noted that they did not appear to be as studious as was expected. Needless to say I was not alone in looking forward to the weekends. My escape was spent in Scotland's capital city of Edinburgh where I stayed with my very good friends, Sonny and Jean Anderson and where I was made very welcome. My presence in their home must at least have been an inconvenience if not much more. Even with a young family of their own they went out of their way to make sure I enjoyed my time in Edinburgh and every weekend another activity was planned.

After a week of purgatory at the Scottish Police College, Sonny and Jeans home was an oasis of calm in a sea of tranquillity. Sonny, now long since retired was a postman at Waverly Station in Edinburgh where he and a number of his colleagues worked transferring the sometimes carriage loads of incoming mail from the trains to the main sorting office and similarly the outgoing mail. I would arrive off the Kincardine bus on a Friday evening loaded down with washing for Jean and make my way directly to Waverly station where I would meet Sonny and the rest of the postie's happily ensconced in the Railway station pub. It was from here that the operation of loading and unloading trains was masterminded, prompted by tannoy announcements alerting Sonny and his pals to the arrival of the most recent train. I suppose I have known anything from six to ten postmen to have been on duty at any one time and I have to say that this would occasionally prove circumspect if one of the number, less hardened than the others, had succumbed to an over indulgence in booze. I have to admit that ever since, anytime I see an electric buggy pulling a snake of cages loaded with bags of mail on a railway station platform, I am inclined to give it a wide berth, just in case!

My weekend visits to Edinburgh introduced me to all kinds of Scottish culture something which I had clearly been starved of in the North. A day at the bookies receiving clear instruction from Sonny on how to understand form and whether or not a particular horse merited an each way bet or was good enough to bet to win was an education in itself. This particular pleasure was only heightened by Sonny's base for his operation, the pub directly next door to the bookmakers from where you could follow all the action on a number of television screens. The real pleasure was, knowing that Jean would have real food waiting for us when we got home. An evening at the Post Office club was a really good night, whether for a dance or an open mike session where frustrated crooners could assault your eardrums with a rendering of "My Way" which in their opinion, but nobody else's, was unlikely to be bettered by Sinatra himself. Greyhound racing, a visit to Ingelston Market and tours of places of Historic interest were all part of my Agenda and I can honestly say that I enjoyed every minute of my time with the Andersons. Sunday evenings came around all too soon and it was time to return to the college where I would arrive with my crisp, clean and freshly ironed white shirts ready to undergo another week of purgatory. My return to the college was always accompanied by a brief period of depression which only lasted as long as it took for my pals to get back, when we would discuss what we had been doing at the weekend.

I suppose I should say that all to soon the eight weeks were up and it was getting towards time to go home except that would be a lie. It couldn't come round quick enough for me. Final exams had been completed and I had slightly more than scraped through, ever so slightly as now I can be completely honest and say I never opened a book outside of classroom time. Again however I was clever enough to leave out the training notes relevant to whichever instructor happened to be on rounds on any given evening and opened at the most current subject he had lectured us on. If not a book then a pair of boots on a sheet of newspaper accompanied by cleaning materials to give the impression that I was either studying or at least industrious. I find it difficult to believe that these guys were so easily taken in but it seems they were. I really didn't give much chance to any of their abilities in interviewing a suspect who decided to lie about their involvement in a crime. I often wondered if a simple "It wisnae me" would suffice to see a criminal released back into the community accompanied with an apology for wasting his or her time. Possibly I am being a bit harsh or overly cynical but sometimes I did wonder.

Our final evening preceding our passing out parade was marked by a formal dinner and dance attended by all students, wives, girlfriends and instructors. In truth I got on particularly well with all but one of the College instructors who for reasons only known to him had taken a particular dislike to me. He frequently went out of his way to get me and I could be fairly certain that any evening that he was on rounds I was likely to find myself on duty team the following evening. Duty team meant no swimming, no bar, no relaxation and you would find yourself patrolling the college grounds, washing dishes or any other demeaning task he could think up. This guy was a real shite, at least to me, and would even go as far as to invent some misdemeanour which I had apparently perpetrated just to show me who was boss. There was no appeal and unfortunately whatever punishment was visited on me was also applied to my musketeer friends. This was particularly hard on Alan Dawson who was more than capable of getting himself into plenty of genuine trouble and was already an almost permanent fixture on duty team. Anyhow, the evening of the dance was accompanied by considerable alcohol intake and as you know alcohol can cause some people to drop their guard.

This was very true of my nemesis who had obviously decided that this would be the appropriate time to make me aware of his feelings toward me. I was, for once, enjoying an evening at the college when he made his approach, obviously the worse for wear and intent on winding me up. I can only assume that because I was leaving the following day and was unlikely to return for at least a year he saw this as his last opportunity to stick one to me. Taken off guard I found myself for no apparent reason being berated by this drunken instructor who very publicly and very loudly announced "Mr Sutherland, I don't like you." Clearly surprised and taken aback at this revelation I felt it was only right to reply, equally as loudly, "Sgt ******** the feeling is totally mutual." Stupid on my part as this only managed to enrage him further and egged him on to vent his fury to a greater degree in my direction. This behaviour had not however gone unnoticed by other instructors present who felt the need to intervene and remove him from my company making no attempt to spare him any embarrassment by calling him all the arseholes under the sun. The following day I did take some evil delight from learning that he had received a reprimand for his behaviour and continued in that delight no less than two years ago when I heard the very same arsehole introduced on a radio station not having progressed beyond the rank of Sergeant.

The pass out parade over, which it very nearly was given the amount of alcohol consumed the night before, I made my farewells accompanied by promises of keeping in touch which none of us really did and began my journey back to Caithness.

I suppose now that I was apparently full of knowledge it was time to start my real policing career.

CHAPTER FIVE

BACK HOME

It won't surprise you to learn that leaving the College was no particular wrench to me and my return to Caithness was in fact a great relief. I was, I suppose back in my comfort zone and raring to get going to put into practice all the knowledge I had gained. "Wrong." With only a few months service I clearly wasn't considered competent enough to be let loose on the general public, certainly not on my own. As much as I may have yearned for my freedom those who knew better made sure I didn't get it and I continued to be closely supervised by officer's senior in service. Amongst these officers there was of course that one Diamond amongst the rough "Joyce." I always looked forward to being on duty with her and it surprises me that I ever managed to get anything done as she was my one major distraction.

As far as I was concerned she was efficient, extremely good at her job, intelligent, the most popular person in the station and absolutely gorgeous to boot and I was in love with her. Joyce really had no idea about how I felt and I didn't go out of my way to tell her in the event that I would ruin a very good friendship although I do feel that she must have had something of an inkling, on the very odd occasion. Travelling salesmen were the worlds worst, they seemed to think that they had a god given right to park their heavily laden company cars wherever they wished with no regard to other motorists or pedestrians. Bringing a reasonably busy town centre street to a complete halt whilst they purveyed their perfumes, jewellery, stationary or whatever to local traders appeared to be of no consequence to them. I offer no apology to travelling salesmen, you know who you were. I frequently found myself standing at a point on the street and noticing that traffic had come to a complete halt only to find on investigation that inevitable travelling salesman ridiculously parked, oblivious to the pandemonium he was causing. This type of scenario may strike you as a bit petty and ridiculous but it gets worse. How often did I encounter this situation when I was on duty with Joyce? The answer is frequently. Those were the occasions when it got worse because the other thing I learned about travelling salesmen was that quite a number of them seemed to think that they were god's gift to women.

As Joyce was the senior officer it became my role to stand in the background and let her deal with the situation whilst I took note of how it should be done. She was always pleasant and polite and inevitably got hit on by these Romeos who would ask her out for dinner or enquire as to when she would be off duty and suggest the possibility of accompanying them for a drink. Maybe I am being a bit hard on travelling salesmen as they were doing exactly what I wanted to do but just hadn't got the guts to ask. As wrong as I may have been these were the occasions when I saw red and felt obliged to step in and leave these guys in no doubt as to what was going to happen if they didn't move that very second. My approach, as harsh as it may have been certainly had the desired effect and before very long we would once again witness the free flow of traffic through the town centre. Joyce did point out to me, a number of times that she felt I had been a bit hard, but what she didn't realize was that I was as nice as nine pence as long as she wasn't with me. It was hard enough trying my best to be as good a policeman as I could be but it was a damned sight harder when I was being love sick at the same time.

I have already said I was never very good with females but I don't want you to imagine that I had no experience in that field at all. Like most young guys I had experienced the very odd sojourn through the minefield of courtship, none of which had amounted to anything nearly permanent or even long term. I was seriously backward at coming forward. The only serious relationship I was, I have to say happily involved in about then was with a female called Nicola who was deeply in love with me and me with her. The only problem was she was about two years old and was to prove by age five just how jealous a five year old could be of an older woman moving in on her territory. After all I was and still remain her favourite uncle. By now I was just, and I do stress just in a position to purchase a small car and barely able to maintain the running costs. What this did mean was that I was able to move back into my parents home and travel on a daily basis to Thurso. The car, a Singer Chamois, cost me £170. I last saw one of these vehicles, an upmarket version of a Hillman Imp, in the Scottish Transport Museum in Glasgow. That sort of experience really brings home just how old you are getting. Although this vehicle served me well, it was first registered in 1966 and given its already considerable age could be prone to the occasional mechanical problem. The fact that the fuel gauge never worked was an added problem which kept me on my toes guessing just how much fuel I did have to keep me going for the week. The majority of my breakdowns could then be attributed to running out of fuel but I did have the good sense (when I could afford it) to keep a spare gallon in the boot.

On one particular occasion I had set out, as was always the case, in plenty of time to make my way the 21 miles to Thurso to start my day shift at 8am. Still within Wick town boundary my little Chamois, not for the first time, gave up the ghost. On this occasion I knew I had plenty of fuel and this was clearly a mechanical problem which I could not deal with at the time so I made my way to my Brother in Laws home and borrowed his Ford Anglia (also to be seen in the Transport Museum) for the day. I made my way to Thurso in time to start my early shift and with every intention of dealing with my cars mechanical problem on my return to Wick. During the early part of the morning I was carrying out a foot patrol of the main street when I received a radio message from the duty sergeant enquiring of me where my car was. I did think that this was a rather strange enquiry but put it down to the appearance of an unknown vehicle in the police station compound. I quickly explained what had happened and identified the Ford Anglia as belonging to my brother in law. The duty sergeant appeared happy with this explanation and I thought no more of it until about an hour later when I was instructed to return to the station.

On returning to the station I was ushered into the Inspectors Office and again asked where my car was. By now I was becoming a little concerned and asked if there was anything wrong. The reply I received was that I should have no cause for concern and to just explain where I had left my car. Once again I went through the story of my cars demise early that morning and the necessity of borrowing a vehicle to make my way to work. The Inspector and Sergeant then began to ask me a series of questions.

Where exactly had I left the car.?

Had I been aware of anyone watching me at the time?

Had I seen anyone in the area?

Was I sure I was telling the truth?

By now it was clear to me that this was an interrogation and I was suspected of something, I just didn't know what. After some half hour of going over my story and answering every question put to me, the Inspector and Sergeant seemed happy with my explanation. I felt by now that I should have some explanation of what was going on and made a very respectful enquiry to that effect. It seemed that an elderly lady of some eighty odd years had been making frequent complaints of the theft of milk from her doorstep and had done so that very day. On Police attending to note her complaint she had pointed out my abandoned car and stated that whoever owned the car had been stealing her milk over all this time. Colleagues in Wick, knowing the car to belong to me obviously followed the next line of enquiry and that was to have me interviewed. This lady continued to make complaints of milk theft and the police continued to investigate to no avail until eventually it became clear that their never had been any thefts and this was just a lonely old lady who craved some company, even if it was just the police. I encountered numerous just such scenarios throughout my police service.

With the exception of the police cadet who could not officially be used for any policing purpose, I was the boy in the station and was very much treated as such.
I suppose that came along with the fact that most of the officers were ex servicemen, married with families and had seen quite a bit of life. I, by contrast, was young, inexperienced in quite literally everything and was struggling to find my feet. This set of circumstances inevitably led to my being the most dispensable person from the shift and consequently any request from a rural based officer for assistance led to their being landed with me. Every new police officer finds themselves in this position until someone even newer comes along, so it's not as if I was being picked on. I very much enjoyed this aspect of the job and found myself

involved in many diverse incidents as a consequence. Derek Oag, as I have already said was the single officer based at Castletown and had previously served with the Royal Air Force. For some reason unknown to both of us to this day we got on particularly well from the very start and when teamed up, worked very successfully together. We would, in fact, plan Derek's requests for assistance pretty much around my availability on shift. This was a particularly surprising friendship for me as Derek was born and bred in Thurso whilst I hailed from the County town of Wick, and neither the twain shall meet. This situation led to considerable light hearted abuse between the two of us but if ever he should happen to read this I want him to know, I meant every word I said. It may be the suspicious mind of a police officer but I suspect he may have meant everything he said as well but was willing to take his thinly veiled dislike of me that considerable bit further.

Derek had requested my presence for covering a Friday night village hall dance and we duly teamed up early evening in order to shepherd the revellers moving between the local pub and the village hall. I would not claim that Castletown, as any other village in the county would cause any particular policing problem, but just as the rest of the villages, the holding of a village dance just could, and frequently was the catalyst for some form of trouble. It was not unknown on some of these occasions to spend your entire shift period ferrying arrests between the dance venue and the cells at Thurso police station. Drunk and Incapables, Breaches of the Peace, Assaults and Drunk Drivers were frequently common place and the truth of the matter was that we could only deal with a part of it. On any other day it wasn't the Wild West but policing a rural dance sometimes felt like it. This was probably the highest profile policing a village was likely to see as in general the local bobby would wander about speaking to everyone, renew Firearm and Shotgun certificates and was everybody's friend and very approachable. A village bobby became an entirely different sort of beast when it came to dances. It was then that he would exercise his police powers, stand for no nonsense and demonstrate to the locals that should they step out of line he was capable of carrying out his duties to the letter of the law. In those days a village bobby was not provided with a with a smartly marked jam sandwich (marked police vehicle) but was expected to provide his own transport, which inevitably meant his own family car for which he was given a small mileage allowance. Derek was then driving a Hillman Minx family saloon into which, after drilling several holes, the police had installed a somewhat antiquated mobile radio of considerable proportions.

The boot space was taken up with a large box containing Police accident signs, reflective jackets, first aid kit, blankets, torches that never worked and the inevitable Kojack magnetic blue light.

We were parked opposite to the village hall making sure that there was no trouble likely to flare when our attention was drawn to a car which passed up the village street not showing any lights. Added to this moving traffic offence it was blatantly clear that the driver had little control of the vehicle and could only lead us to the conclusion that he was likely to be drunk. Activating the quite frankly, pathetic blue light which may have flashed every two seconds or so, we took off in pursuit of the offender who clearly had little intention of stopping despite Derek's additional efforts of flashing headlights and sounding of the car horn. On approaching the village boundary the pursued driver finally lost control of his vehicle, mounted the grass verge and partially entered a shallow ditch bringing to an end, at least the motorised aspect of the chase. As Derek was bringing his car to a halt the drunk and uncatchable jumped from his vehicle and leapt a low fence into an open field sprinting away into the darkness as fast as his somewhat unsteady legs were capable of taking him. "Get him Snowie" was sufficient instruction for me to take off in the same direction as the fast receding form of the potential accused. Long wet grass, mud and smooth soled uniform shoes are not conditions and footwear that lends itself to efficient pursuit but then again changing into the appropriate attire is not really an option under these circumstances. I could see that I was slowly gaining ground on my quarry and made one final monumental effort to close the gap and at this point threw myself forward and carried out what I believed to be the perfect Rugby tackle. I really felt that it was a shame that Derek wasn't there to witness my athletic take down but he was some considerable distance behind expending as little effort as possible ambling up the field. Following a somewhat token struggle punctuated with numerous expletives the prisoner lay on the grass gasping for breath whilst I sat on top of him to prevent any further attempts at escape and settled back to await my colleague's belated arrival. Quite frankly I just wasn't up to any form of struggle and further expending of energy at that precise time as I was every bit as shattered as my prisoner. I became aware of a dull glow which I knew had to be Derek picking his way through the field avoiding the numerous cow pats which neither I or my prisoner had time to consider, the evidence of which was adhering to parts of my uniform and shoes and likewise that of my captives.

On his arrival Derek's first comment was "Well done Wicker" (pronounced Weeker) and continued to inform me that it was just as well that I had managed to catch the fugitive at that point as had I run a further ten yards I would have gone straight over the edge of the local quarry. This, as it turned out was indeed the case and just a few more strides would have launched me into space over a 40 plus feet drop. Needless to say this particular piece of information did cause me some degree of annoyance which resulted in my hurling some considerable abuse at Derek and berating him for not having warned me about this obvious danger. Derek's only response to this tirade was "You'd have been alright you would've just bounced." This couldn't care less, attitude from someone I thought was a friend angered me even more and I rounded on him again and accused him of making no effort to assist in the chase. His response, "You didn't really expect me to chase him up here it's to dangerous, that's the benefit of local knowledge." How do you respond to that? The truth is you don't and Derek and I had many a laugh about that particular incident over the years although I did wonder at the time.

After all, it could have been the perfect murder.

I had by now decided to grow a moustache for two, what I considered to be valid reasons at the time. The first was to give the impression that I was in fact older than my years and dispose of my baby face sort of image, and the second, a more vain reason, to hide a rather broad upper lip. I also imagined that the growth of facial hair gave the impression of being that little more mature and might just make me that little more attractive to the opposite sex, in particular, Joyce. The style of the day was known as a Zapata which basically reproduced the look of a Mexican bandit which I suppose, on reflection, was inappropriate for a police officer. Being somewhat indecisive, (not very good for a policeman) I couldn't decide whether I would wear a moustache or not and dependent on my mood on any given day I would shave it off and then decide to grow it again. What I didn't know was that my indecision on this matter was causing the Station Inspector some disquiet and I was duly summoned to his office. Any such summons, no matter who was on the receiving end always generated discussion amongst your colleagues and comments such as "Your in the shit" or "He was in a foul mood when he came in today," was I suppose designed to offer some sort of reassurance. Trust me, that was as sympathetic as you could expect. Previous experiences in the Inspectors Office left me in little doubt that I had not been called in to be commended for good work and his immediate demeanour verified my assumption. On entering his office I came to attention in front of his desk and mumbled "You wanted to see me sir." "Yes, show me your warrant card." This request, no, order, caused me quite a panic as a request to hand over your warrant card was likely to be followed by the words "Your suspended" and I hadn't a clue what I had done wrong.

On presenting my warrant card the Inspector went on to point out that I was not wearing a moustache and that he would be grateful if I would please make up my mind on this subject as he could then make arrangement for a new photograph and warrant card to be produced. I was duly provided with an updated card and I have to say the contrast with that which I had first been issued was like night and day. Instead of a scared looking immature young boy when requested to produce my identification I could now at least present an image of a reasonably mature young man. It would be wrong of me to finish this aside leaving you with the impression that the Inspector was something of an Ogre; in fact nothing could be further from the truth. Inspector Ken Aird was an absolute gentleman who would never do you a bad turn if he could do you a good one and I am happy to say, one of the finest Inspectors I ever had the privilege to serve under.

By now I was probably becoming proficient in dealing with some of the bread and butter aspects of policing and my senior colleagues were allowing me to take the lead in dealing with such things as minor road accidents, Drunk and incapable reports, minor breaches and assaults and other fairly mundane issues which frequently arise. I was still taking a less active part in the more serious incidents and I suppose to some degree I, just like every other probationer was considerably cosseted at this stage of my service. This set of circumstances was however to change dramatically when I was called once more into the Station Inspectors office to be told that I had been temporarily transferred to the Shetland Islands. This piece of news was quite frankly devastating. I had not long gotten over my enforced absence from the County of my birth when attending the Scottish Police College, and this move by contrast, appeared at the time to be even worse. Shetland, after all it was the end of the known world, maps of the area still showed the words "Here be monsters," how did you get there and worst of all, Joyce wouldn't be there. A small ray of sunshine was however thrown into the package with a promise that I would return to Thurso on completion of my term of secondment and I was determined to hold on to that promise even though I knew that the police weren't very good at keeping them.

So it was I was obliged to take my remaining leave entitlement as I had been told in no uncertain manner that there would be no opportunity for leave while I was on the Shetlands and consequently six months was six months. Accepting my fate I made my farewells and steeled myself for what I could only imagine, was the commencement of a prison term.

I got that one wrong too.

CHAPTER 6

SHETLAND

I had packed my cases and found myself even more laden than when I had gone to College.

Well, it was for at least six months and I needed lots of clean clothes as I hadn't got a clue where to start with washing them and as for ironing, I just knew that one was going to be well beyond my limited capabilities.

I blame my mum for that and if I come across as at all chauvinistic, I also blame my mum for that and take my word for it, if you know any chauvinists, blame their mothers.

I just knew I was going to be dressed like a tramp, would most probably starve, and it would be all her fault.

I had concluded that my only hope of survival was to befriend some older women who would want to mother me, or alternatively some married policemen's wives.

I was heading for Shetland with a plan.

Getting to Shetland was another matter.

Travel options today are no different than they were back in 1976 except now I can fly directly to Shetland on a daily basis with an option of ferries from both Aberdeen or nearby Scrabster passing through the Orkney Islands.

Not so in 1976, if you were lucky, weather dependent, two ferries a week from Aberdeen or a short flight from Wick to Kirkwall, overnight stay and onward flight to Shetlands Sumburgh Airport. Luckily I was given the latter option as the alternative was just too terrible to contemplate.

An almost six hour train journey to Inverness with a few hours wait for a connecting train to Aberdeen where after another four hour train journey I would have been obliged to stay overnight before a further twelve to fifteen hours on a ferry.
No thank you!

So it was that I set off, less than enthusiastically on the first leg of my journey. I was met at Kirkwall airport by a local police officer and ferried to Kirkwall Police Station where I was met by the duty sergeant. For once, a young fellow, who was a long way from retirement and just happened to be a Shetlander. John Ratter, although I didn't know it at the time, was to figure quite heavily in my later policing career but for the moment was taking the time to reassure me that I would enjoy my time in Shetland.

I wasn't about to believe him, neither was I willing to believe him at that time. I was quartered for that night with the most wonderful elderly retired couple who lived directly to the rear of the police station. She was an amazing cook and I relished every morsel of the meal she placed in front of me as it was unlikely I would see this standard of meal for quite some time. Her husband also supplemented his pension by producing hand made Orkney chairs and took the time to demonstrate the art of weaving and forming the trademark hooded cover which makes the Orkney chair so unique.

Today these items can easily fetch in excess of £1000 which is some acknowledgement of the hundreds of hours it can sometimes take to produce one. The following morning I was presented with a first class breakfast and shortly after a police vehicle arrived to take me to the airport. The old lady quickly went to fetch her husband with the words "Come along dear, our boy is leaving," which I have to say I found quite touching.

The onward flight to Shetland lasted about 40 minutes passing over vast empty tracts of the North Sea occasionally punctuated by the odd fishing boat battling its way to some port or another. The approach to Sumburgh and passing over the picturesque Fair Isle did however present an entirely different picture as now I could see numerous fishing boats and oil supply vessels plying the seas far below. Surely this was an indication that Shetland was not the backwater that up to now I had very much believed it to be.

The landing and approach to the runway, I have to admit I found quite scary, passing over the lighthouse jutting out on the headland and gaining the impression that you may well clip the light itself followed by an even stronger impression that the aircraft wing tip may gouge a trough in the sloping hillside can be quite unsettling on your first visit. I know that this impression was very much exaggerated in my mind but offered me small comfort at the time.

A successful landing and disembarkation of the aircraft revealed a thriving airport which had long since outgrown its available resources and was crying out for a new terminal building to adequately cope with its fast growing daily business. Helicopters of all shapes and sizes and numerous aircraft, a number of which emblazoned with company names I had never heard of either loading or offloading oil workers was the first real indication that Shetland was buzzing.

I made my way to what I can only describe as a conglomeration of Portacabins joined together creating a considerable enclosed area which housed carousels, boarding gates, offices, booking in desks and a cafeteria, in fact everything you would expect to find at an Airport. I had picked up my very heavy suitcases, made my way to the main concourse and was wondering "What do I do now" when I spotted two police officers standing scanning the crowd. Struggling with my luggage I made my way towards them and identified myself.

"Hello I'm Robert Sutherland, are you looking for me?"

The older officer responded and I immediately identified by his accent that he was most definitely a local. "Doo iss da new polisman, I am Constable Slater and dis iss Constable Porter."

At this point I make immediate apology to all Shetlanders as it is not my intention to show any disrespect to the local dialect with my inability to reproduce it in a written form.

"Right, follow us da car iss outside."

Two things immediately struck me, firstly, they both had the same Christian name "Constable," and secondly I was going to have to transport my own, not inconsiderable luggage some unknown distance to a waiting police vehicle. Nice start!

I settled down in the back of the police car for what I discovered to be a 26 mile journey to the main town of Lerwick during all of which the two officers argued with each other with absolutely no remittance. One half of the argument I could understand as Constable Porter was, by his accent, clearly English whilst the other half of the argument presented by a Shetlander in a somewhat agitated state may as well have been in Greek. I am led to believe, and I am quite willing to apologise if I have been misled, that the Shetland dialect is not too dissimilar to that of Norway and after all that is where you will find the nearest Railway Station. It was going to take me a couple of months before I was completely comfortable with my understanding of the dialect.

At least I managed to take in the spectacular scenery during that journey and I found that it very much reminded me of my home county of Caithness which I was already missing very much. The scenery did little however to quell my sense of foreboding and the thoughts flooding through my head asking "What the hell had I gotten myself into?" I couldn't fail to notice the vast amounts of ongoing construction works, which took on the form of new roads and road layouts, council and private housing and commercial builds.

My arrival in Lerwick was as surprising as my first impressions of Sumburgh Airport.

Here was a clearly thriving and fast expanding town of some 6000 inhabitants with a busy fishing port serving all kinds of nationalities, Hotels, Pubs and an unfortunately limited shopping area at that time.

I arrived at the Police Station, which I learned had, many years before been the island prison and its external façade certainly indicated that this would have been the case. On entering the building I was struck by the sight of what I believed to be the oldest policeman I had ever seen.

John Isbister, pronounced (eyesbister) was seated in a small enclosed cubicle which housed the station radio and telephones and from my perspective his head was perfectly framed in a small window displaying a perfect profile as If he were a picture hung on a wall.

This initial impression was effectively added to by a receding hairline, prematurely greying hair and half lens spectacles perched on the point of his nose. John, I was later to learn, was a highly respected and extremely talented Shetland Fiddler who gave freely of his time to teach his wonderful art to the younger generations of the island. I was then introduced to Sergeant Isbister who in turn introduced me to the other officers on duty all of whom were introduced as Constable or alternatively introduced themselves as Constable. I did however retain my Christian name as I felt that over the previous 21 years I had come to treat the name Robert as an identifying feature somewhat unique to me.

Having been informed of my duty shifts I was then transported to Carlton House, previously the home of the Zetland Constabulary Chief Constable and at that time still in the process of being converted into a hostel for single Police Officers. Quite literally being abandoned at the front door (well what did I expect) I rang the doorbell and the door was opened by a chirpy young fellow with the words "Hi I'm Andy Thomson let me help you with your cases."

I couldn't believe it, here was a guy with a Christian name, just like me, and he was extremely friendly. Andy had just arrived a week prior to me in Shetland and immediately confided that he was finding things rather difficult. He told me that he found the officers he had been working with to a considerable degree, reserved and in his opinion hard to get to know. Needless to say, given my initial observations, I had no difficulty in accepting Andy's insight with regard to what I may expect. I think I was already suffering from a degree of depression, after all I didn't want to be here and early indications were that I wasn't wanted.
"Great Start!"

So it was that I found myself commencing a late shift the following day suffering all the same doubts and trepidations I had experienced on my very first day. Once again I was brand new and faced with the prospect of either being accepted as one of them, or possibly not. John Isbister was the duty sergeant and informed me that I must first meet with the Station Inspector before commencing my duties. Ushered to the Inspectors office door John Knocked and announced my presence. I was surprised to find yet another young sergeant seated behind a large imposing desk and my first thought was "Where's the Inspector." "Ah, Mr Sutherland, we were expecting you three weeks ago." Here was a surprise, firstly the Sergeant spoke with a broad Caithness accent and secondly, not for the first or last time, I hadn't a clue what he was on about. "Where have you been?" What could I think, first day in a new station, already apparently in trouble and once again I knew I was innocent.

Pat Douglas, to retire Chief Superintendent was clearly looking for an explanation and he wasn't cutting me any slack just because we were both Caithnessians. I explained that prior to transfer I had been instructed to take all leave due to me and my transfer date had been set to accommodate that.

Pat seemed to grudgingly accept my explanation but not before making me aware that Shetland had not been informed of this decision and at that time they needed every policeman they could lay their hands on. Innocent as I was I was feeling unjustly guilty and felt obliged to make profuse apology. Having made his point Pat now brushed the matter aside and outlined what he expected of me during my time in Shetland. He painted a picture of an extremely busy undermanned station and left me in no doubt that there was no room for passengers. I was expected to buckle down and get on with the job to the best of my ability. Somewhat reeling from this first interview I was released for my meal break and took that 45 minute period to further reflect on my destiny.

It had by now grown dark before I was instructed to accompany one of the local officers who was enquiring into the theft of a motorcycle. As we commenced our journey to the Shetland Observatory some short distance out with the town's boundary, my colleague detecting my obvious sullen mood decided to make some small talk. "Doo knows, we don't really want you Sooth fella's up here." As an opener for enjoyable conversation this initial remark didn't really rock my boat, certainly not in a positive sense.

That was it, I had enough and this guy was doing nothing to endear himself to me, young as I was both in age and service I let rip with both barrels. "Look pal, for your information I don't want to be here. There are lots of other places I would rather be and I don't need to hear comments like that from the likes of you. I was sent here I didn't ask to come." The aggression with which I made this delivery ensured silence for the rest of our journey and allowed me to seethe without further interruption. Arriving at the Observatory we went directly to the accommodation block where my colleague knocked the door and awaited an answer. When the door was opened a bright light from an uncovered bulb spilled out onto the front area, and from where I was standing did a most effective job of placing the respondent in silhouette.

Although I couldn't see him I once again detected a Caithness accent and strained to make out his features whilst my colleague began to enquire of the whereabouts of his complainer. The guy at the door appeared equally interested in my presence and after a few moments of clear disinterest in my partners enquiry exclaimed "Robbie Sutherland"! It was now I recognized him as an old school pal and one time neighbour Colin Richard. Here was an opening for the usual "What are you doing here?" exchange of demanded information on both our parts and arrangements for later socialising. Things were looking up and I left in much better spirits than I had arrived in. My change in demeanour was not lost on my colleague and resulted in an apology for his initial remark and the beginnings of what was to become a firm friendship. I finished that first evening's duty on a very positive note and although I didn't realize it at the time I was going to enjoy my period of duty in Shetland.

I have already said that Shetland very much reminded me of my home county in relation to its geographic features but not only this, there is also a commonality in place names, surnames and staple employment, fishing and agriculture. This clearly relates back to our common Viking heritage and both island groups and Caithness display ample evidence of Viking sites from the days that Scotland was ruled by this warrior nation. The surnames Sutherland and Sinclair are equally as common in Shetland as they are in Caithness.

I was a Sutherland and my mother had been a Sinclair, added to which one of my many aunts was a Shetlander and her son had served with the Zetland Constabulary in the early sixties and fondly remembered by the older officers. Once all of these facts had been uncovered by my enquiring colleagues it seems I found myself almost immediately accepted into the fold and although still a "Sooth Moother" I now began to find Shetland a very friendly and inviting place.

I was on duty with one of two Sinclair's at the station. Brian and Alan Sinclair were as different as chalk and cheese, one extremely tall and dark and the other much smaller and blonde. In common however I found them both to be extremely fine fellows. Alan Sinclair and I had been instructed to attend the scene of a road accident at the North end of the main island in the direction of the Sulom Voe oil terminal. Road accidents were ten a penny and rarely reported to the police, it was an extremely common sight to see brand new hire cars written off at the side of the road whether as a result of road conditions, drunk driving or whatever and the first we would know about it was when we came across the wrecked vehicle. In this instance what we encountered was a three vehicle accident which had occurred at a junction and the only reason it had been reported was that one of the vehicles involved was a taxi.

Normal practice in these situations is to separate the drivers of the vehicles for independent interview to first assess what has occurred and based on your observations and information gleaned, decide on a course of action. Alan, being the senior officer present, instructed me to speak to the driver of the taxi to get his side of the story. Not anticipating any problem I approached the taxi driver and asked him what had happened.

"I was been to Vidlin."

What was he saying, I hadn't got a clue.

"I'm sorry, could you repeat that? "

"I was been to Vidlin."

No, didn't register that time either.

"I'm really sorry; could you say that again slowly?"

"Yes,…..I…..was…..been…..to……Vidlin."

Yes it was definitely what he had said but I hadn't got the slightest idea how to interpret it By now I was becoming slightly agitated as no doubt the taxi driver was and I was debating how I would once again broach the subject without appearing rude. "I'm terribly sorry but I am new here and I am having terrible difficulty in understanding the dialect, I wonder could you say that one last time?"   My difficulty had by now attracted Alan's attention, I gather, either by my transmitting of sub conscious distress signals or it could have been the agitated taxi driver shouting slowly at the top of his voice

"I……WAS…..BEEN….TO……VIDLIN."

Totally frustrated by this point I became aware of Alan's presence and asked him

"Can you tell me what this guy has just said?"

"Yes, he said, I was been to Vidlin."

The taxi driver had obviously reached the conclusion that he had been talking to an idiot and maybe he was. What you had to know was that Vidlin was a village on the island and the term "I was been" meant "I had been to". There you go, not so difficult when you understand but I quite simply just didn't understand and was of absolutely no help to Alan during the course of that enquiry.

Just to finish on the point of dialect I suppose it did take me a good couple of months to become comfortable in conversation and for that initial period I quite frankly refused to answer the 999 emergency telephone. Emergencies cause most of us to become agitated and as I have already said an agitated Shetlander talking quickly was totally lost on me. On the other hand it wasn't terribly long after when the local Detective Sergeant invited me to accompany him to lunch, I responded, without thinking,

"I was been!"

Living in Carlton Place at the Braehead in Lerwick was a pretty much solitary existence as Andy was inevitably on an opposing shift and our paths crossed but rarely. Watching television was not really an option as Shetland, in 1976 only received BBC 1 in black and white and interference from foreign radio stations was so bad that the TV programme dialogue could only be heard faintly in the background.

Any other form of entertainment, unless you were a drinker, was extremely limited and not only that, my limited wage, barely saw me from pay day to pay day. At that time, after deductions, I was receiving the princely sum of £55 a fortnight and a further £5 was deducted for my free accommodation. Without the free accommodation we quite frankly couldn't have survived as the cost of a bed sharing a room with another five was £35 per week, and that didn't include breakfast.

This was only part of the price paid for the discovery of oil in the North Sea and undoubtedly made wealthy people of a number of Shetlanders. Oil wasn't all positive, the large wages paid by the oil companies took a massive toll, certainly on the police who were leaving the service, some with a considerable number of years service to get their share of the big money. Local Bakeries and other small shops had also been forced to close through staff being attracted to the potential of big earnings, and you couldn't blame them. I won't say I wasn't tempted myself.

Police discipline regulations prevent a serving police officer from owning or running a business or taking up any other form of employment and this regulation was strictly applied in any other area of Northern Constabulary, with it seemed, the exception of Shetland. Although not officially condoned the powers that be actively turned a blind eye to officers taking up part time jobs as without this flexibility there was every likelihood they would leave and seek employment with the oil companies or numerous associated businesses. Jobs were in abundance and just everybody paid more than the police.

One of the officers, a married man with children, cashed in a long term insurance policy and was able to pay £200 for a second hand mark 1 Ford Escort which he promptly fitted with a taxi sign. Eight hours work on a Friday and Saturday night attending country dances would net him upwards of £60 a night. The mathematics wasn't hard to work out, two nights work could net him the equivalent of a month's police wage. This arrangement worked fine when he was on day shift or weekend off but both Andrew and I found ourselves agreeing to work additional hours to cover his much more lucrative activities.

Back shift was 4 till midnight and night shift was midnight until 8 in the morning. This meant that on Friday or Saturday nights Andrew or I would either turn out 4 hours early or remain on shift an additional 4 or sometimes 5 hours to cover his absence. It didn't take long for the bosses to start grumbling once they realised that this officer was never working a Friday or Saturday night Backshift and very little of these two same nights of night shift. The irony of this particular situation was that although Friday and Saturday nights were the most lucrative for his business it was also the two nights which made the most demands on policing resources. It was then that the oil workers although working a seven day week let their hair down and quite literally took the island by storm.

This situation frequently required that officers remain on duty or start early and every hand was needed. Inevitably, the taxi driver was called in and faced with an ultimatum, the police or taxis and there was never really any competition. Before long he was running a small fleet of taxis, employing drivers and making an excellent living. The success of this business allowed him to further expand and for some years he ran a very lucrative haulage business.

The police station was joined on to the Sheriff Court building and a connecting door allowed us to take prisoners directly from the cell block into the court. This was a very convenient arrangement not purely from the practical point of view of transportation of prisoners but also made for an excellent relationship between court and police station staff. A day shift would find one of us fulfilling the role of court officer which I did on a number of occasions. The purpose of the Police court officer was to record the Sheriffs findings for our record purposes, be present in respect of any possible disturbance and at any later date prove the conviction of an individual which has been denied in a subsequent court.

I only ever witnessed the need for the latter requirement once during my service in Orkney when we had to take a Metropolitan police officer up from London to

Kirkwall to prove that an accused person there had been convicted of an offence in London. On this particular day I had been designated duty as court officer and settled down to deal with the mundanity of the task, expecting the usual Breaches of the Peace, Motoring Offences etc. The court procedure was going as expected and the reasonably anticipated fines and sentences were being passed down by the Sheriff up until the point that a usually straight forward drunk and careless driving case was called.

An elderly man in his seventies, who looked like all of our granddad's was called to the dock by the Sheriff Clerk. This old fellow had to be called twice as he was quite deaf and had to be assisted into the dock as he also appeared to be to some degree infirm. The court was as usual packed and the sight of this poor old man being subjected to this indignity drew a murmur of sympathy from the observing officials and miscreants alike. The Sheriff, aware of the situation, immediately instructed the old fellow to sit down and due to his deafness the instruction had to be relayed not once, but twice at greater decibels by the Sheriff Clerk. The Sheriff Clerk, now aware that he was going to have to shout tried to confirm the accused's name and address.

"YOU ARE ***** NEWLANDS (in Shetland pronounced Nowlands) AND YOU LIVE AT *******"

"Uh."

The Sheriff Clerk has by now moved from his desk and is standing looking up at the old fellow in the dock shouting the same question to him. The undignified scenario which was beginning to unfold in this bastion of Law and Order was now beginning to draw low chuckles from the onlookers, including myself. On eventually confirming his identity the Sheriff then asked if he understood the charges against him.

"Uh."

By now leaning well forward and shouting his questions over the court officials located below, who in turn were assisting to relay these same questions to the accused, the scenario was beginning to descend into pantomime.

"Do you understand the charges against you?"

"No."

"Haven't you read the charges Mr Newland's?"

"No"

"Why haven't you read the charge's!"

"I can't read."

The court "Aaaaaaaaaah.!"

"Couldn't you get one of your family to read it to you?"

"No."

"Why not?"

"They never learned either."

The court, "Aaaaaaaaaah!."

These revelations now led to the unusual circumstance of the charges being read out in full to the court, shouted. Looking around the courtroom I could see lots of people covering their faces and stifling laughter and I have to say I was having exactly the same problem.

Eventually we had reached the point where the accused was required to plead guilty or not guilty and he duly pled guilty making the point that he didn't want to waste the courts time. Prior to the Sheriff passing sentence the accused had an opportunity to disclose his circumstances in order that the Sheriff could impose an appropriate penalty. His only income was his old age pension.

The Court, "Aaaaaaaaaah!"

His wife who was also infirm would be virtually housebound if he was disqualified from driving.

The Court, "Aaaaaaaaaah!"

He had never been in trouble in his life before and he was terribly ashamed at his age to be in court.

The Court, "Aaaaaaaaaah!"

This old guy had clearly won the sympathy of all the onlookers who without exception were rooting for him. His offence was in fact quite severe, driving at more than three times over the legal limit, crashing his car into a wall which was totally demolished and writing off his car as a consequence. The Sheriff passed down his sentence. "On the charge of careless driving I can't fine you less than £10 and endorse your driving licence"

The Court, "Aaaaaaaaaaaah!"

"On the charge of drunk driving I am obliged by law to ban you for the minimum period of 1 year and I will fine you £30."

The Court, "Aaaaaaaaaaaah!"

The Sheriff couldn't have been kinder to this old guy and the whole court was happy.

"You will need time to pay Mr Newland's."

Surprisingly, this final comment did not require to be relayed to the old guy and he pulled from his pocket a wallet absolutely stuffed with notes.

"I'll pay now your honour."

Again, without any requirement for repeating final instructions on payment the old guy almost sprang out of the dock and briskly left the courtroom. The whole court now erupted into gales of laughter while the Sheriff, for a brief period, sat with his head in his hands. Everybody had been most efficiently conned.

Over the years I was to find myself dealing with all forms of death and the saddest of these, with the exception of the passing of children, was suicide. Suicide, in whichever form it took was never pleasant and whether the method of death was by firearm, drug overdoses, hanging or whatever it almost inevitably brought with it questions that could not and frequently would never be answered. More often than I care to recall I have been asked the question "Why?" and never once have I been in a position to adequately answer.

A number of reasons such as, Mental issues, financial problems and lost loves are frequently cited in these cases but you have to ask yourself "surely there was another solution." The reason that I bring this up is that this shadow has passed my own door and with a family the size of my own all sorts of tragedies are as I have experienced not unlikely. Lies, Damned lies and statistics is an expression I have frequently heard and the bottom line is, at least in my opinion, and I don't think I am alone, a statistic can only be treated as a guideline.

The accuracy of any statistic is dependent on how the subject is analysed and I have seen many examples of statistics presented in both the negative and positive, depending on what you think your audience wants to hear. In short, clever manipulation can make a statistic read any way you want it to. By the way, I am pointing the finger at every organisation which makes use of statistics and not the police in particular. So, what has this got to do with Suicide?

One of these statistics which frequently rears its head is that the Highlands and Island's of Scotland has the highest suicide rate in the country per head of population.

This may well be true and there is every possibility that I am about to talk through a hole in my head, but a considerable number of the suicides I have personally dealt with were not native to either the Highlands or Islands.

I am now going to relate to two of these incidents, both of which occurred in Shetland, one of which I had some minor involvement with and the other which was related to me by colleagues. We received an emergency call at the police station informing us that a body had been discovered in the public toilets at the pier head in Lerwick and immediately on receipt of this information went directly to the given location.

On arrival at the public toilets we were met by a minor harbour official who was clearly shocked and directed us to one of several toilet cubicles within the toilet block.

The toilet block was, I suppose, of a fairly typical layout with a row of urinals along one wall and a number of partially enclosed toilet cubicles running along the length of the opposing wall. All of the toilet cubicles with the exception of one was lying wide open. It is difficult to forget what we encountered behind that one door.

A young man, a university student in his late teens from the South of England had made his way to Shetland eventually sailing from Aberdeen on the St Claire ferry and arriving in Lerwick at about 7 or 8 o'clock that morning. On disembarking from the ferry he had made his way along the pier directly to the toilet block. On entering the toilets he went directly to one of the cubicles, closed the door and laid down his belongings. From this point I can only surmise the rest of his procedure but from the position in which he was found I suspect the supposition to be reasonably accurate.

I believe at this point he secured a belt to the coat hook fixed to the back of the door and then slipped the loop over his head. With his back to the door and facing the toilet pan he then placed both feet on to the toilet pan itself and lowered his body down the back of the door effectively slowly strangling himself to death. Having the ability to do so, the urge to save himself as he slowly moved into an unconscious state must have been great but the determination to end his life must have been even greater.

We now had to find out who this young man was, where he was from and then make the appropriate arrangements to inform a mother and a father that their son had taken his own life. They would never have an answer to the question "why?" and we were not in a position to explain this tragic act for them.

The nature of this death was unusual enough to prompt some discussion in respect of similar suicides which had occurred on the island. Story telling, no matter what the subject is a past time in which all officers engage and today I believe such a method of passing on information is known as Living History. Living History, I can assure you is, alive and well within the police service.

Frequently you will come across attempted suicides which those who know better and have a much better understanding of the human mind than I would make claim to, categorise, a cry for help. These "Cry's for help" generally, and in my experience most commonly, take the form of drug overdoses. A trademark of this type of attempt is the informing of a second party of the victims intention to take their own life. In most cases this results in some form of intervention, whether by the police or medical authorities and the general upshot of the intervention is that the victim enters a programme of mental health care. This is however not the case with far too many suicides where it is clear that the intention is to, not only take your life, but to be sure that you do.

Although not involved in this incident, the determination of the already described death prompted the telling of another some short time previously. Colleagues had been called to an address in Lerwick following the discovery of a body. On arrival at the address they had been directed to a bedroom within the establishment and here they encountered a method of suicide previously unseen. Within the room they found a large double bed with high headboard and footboard. A rope had been passed around both the headboard and footboard. The rope from the footboard was tied around the victim's legs whilst the rope from the headboard was looped around his neck. The victim then quite simply lowered himself over the side of the bed. Again, the ability to save himself was obvious but the urge to end his life must have been great indeed. I was to encounter a much more horrifying scenario some years later during my service in the Orkney Islands.

Shetland really was, quite a place, here you could find almost every nationality under the sun. A busy fishing port played host to Norwegians, Danes, Russians, Spaniards and several other nationalities including vessels from other Scottish and English ports.

Added to this mix you would find oil workers from all over the world and off course the heavily outnumbered locals. Normal weekdays kept our rapidly dwindling police resources busy enough but weekends, unlike the country dances in Caithness which sometimes felt like the Wild West, this was the real thing. I cannot help but admire the Shetland people for being as tolerant as they were in seeing the crime rate soar and having their normally peaceful existence seriously interrupted.

Local hotels and bars saw their businesses booming and hostelries such as the Excelsior, Queens, Lerwick Hotel and Thule Bar were frequently filled to capacity. As I found on some of my rarely uninterrupted weekends off a visit to the Excelsior bar meant a battle and long wait to get through the often 4 or 5 deep crowd with no hope of a seat at the end of it. I personally found it impossible to have a pleasant evening under these circumstances and conversation with a pal was equally impossible. Maybe I was growing old before my time but I quickly learned to avoid these establishments at weekends.

One particular weekend off I was sitting alone in Carlton House when I received a phone call from the police station trying to contact a couple of dog handlers who had come up to the island to do a display as part of the Lerwick Gala week. Knowing that these two colleagues had gone for a pint to the Excelsior bar and given that the message was urgent I agreed to find them and pass on the information. On entering the bar it was as usual packed to the door and it took me some time before I spotted my quarry squeezed into a corner surrounded by a number of locals. On approaching the group I was to my surprise, immediately identified by a number of females present as the "noo polisman". I was not aware until that moment that I had been subject to some scrutiny by a number of female inhabitants, and my potential merits had been discussed at some length in various quarters. I was most definitely not in my comfort zone as I was feted by a few of these girls, all of whom were vying for my undivided attention. I had never found myself in this position before and I have to admit I found it a bit scary.

The dangers associated with paying a little more attention to one rather than another became apparent when minor tiffs began to break out and I was finding myself playing the part of peacemaker. I began to ask myself, "Were they blind" or maybe they were doing it for a bet, all I did know for sure was that my safest course of action was to get myself out of the situation. I only wish that Joyce, who I was missing terribly, had shown me just a part of the attention I was receiving here.

Not to put too fine a point on it, I am not now, and never have been any sort of oil painting and I put this incident down to the first comment.

"Noo polisman"

I was a stranger to the island as thousands of others were but I was a stranger with a difference. I wore a police uniform and as I have discovered quite a lot of women are attracted to that fact alone and looks just don't enter the equation.

My two dog handler colleagues had been invited to a private party which was being run by the Gala week committee in the pavilion at the local Nicolson Park and I was invited to accompany them. Seeing this invitation as an opportunity to sensitively extract myself from a situation which I was fast becoming extremely uncomfortable with I eagerly accepted. This arrangement was met with a howl of protest and these girls tried their best to convince me to stay with them. I knew I had made the right decision, "I think!"

Anyhow, we set off to make our way to the park and on our arrival there was met by a locked, and apparently empty pavilion. A few groups of locals were hanging about and were without doubt viewing us with some degree of suspicion. A few cigarettes later we had reached the conclusion that we were probably at the wrong venue when a large group of people arrived carrying trays and copious quantities of beer and alcohol. The leader of this group approached us and said "Glad to see you could make it boys" and clearly being at ease with our presence this welcome encouraged the others, previously uneasy with our being there to approach and make conversation. I suppose it was still the early days of the oil invasion and the locals, at that time were still jealously guarding their private celebrations from gate crashers which they had suspected us to be. The party which took place inside was shaping up to be an excellent night with fiddlers, accordion players and no shortage of food and drink. The crack was excellent and I was seriously enjoying myself. I had already managed to extract myself from the earlier situation in the Excelsior bar and thought I had made the correct decision when I very quickly found myself in a worse one.

A very attractive older woman of, I would guess about 40 years of age began to take a particular interest in me.

Even at the then age of 21 I could most definitely appreciate her attributes and was initially flattered by her interest which I considered to be an older woman's mild flirtation with a young man. My two older colleagues clearly identified an opportunity in this situation which I had not even considered and made their individual unsuccessful plays for my by now admirers attention. They were much more men of the world and I was still just a boy, a very naïve boy. As the evening progressed this woman quite literally attached herself to me, wrapping her self around my arm, leaning her head on my shoulder and gooing at every opportunity into my face. As naïve as I may have been even I began to realise where this woman thought this meeting was heading. My attempts at polite conversation only succeeded in making the situation worse when I discovered she was married, had a son and daughter not a great deal younger than me and then went on to introduce me to a man seated nearby as her husband.

I was horrified, had I put myself in the way of a serious kicking, needless to say I had to find some way out of this outrageous situation, not of my making. She then introduced a young girl of maybe 17 or 18 years of age seated next to her husband who I assumed, prior to introduction, was her daughter. Got that one wrong, this was her daughter's friend and her husband's current girlfriend. The husband appeared to be a very amiable fellow and went out of his way to put me at my ease, explaining that although he and his wife still lived in the same house and got on very well, they had both gone there separate ways in respect of relationships and his girlfriend actually lived with him. I have to say, these revelations did little to ease my concerns and if anything had actually made them worse. My admirer, now convinced that I must be at ease with the situation, took the opportunity to leave me in no doubt what she had in mind for me for the remainder of the night and pulled no punches when describing her sexual prowess. Let me assure you, these were not the erotic imaginings of a young man, this was for real. I was wishing I had stayed with the girls at the Excelsior. The police, being a disciplined organisation, took a dim view of any sort of scandal in those days and a young probationary officer becoming embroiled in an affair with an older married woman, no matter how enlightened she and her husband may be, could lead to a charge of "Bringing the force into disrepute."

I was having visions of an early end to my police career while at the same time pondering how I was going to escape from this man eater. After all, I could have been scarred for life. My two colleagues had settled down, taking full advantage of the Shetland hospitality and were by now very much the worse for wear. I, on the other hand, had been very careful regarding my alcohol intake as I knew I had to stay sharp to make my escape. "I was on duty the following morning."

"Lie," that didn't work.

"I was shattered having taken too much drink."

"Lie," that wasn't accepted.

"I was already in a relationship with a local girl."

"Lie," that didn't matter.

No matter what excuse I offered, she wasn't having any of it and my immediate future was clearly mapped as far as she was concerned. When, where and if my opportunity to escape was to arise, I hadn't got a clue and I was once again seriously shitting myself. We left the party in a group of a dozen or more and I found myself being steered in the opposite direction to which I wanted to go. As luck would have it, one of my colleagues had seriously over indulged in the Shetlanders generosity with drink and was being violently sick at the side of the road. Progress was considerably curtailed as a consequence and it rapidly became clear that we had to get him home to bed. A passing taxi was hailed and I grabbed the opportunity to leap aboard with my two friends, making the excuse that they didn't know where to go and I was the only one that had a key to get in. Needless to say this didn't go down too well with my friend who made numerous protests and virtually pleaded with me to stay. I couldn't get away quick enough and thanked my lucky stars for a near miss.

I did on the odd occasion see this woman on the main street when I would be out on foot patrol and it was then that I would make a diversion down a lane or about turn and move away as quickly as I could in the opposite direction. I wasn't in any kind of hurry to renew my acquaintance here.

I have already said that Shetland was an extremely busy police posting and we quite frankly just did not have the time to carry out the more mundane police duties. The demands on our resources just kept increasing whilst our numbers continued to dwindle. Frequent day shifts found us carrying out, an almost shuttle service between Lerwick and Firth camp at Sulom Voe where we made inevitable arrests with the minimum of enquiry time. No matter what penalty the Sheriff decided to impose it could not compete with the Double Jeopardy imposed by the management of Firth Camp. The camp offered all the facilities you would expect of a very high standard hotel of the day and chief among these was the most excellent standard of cuisine I had to that point ever encountered. Any visit by the police was accompanied by an invitation from the security staff to partake of this excellent facility and I, being single and a totally incompetent cook, found myself in heaven.

The oil companies had a strictly imposed rule, any form of misbehaviour or get yourself arrested and you were out on your ear. Added to this was a second rule, no accommodation, no job. These guys could earn as much as £500 a week and maybe more. Even by today's standard that is a very good wage and this was 1976. How many times did I see men throwing away a fortune through an alcohol fuelled moment of stupidity? Little wonder then that we were losing officers hand over fist to the oil companies or associated industries, the police, quite simply couldn't compete.

If we weren't at Firth camp then we were down at Sumburgh Airport checking on arriving and departing Irish flights. The I.R.A. were extremely active at that time and the Prevention of Terrorism Act obliged us to check every departing or arriving passenger, carry out body searches and luggage checks. I have to say, I love the

Irish and Ireland and spent a wonderful fortnight there as recently as September of 2005 travelling throughout the South and a short spell in Belfast admiring the architecture.

Dependent on when you find yourself reading this story, you can replace the word recently with "a long time ago" or whatever you consider relevant. I have every intention of going back.

Anyhow, this process also required that each individual present us with an information card which they completed prior to presenting themselves to us and which we retained for record purposes. This card asked for all the usual information, name, address, date of birth etc and was a simple enough document to complete but clearly not simple enough for some. More than once I came across,

Christian name............Patrick

Maiden name..............John

Surname....................O'Reilly

That wasn't so bad and easily sorted, but then there was the Smart Alec's who would enter their name as Donald Duck or enter their title as Reverend followed by Ian Paisley. I knew who Ian Paisley was, who did they think they were trying to kid, I wasn't nearly as green as I may have been cabbage looking. This little prank may have seemed a good idea at the time but inevitably led to delays in having the offender re complete another card there and then which drew numerous comments of "Arsehole" or other such well chosen expletive from his waiting workmates. Some of these workers had been on the island for three months or more and desperate to get home to their families so I wasn't surprised when on one occasion I witnessed one of these time wasters being fired on the spot by his frustrated foreman.

Justice was frequently swift and often harsh.

I was on night shift when we received an automatic alarm to the police station informing us that the alarm had been activated at the local jewellers in the main street.

Back then, these calls could be routed through the 999 system which has not now been the case for a considerable number of years and with the exception of the rare high priority target all alarms are monitored by central control stations. This demanded an immediate response and I, along with a colleague was instructed to attend. Within two minutes we were standing in front of a smashed plate glass display window where we found various items of jewellery strewn about on the roadway. This was clearly a classic smash and grab and at this point we hadn't a clue what the perpetrators had made away with. Our first priority was to inform the station of our initial findings in order that they could rouse the owner from his bed and then to make a search of the immediate area for any clues.

This was real police work calling for sharp wit and deductive reasoning, just like I had seen on the telly, this was a challenge, this, was the sort of thing I had joined for. Sherlock Holmes had nothing on me. My colleague stood guard over the broken window whilst I commenced a cursory examination of the immediate area. I hadn't taken more than a few steps around the corner when I spotted a young man in a more than adequately lit public telephone box. Something drew me to the conclusion that I should check this guy out. I would like to think that my suspicion was peaked by my gut instinct as a natural police officer but it was more than likely the fact that it was the middle of the night and there wasn't another soul in sight.

As I approached the telephone box the object of my attention turned his back to me and was making frantic attempts to hide his face. I needed to speak to this guy. Opening the kiosk door I was met with a polite enquiry "Yes officer how may I help you." Clearly under the influence of drink and trying his level best to act as normally as possible, without success, he told me that he was trying to contact a taxi and asked if I could possibly help him. At least three items of jewellery lying on the kiosk floor, plus others hanging out of his pocket very much ensured that I could, but it wouldn't be the sort of taxi he particularly wanted. I couldn't help but imagine that this was the sort of scenario you would expect to find in a cartoon but it did happen. Imagine, hiding in a phone box, how stupid was that, it was a bit like an Ostrich sticking its head in the sand, imagining it self to be invisible.

I must have been inspired with this capture and decided to take on a theft that had been reported a few days previously. The skipper of a Hull registered trawler which had been harbour bound in Lerwick awaiting spare engine parts, reported the theft of a number of coils of rope valued at several hundred pounds. I felt fairly safe in making two assumptions. Given the length of time the trawler had been in port, it was a fair bet that the crew had run out of drinking money and one or more of them had taken the rope and sold it on. If I was right, then I supposed that it was most likely that the coils of rope had been bought by a locally based fishing boat. I could have been entirely wrong in both assumptions but based my initial enquiry around these suppositions. My first approach was to the trawler skipper who, although keen to have the matter cleared up in order that he could make a positive report back to the company, took serious umbrage at my suggestion that a member or members of his crew were the most likely suspects.

This, initially cooperative and I would have said reasonable man became so incensed at this that his demeanour totally changed and I found myself dealing with what we termed, a hostile witness. I had taken the lead in this enquiry and he clearly wasn't impressed by this young upstart policeman. Where was his crew? Stupid question, off course they were in the pub getting drunk. Although there were a number of pubs in Lerwick, their most likely watering hole, I reasoned, would be the Thule Bar and that is where I found them.

Trying to interview this lot was no picnic and they left us in little or no doubt that they had little regard for the law and even less for those who enforced it. One of the number, particularly, stood out and was seriously aggressive in his responses to us making thinly veiled threats as to what may happen if we didn't leave him alone. Having taken the measure of these nice gentlemen I have to say I was getting some vibes about Mr aggressive and concluded that he would not win any popularity poll, certainly not with us, and I had detected a slight glimmer that he wasn't so popular with the rest of the crew either. I was obliged to look elsewhere for relevant information and decided to have a discreet word with the barman. Under normal circumstances, speaking to the barman would have been a real shot in the dark, after all these guys are putting money across the bar and that's what business is about. I really wasn't expecting to get anywhere, and probably wouldn't, if it weren't for Mr aggressive.

Seems I had gotten at least one thing right, Mr aggressive had succeeded in making himself unpopular with absolutely everybody including the barman and he was more than willing to land him in the shit. This crew had been good customers, and were spending considerable quantities of cash in the pub every day, with the single exception of our man who was scrounging drink from the rest of the crew. He had apparently run out of cash very early and been a hanger on scrounging drinks wherever he could get them which included approaches to some of the local regulars. Not only that, he had also mysteriously come into some cash and was buying his way back into the rest of the crews good graces. You don't need to think too hard to imagine where my thinking was heading now and I pumped the barman for as much information as I could get. Yes, he had been in the company of two local fishermen quite frequently and the barman was even able to tell me the name of their boat. It was beginning to look like I might just crack this one.

I made my way to where this vessel was docked and spotted two young men working on deck who answered the descriptions I had been given by the barman. On speaking to them I couldn't miss the fact that they were immediately nervous and their whole demeanour was screaming out to me that they were guilty before I had even gotten round to asking them any questions. Take my word for it, it doesn't always work this way but just occasionally it does. Some people just shouldn't get involved in crime and these two were rank amateurs. They were clearly shitting themselves so I decided to approach my enquiry in as gentle a fashion as I could to put them at their ease, gain their trust and assure them that they were not about to be hanged. That was a mistake, me playing Mr Nice Guy only succeeded in giving them the impression that they had a soft touch and as a consequence their confidence grew and they were not about to give anything away. I didn't have a warrant to search the boat and before I would be able to get one there was every possibility that the stolen rope would be gone prior to my return.

The high I had been operating on was fast becoming a low and the thought of giving Mr Aggressive his come uppance was beginning to dwindle in my imagination. Salvation was quite literally just around the corner as the skipper of the fishing vessel appeared and demanded to know what was going on. He was off course quite within his rights and as I began to explain I was hurriedly interrupted by both crew members pleading their innocence to the skipper. These two guys were a damned sight more scared of their skipper than they were of me and I made a decision right then to exploit that fear. The skipper was clearly angry and just looking at him I knew he was a law abiding citizen who wasn't happy with what was going down and not only that, I got the impression that they hadn't convinced him. I continued the, softly, softly, approach with the skipper, apologised for my presence on his boat but told him that I was sure he would understand why it was necessary.

Outlining the circumstances to him I could sense that he was in accord and when I suggested that he should instruct his crew members to recover the stolen property from where it may be concealed he complied immediately. Turning to his crew members he gently instructed them to get the rope and I could see that he was having great difficulty in controlling his temper. A last ditch attempt at pleading their innocence was enough for this man to explode and he now shouted extremely forcefully at these two to get the rope. Both men, heads down, shuffled away and returned in a few minutes with four brand new coils of rope.

Now they were trying to justify their actions to the skipper and he was having none of it and told them that they shouldn't worry about what I was going to do to them but to be more concerned about what he was going to do once I had finished my enquiry. I very much believed that he was going to make them suffer much more than I was ever going to achieve. I was delighted, I had recovered the stolen property, I had arrested the two men who had bought the rope, knowing it to be stolen, all I had to do now was find out who they had bought it from. A final word with the skipper ensured I would be given all the information I required as he instructed his two crew members in how they would deport themselves at Lerwick police station. I was making use of my best and available resource in the shape of the skipper. Back at the police station, a very short interview revealed the single culprit from among the crew of the trawler and there are no prizes for guessing who that may have been.

My colleague and I returned to the Thule bar where the trawler crew had been getting steadily drunker and had by now been joined by their skipper. On approaching the group we were not unexpectedly met by less than complimentary grumblings and veiled threats of violence. I have learned to my cost that police officer or not you disregard this sort of situation at your peril and knowing that I was just about to arrest a member of this crew I knew I had to treat the situation with kid gloves. Shouting over the noise being made by the crew, not least Mr Aggressive, I addressed myself to the skipper and told him that I had recovered the stolen coils of rope.

Revealing this information caused the group to quieten considerably and allow me to carry out a less than shouted conversation with the skipper. I knew that my next revelation, the unveiling of the culprit in the best Hercule Poirot fashion was not unlikely to spark a riot that I might have considerable difficulty in extracting myself from in one piece. I won't say I wasn't afraid, only a fool would claim not to have been, the only thing I did know was that I couldn't afford to show it.

I didn't know how I was going to deal with the consequence of my next action or whether it was the sensible thing to do given the circumstances but I decided to take the bull by the horns anyhow. Here I was in the nearest thing to a Wild West stand off I had experienced up to that point in my police service. Identifying Mr Aggressive as the culprit was met by a loud roar of disapproval, and announcing my intention to place him under arrest found the group rising from their seats and daring me to do my worst. What could I do, I couldn't afford to back down, if I did I could resign as soon as I liked and I had no intention of doing that. I must have had a bit of a death wish in those days but the thought of a severe kicking was much more welcome than to be considered a coward and spoken about by your colleagues who would question if they could trust you to watch their back in an awkward situation. "Oh well, hey ho," it would only hurt for a while, I hoped!

Moving amongst the group I addressed Mr Aggressive and told him that he was now under arrest and he was coming with me to the police station. He had decided he wasn't going and I had by now more than made up my mind that he most definitely was and damn the consequences. In police reporting terms, a violent struggle ensued punctuated with lots of shouting and swearing and most worryingly, lots of jostling and threats being voiced by his crew mates.

I know I received a few half hearted blows throughout the course of this melee but I was not in a position to identify their source and my one concern at that moment was to get my prisoner hand cuffed and out of there. By now we were virtually dragging our prisoner from the bar and although handcuffed he was still managing to kick out and score the occasional hit. We now found ourselves in the middle of what I can only describe as a rugby scrum holding on to our prisoner for all of our worth whilst his crewmates were making every effort to deny us our prize. Preceded by some of the baying crew, we virtually fell out of the bar door followed by the remainder and I shouted to my colleague to draw his baton, which we both brandished with obvious intent at our protagonists. Getting our prisoner into the back of the police car was fraught with difficulty given his intense struggling and the added danger of his mates looking for an opportunity to pounce. I made a few unchecked swipes in the direction of our attackers which although failing to connect left them in little doubt that I was more than willing to open a few heads if I was forced to. This action proved sufficient for them to back off just long enough for us to get in the car but before we could get the vehicle started we found ourselves surrounded on all sides and the police car being shaken from side to side.

My colleague was in some doubt about what he should do next and I suggested that it may be a good idea to "Get us the **** out of here." Mr Aggressive was meantime engaged in kicking the backs of seats and the rear passenger door while shouting for the others to get him out of the car. Gunning the engine we managed to extract ourselves with a considerable squeal of burning rubber and left our adversaries shaking their fists, cursing, and shouting threats of revenge.

Adrenalin pumping through my body I found the time to congratulate myself on a job well done whilst at the same time thanking my lucky stars that I had just managed to get away with it. Arrival at the police station was just the signal for our prisoner to start up again and we had a real struggle getting him in through the back door to the cell area. On entering the building he must have realised that he had lost the fight and settled down somewhat but he wasn't about to give in gracefully. Standing between me and my colleague on the prisoner's side of the charge bar our prisoner was still managing to exude an air of contempt which he was about to voice quite forcefully.

Big mistake! The duty sergeant approached from the opposite side carrying the lock up register and seeing our somewhat dishevelled state, asked what had happened. I outlined the circumstances and the sergeant, who had dealt with our first two arrests, set about the normal lock up procedure.

Given that our prisoner was in the custody area I was instructed to release him from the handcuffs which I have to say I didn't think was a very good idea but orders are orders. The duty sergeant, very methodically placed the large lock up register onto the charge bar and opened it up at the appropriate page, took a number of pens from his pocket and placed them neatly to the side and then very deliberately donned his spectacles. Looking over the width of the charge bar he then very politely and very softly said "Now boy, fits doo name."

"**** off." I immediately cringed and thought to myself "This guy has got a bigger death wish than I had." He had no idea what he was dealing with. "Now, now, boy, dur iss no need for dat sort of language, fits doo name."

"**** off."

I couldn't believe it, he had said it a second time, he was clearly mad.

"Now look boy, I am normally a very reasonable fellow, for da last time, fits doo name."

"**** off you old B******."

I had not a clue about what was going to happen next but I did suspect that Mr Aggressive may shortly be regretting his foolishness. The sergeant removed his glasses and placed them in their case, picked up his pens and placed them in his pocket, closed the prisoner lock up register, which he then raised above his head and brought it crashing down on top of the prisoners head. This last action occurred so quickly that all that I saw was the prisoner slide down the wall directly behind him where he sat for some moments obviously dazed. Meanwhile, the sergeant replaced the lock up register, took the pens from his pocket and neatly placed them as before and then put his glasses back on his face. Now leaning over the charge bar and peering down at a somewhat subdued prisoner, he very calmly said.

"Now boy, fits doo name."

No further problems there then.

The following day the skipper of the trawler was summoned to attend at the police station where he was left in no doubt that he was very lucky that both he and the remainder of his crew were not being arrested and the sort of behaviour they had displayed would not be tolerated. A letter outlining the circumstances was also sent to the vessel owners. I felt I had done a good job and that was acknowledged by senior officers but it didn't prevent the age old practice of a good capture being hijacked by C.I.D. Life can be very unfair at times.

It wouldn't be fair of me to close this chapter without acknowledging some of the laughs I had when I was up there, because believe it or not my period of secondment to Shetland was one of the best things that happened to me and was responsible for shaping me into the confident policeman I believe I became. As I have said I was living in Carlton Place and during my tenure, and that of other colleagues who had lived there before me, had become known as a bit of a party pad.   Young, single policemen, and strange goings on, much of which was extremely exaggerated, not by us, but people who for one reason or another were interested in what we got up too. We decided to do nothing to harm the mystique which we felt gave us that little extra interest. Andrew Thomson, myself and by now David Inglis, a new recruit, were living permanently at this address and played occasional host to visiting officers from elsewhere in the force. Any such visit almost inevitably signalled either a full blown party or at least a lively drinking session, but I have to say that the liveliest event I was involved in was my own leaving bash.

A number of young and old colleagues from the police station, an indication I hope of my acceptance as one of them and a number of my own friends and quite a few nurses from the Gilbert Bain hospital had all made the effort to turn up to wish me farewell. I should maybe say that I had been interviewed by the Chief Inspector prior to my leaving in an effort to convince me to stay in Shetland. Although I had seriously enjoyed my time there, I had very much decided to cut my nose of to spite my face when I discovered that every other officer who had been there prior to me had been allowed at least one flight home during the secondment period. I had been told that I wasn't entitled to any so I suppose I was bristling a bit and had decided I was going home. Anyhow, this party took place the night before the morning I was due to leave.

Not the best idea ever conceived.

The party was going extremely well, there was no shortage of booze and some of my colleagues had provided, or at least their wives had provided loads of snacks to soak up the drink. As the evening progressed, the older married couples began to drift away eventually leaving all of us young ones which must have numbered in the low teens.

We were having a great laugh and people were beginning to disappear, I assumed because they were pairing up and having a good time. Without realising I soon found myself drinking, accompanied only by my good pal Colin Richards when somebody shouted, "Come here Robbie." I made my way out into the corridor and found it packed with my male friends and a number of young nurses who had decided to give me a bed bath, except not in a bed. Escape wasn't an option as my only escape route was being blocked by Colin.

Now I realised, he was the Judas, the one you would least expect, what are mates for. What made it particularly hard to bear was that he hadn't even demanded thirty pieces of silver. I now found myself being dragged into the bathroom where I could see that the huge bath was all ready and filled with water. It was the middle of winter and it was cold water. I had decided that there would be no point in struggling and the sooner I let them get on with it the sooner it would be over.

The next thing I knew I was hoisted up and unceremoniously dumped fully clothed, into the bath. I hadn't anticipated just how cold the water was, it was freezing and as soon as I hit the water I was gasping as it had driven all the breath from my lungs. I began to thrash about while they kept ducking me under and water was being spilled over onto the bathroom floor, were they ever going to let me out. After what seemed like an eternity, probably only a few seconds, I managed to get out of the bath and stood dripping and freezing on the bathroom floor, begging my friends to let me pass in order to get dried and changed. I was so cold I could hardly speak. They had no intention of letting me pass and everyone was just standing there laughing hysterically.

Yes, off course, from their point of view it was hysterically funny but I, in the meantime was very likely to die of hypothermia. My friend Colin must have felt a moment of compassion and threw me a large bath towel and my only other option was to strip there and then. More howls of laughter which was doing nothing for my macho ego, what was so funny about me trying to get dry. Andrew Thomson seemed to be taking a particular delight at my obvious discomfort so I felt it was only right that he should experience the moment. I grabbed Andrew and dumped him in the bath and I have to say he looked like he was enjoying the experience every bit as much as I had. Now that I had somewhat recovered I could see why all my friends had found the whole thing so funny, I thought it was hilarious, Andrew on the other hand wasn't laughing so much now.

David Inglis was the next one in and all of a sudden it began to dawn on the others that they were all going in, girls as well. People were running away and hiding in the various bedrooms whilst being searched out by a rapidly growing, very wet revenge squad, and delivered to the two baptisers. It was becoming a little bit like a conveyor belt operation and friends were turning on friends, you couldn't afford to trust anyone.

Girls hiding in cupboards or under beds were being enticed out by their best mates who were assuring them that the whole operation had stopped while the revenge squad silently waited to pounce and deliver them up for immersion. It went on for hours, punctuated by more drink to strengthen our resolve to get everybody. Carlton Place was populated that night with loads of 20 plus youngsters in considerable undress lying where they had collapsed as nobody could go home until they had dried their clothes.

That's how I left the place the following morning when I was picked up by a police vehicle to drive me to Sumburgh Airport. It had been a great party, I had pretty much loved every moment of my time in Shetland and I was sad to leave.

Just like the Terminator "I would be back."

CHAPTER 7

BACK TO THURSO

Every bit as much as I had enjoyed my time in Shetland I was delighted to be home and even though I had forced myself to learn to wash and iron clothes and was becoming something of a passable cook I was more than happy to let my mum regain her rightful role. I had accumulated some leave and time off for overtime worked so I had at least a fortnight before I was due to recommence duty at Thurso. I needed it all when I visited my poor little Singer Chamois which had been garaged for six months and was showing considerable signs of neglect. It was going to take me a fortnight to get it fit for its M.O.T. and back on the road.

My dad was desperate to hear about my time in the islands and I was able to keep him entertained with loads of stories that I haven't put down in this, as I write, hopefully, book. The experiences of 31 years are quite considerable and I could probably fill three books with stories so I had to make a decision to be selective.

By the time I returned to Thurso I discovered that they had introduced a new shift system. The duty times had remained the same but instead of a bit of a lottery as to whom you may have been working with we were all now teamed up with three other officers and a permanent shift sergeant. I suppose it was the Sergeants who had come of the losers as previously they had not been required to work beyond 2 in the morning other than in an emergency. Now they were working the same patterns as the Constables.

I was no sooner back on duty than I received the by now, not unexpected summons to the Inspectors office. What had I done this time? Ken was sitting behind his desk and I did the usual come to attention accompanied by "Sir you wanted to see me?" "Yes Robert, I've been hearing great things about you from Shetland."

By Kens account I was apparently the man, and they had been sorry to lose me, but Ken wasn't about to let me rest on my laurels and left me in no doubt that he expected the same level of commitment in Thurso. I had become confident enough now to pretty much assure him that was exactly what he would get. For once I left the Inspectors office with a bit of a spring in my step and when quizzed by my colleagues about what level of shit I had landed myself in this time, I disappointed them by saying "He told me I was wonderful." Stick that one in your pipe and smoke it boys.

During my time in Shetland I had managed to speak to Joyce a couple of times on the telephone but it didn't prepare me for meeting her once again in the flesh. I knew I was still in love but she still didn't know that she was meant to be in love with me. How frustrating was that?

I was manning the front office, writing reports while taking telephone calls and responding to radio messages when, what I believed at the time to be a fairly old guy was shown into the front office. This old guy was waiting to see the Inspector and knowing that a new Sergeant had been appointed to Thurso I assumed that this must be him. Being as young as I was I thought this guy must be nearly dead as ageism was as rife in the mid seventies as it is today except it hadn't been given a name yet. Being alone with him I felt it only polite to introduce myself.

"Hello I'm Robert Sutherland are you the new Sergeant."

"Yes, how are you doing Robert, Donald Mackay," was delivered in a broad Caithness dialect.

Donald was to be my new shift Sergeant, and without exception was the best I was ever going to work with throughout my service and I worked with a lot of good guys.

A number of years after Donald retired I met him at a local County show in Wick where all the retired bobbies would accumulate in the police incident caravan for a cup of coffee and a gossip about old times. I loved these impromptu meetings and would be absolutely transfixed by the stories they would tell and never wanted them to leave. I chose this venue to reveal to Donald exactly what I had thought the first time that I had met him and asked what great age he had reached at that time. "I was 38 Robert." I was 40 the day that I asked the question.

My shift colleagues were my old friend George Douglas, John Henderson and Ronnie Gunn. Ronnie and I had served our time as fitters together although I had been at Dounreay and Ronnie at the neighbouring HMS Vulcan, Nuclear Reactor Test Establishment. I was to serve as Ronnie's best man some time later when he wed his long time girlfriend, Kirstie. Ronnie had been brought up in Castletown and although at that time the small harbour there still saw some shellfish boats operating he had never really gotten into that type of cuisine to the degree that I had. I had been reared on it.

All kinds of fish, even Whale steaks on the still odd occasion that we saw Whalers enter Wick harbour, Crab, Lobster, Scallops and Whelks, if it came out of the sea I ate it, and still do to this day. Ronnie and I were on night shift and as we walked the streets we would frequently meet a particular group of local fishermen who would congregate in the town centre. Angus Macintosh, (Angee) and his crew, most, if not all of whom have long since passed away would be standing having a final blether before making their individual ways home to bed after a hard days fishing. I always enjoyed getting the crack with Angee and he always took the time to have the crack with me.

He was one of the most unassuming men I had ever met and you would never have guessed that he was a real war hero. Angee would, only when pressed, tell me of some of his adventures during the Second World War, and I, as usual, was enthralled to listen. Unusual, even back then, Angee was a prolific user of snuff, and his stories were frequently interrupted to allow him to delve into his pocket, withdraw his snuff box and take a deep draw of the powder. He had been a Royal Navy diver during the second war and highly decorated, even receiving the Croix De Guerre from the French Government at the cessation of hostilities. Angee would never tell you that, and it was something I had to find out for myself. I had a great admiration for Angee Macintosh

Anyhow, I had as usual met Angee during the course of my wanderings and he, knowing my fondness for seafood greeted me with. "Robert, the biggest crab I've ever seen in my life is lying in the wheelhouse of the boat. We pulled it up in the net tonight. If you want it go and help yourself." I didn't need to be told twice and thanking Angee I quickly made my way back to the police station. I did wonder, if it was the biggest crab that Angee had ever seen it must be some monster. Ronnie and I made our way down to Scrabster harbour to where Angee's boat was tied up and I climbed down the pier ladder and entered the wheelhouse. He hadn't been exaggerating, here was the biggest crab I had ever seen and was ever likely to see. It was huge and took up the full area of a fishing box. I could hardly believe what I was looking at and neither could Ronnie but all I could think about was how delicious it was going to taste.

We didn't have much of a kitchen in the Old Police Station and the first problem I encountered was that we didn't have a big enough pan to boil this thing in. Not to be outdone I began a search for a suitable receptacle in which to cook my crab as I wasn't about to be beaten, I was eating that crab come hell or high water. I eventually found myself outside in the garage and here I had my Eureka moment when I spotted a very large fire bucket. This was the beast that was going to do the business. Back in the station I frantically scrubbed the bucket until I had the interior as clean as I could possibly get it and began boiling kettles of water with which I filled the bucket and placed on the cooker ring at full belt.

It must have taken me half an hour before I had a suitable quantity of water boiling on the stove, and I can't believe that this operation was doing anything for the efficiency of the stove itself, but I had a single minded purpose and it was eating that crab. Eventually, I dumped the crab into the boiling water, cruel I know but that was how you cooked them, and waited impatiently for the feast to be ready. Let me give you a little advice; never eat a hot crab, it should first be allowed to cool before you indulge. Although this very concern had been expressed by our colleagues neither Ronnie or I were about to listen, and very quickly set about devouring this monster.

I savoured every mouthful and Ronnie just didn't seem to know that he had had enough and I still have memories of him sitting there, surrounded by broken crab shells with his uniform heavily decorated with crab meat which had been dropping from his chin. Although having been offered their share of the bounty our other colleagues had chosen to refuse our generosity whilst at the same time predicting that the whole thing would end in tears. I, and Ronnie in particular, felt we had a duty to eat the lot.

The following night I turned up for duty as usual only to find that Ronnie had phoned in sick.

He spent three days being violently sick accompanied by a severe case of the runs, he obviously didn't have the constitution that I had, but then again I had been eating the stuff for as long as I could remember. Both of us were obliged to listen to lots of "I told you so's," and "You wouldn't listen you got what you deserved." They were right, I got what I deserved, a lovely crab and I enjoyed every bite.

I saw what seemed like countless tragedies over the years, some of which I had a direct involvement with and others where I found myself engaged on the periphery of the necessary enquiries. I was on duty in Thurso and if my memory serves me correctly it had to have been a Sunday or Monday night. My reasoning for reaching this conclusion is that there were only two of us on duty and some rest days between shifts were staggered. Information we were receiving over the radio indicated that some fairly serious road accident had occurred on the opposite side of the county somewhere in the Wick beat.

As the situation began to unfold it became apparent that some form of articulated vehicle had driven off the road and over the cliffs at the Ord of Caithness. The Ord of Caithness is the natural and obvious geographical boundary which separates the two counties of Caithness and Sutherland and at its highest point must be some four or more hundred feet above sea level. I don't know the exact height but for the purpose of this story it isn't really relevant other than to say that this is the very point at which the lorry had left the road.

Officers were being recalled to duty and further assistance was being sought from Thurso where we began to make the necessary arrangements to send more men to the locus. Needless to say, this was a major incident and it was a case of all hands to the pump, including the other emergency services and a real need for the expertise of the Coast Guard. Although I didn't attend at this particular incident I listened intently to all the radio traffic and followed the progress of the event as it continued to unfold.

It must have been about 5 o'clock in the morning when I received a telephone call from the control room at Wick. I was informed that this accident was a triple fatality and all three deceased appeared to have been identified. It seemed that two of the deceased, although belonging to the Aberdeen area, were working in Thurso and living in lodgings at an address in the town. Provided with the names and other necessary information I was instructed to attend at the given address in order to confirm that these two men did live there and had been expected to return that night. This sort of duty is never nice and certainly not easy but at least in this case I could find a little comfort in the fact that I wouldn't have to give terrible news to a parent or husband or wife.

In that sense, it appeared, on face value that this was probably the most clinical duty of that sort of nature I had so far been instructed to carry out. At that time of morning, you won't be surprised to learn it is necessary to wake the household and I found myself hammering on the door for some time before I succeeded in gaining a response. The enquiry was urgent and I couldn't leave without obtaining the information I required. The front door was opened by a youth of probably eighteen or nineteen years of age who not unsurprisingly was struggling to comprehend what was going on through the haze of recent sleep.

I asked if I could come in and he showed me through to the sitting room where he enquired of me if anything was wrong. Until such time as I could confirm that he did know these two men I was not in a position to reveal too much information. A short conversation confirmed that both men were in lodgings at this address and they had gone home for the weekend with the intention that they would return to Thurso the previous evening. He had thought it strange that they hadn't arrived but put it down to a delay of some sort and had thought little more of it. Satisfied that I was at the right address and fairly certain that I had enough information to confirm identities I then told the youth what had occurred.

His reaction was, as I would have expected, shock, but otherwise he took the information very calmly and he gave me no reason other than to believe that these two men were nothing more than two casual lodgers. "You had better tell my mum, I'll get her." A couple of minutes later a woman of maybe 45 or 50 years of age just risen from her bed, came into the sitting room and enquired if anything was wrong. I once again asked if these two men were lodgers at that address which she confirmed.

"Has anything happened?"

I told her that I was sorry to give her bad news but both men had been killed in a road accident at the Ord of Caithness earlier that morning. Over the years I have seen various reactions to news of a tragedy ranging from stunned silence to hysterical screaming, all of which is entirely understandable and you have to try to put yourself into the shoes of the person receiving the news. This poor woman screamed and then collapsed on the floor at my feet. Both her son and I immediately went to her aid and assisted her to get to a seated position on the couch where she sat with her head in her hands sobbing. My surprise must have been apparent when I looked at the son who said "Maybe I should have told you, my mum was getting married to the older guy next month." Yes, he should have told me. I swore that I would never be caught out that way again.

As the story of that night began to reveal itself it seemed that the two men had indeed been returning to Thurso. They had driven up from Aberdeen in their company van which had broken down in the village of Helmsdale some 40 miles from Thurso and given the lateness of the hour they decided to hitch a lift the rest of the way with the intention of returning the following day to pick up the van. Having managed to get a lift as far as the Causewaymire (the link road between the then A9 and Thurso) it seems they had failed to make the remaining 20 miles and decided to head back to Helmsdale. An articulated lorry heading South had picked them up, and unfortunately for them the driver was drunk. The lorry left the main A9 at a parking area at the top of the Ord, ploughed through the heather and down the steep slope of the brae before plunging to the beach below.

I can't even begin to imagine the horror of these last few short moments, but the memory of that incident stayed with everyone for many years until the scar of the lorry's descent was erased from the hillside when it was eventually overgrown with heather.

As much as the fixed shifts was designed to ensure a minimum staffing level we frequently found ourselves with only two officers on duty. This circumstance would arise because officers were on leave or attending work related courses or indeed sick.

The fact that at that time our secretaries didn't work nightshifts, meant that one of us had to remain office bound.

Another night shift, and again only two of us on duty. My colleague for that night was Jimmy Scott a great big fellow who you would never have guessed was the son of a fairly fire breathing and much respected local minister. I didn't know what a minister's son should look like but if asked to imagine one I would never have visualised Jimmy. Jimmy or Crusher as he had been dubbed by the rest of us was a gentle giant but more than capable of displaying the benefits of his size if the need arose. He was also the training constable and had responsibility for ensuring that the likes of me stayed in line and did the job properly. The poor guy certainly had his work cut out with some of us and I probably counted amongst that number. Jimmy was also one of the most generous people I met in the police, he would never see anybody stuck and he would give you his last. I know that my last remark is something that you may hear about a lot of people but it was so true in respect of Jimmy. More than once I had seen him taking the last of his money from his pocket and giving it to someone who he felt was in greater need.

Jimmy was in the office and I was out on patrol checking the night beat premises when he radioed me to say that a 999 call had been received reporting a disturbance in the Spring Park area of Thurso. Spring Park is a fairly large, at that time, council owned estate inhabited mostly by locals and rarely required police attention which remains very much the case today. Spring Park is a nice area to live in but occasionally even the best of us can have an unexpected reason to call for the police.

Obviously emergency calls do get a priority response and I attended immediately at a street where every house was in darkness with the exception of one which was lit up like a Christmas tree.

The front door was lying wide open and as I approached the woman of the house, on spotting me, began screaming, "He's going to kill him." Who was going to kill who, thank god she wasn't shouting "He's killed him," as that would have meant I was too late. Pretty much all of these houses have a very small front porch just big enough to hold a small table or maybe chair and on entering the porch a 90° turn brings you directly to the bottom of the staircase. Here I encountered a scene that did nothing to answer the question; who, was going to kill who. Framed towards the top of the narrow staircase and clearly attempting to make his way forward I saw the back of this very large man who by his demeanour and clear threats of violence was in a very aggressive frame of mind. At the top of the staircase I could see a very slightly built man at least half the size of the other who was brandishing a very large piece of wood which was hovering ominously, directly over the big guys head. You may understand my confusion but based on the little guys screams for the other to "get back," I formed the opinion that he was most likely to be the victim.

I immediately ran up the stairs and forced my way in between the two protagonists and standing with my back to the little guy I ordered the big fellow to back off while at the same time shouting at the little guy to put the wood down. The big guy was staring directly through me and growling which I should have realised was an indication that he wasn't about to comply, but I didn't. The next thing I knew the big fellow stretched out his arm, which he wrapped round the right side of my body and quite literally flung me aside back down the staircase where I ended up in a heap having landed on top of a telephone table which came off second best.

It was at this point that I realised that my commanding presence wasn't about to resolve the situation and decided that a more basic approach was going to be required.

"Ho hum" here I went again, but at least this time the odds were shortened. I drew my baton and shouted at the woman to phone the police station and tell Jimmy that I was in serious need of assistance. I ran up the stairs again and once more forced my way in between the two. This time I was brandishing my baton over the big guys head and most worryingly the little guy was brandishing the wood over mine. I wasn't about to be caught a second time and when the big guy made another lunge at me I lifted my leg and kicked him as hard as I could with the soul of my boot. This did the job and he fell backwards down the stairs landing in the porch and I ran as fast as I could after him.

As he began to rise and was trying to regain his balance I took the opportunity to kick him again which succeeded in propelling him out through the door to land in a heap in the front garden. Running after him I shouted to the woman to close and lock the door as I adopted a position with my knee in my prisoner's side, a firm hold of his shirt collar and threatening him with as hard a bashing as I was capable of delivering if he dared to move from his prone position. This was the situation Jimmy encountered on his arrival and as he ambled up the path he asked me what had gone on. I quickly explained to him, in between gulps of breath exactly what had happened to which he replied, "That wasn't really necessary, look!" At that Jimmy bent down and plucked the guys glasses from his nose which resulted in the most incredible change.

All of a sudden he was pleading for the return of his glasses and swearing that he wouldn't cause any more trouble. He came along like a lamb. It seems that without his glasses he was blind as a bat. Well, I didn't know, did I! Yet again, another lesson, in the value of local knowledge.

There were two fairly major changes about to occur in Thurso. The first and in my view the least important was our pending transfer to an all new, all singing, all dancing police station that had been built in the grounds of the existing station. My initial thoughts during the run up to this move was, was it really necessary and what was wrong with the station we were in. It struck me as just a big waste of public money and we were absolutely fine where we were. It would have been more appropriate for the powers that be to have replaced our ageing police vehicles which were in my view, very much an embarrassment at the time.

Our general purpose vehicle was a mustard brown Hillman Avenger estate car fitted with a large blue globe that gave the impression that it was growing out of the roof. It was also fitted with two tone horns that unlike the sirens of today gave of a loud "Bee Baw" sort of sound. It was very unusual to hear any form of siren in those days but if you did it was a fair bet that it either belonged to an ambulance or a fire engine. The police were definitely not guilty of indiscriminate use of any form of emergency signalling device other than in the most extreme circumstances.

Our Avenger was another reason that we didn't use the horns as on the rare occasion that we did a historical and apparently untraceable short in the wiring system was pretty much guaranteed to kick in. Now you would find yourself driving through the town with the blue light flashing and instead of the expected "Bee Baw" drone of the horns it was either a "Bee Bee Bee Bee" or a "Baw Baw Baw Baw" dependent on which note it had decided to fail on. However I digress, it wasn't until we were in the act of moving into the new police station that I realised just how bad a state of repair the old one was really in. As the building emptied and the ravages of time became much more apparent I could only conclude that I had been wrong and it was only fit for demolishing.

Just prior to our move the second bombshell struck. Wick, being the divisional headquarters and having responsibility for Caithness, Orkney and the Shetland Islands very much merited the presence of a Chief Superintendent, a role that was filled by a very imposing man who hailed from the Strath of Kildonan, Bill Mackay. I always got the impression that the higher up the promotion tree you rose, the more approachable as an individual you became and in my opinion Bill Mackay was very approachable. He had commended me to the Station Inspector on his first unannounced visit to Thurso when he had called at the front hatch dressed in plain clothes introducing himself as the newly appointed Divisional Officer.

I didn't know him from Adam and I wasn't about to let him over the threshold until he had shown me his warrant card, which he did. It wasn't that I was particularly security conscious but what were the bets if I hadn't asked him for identification that I would have got a severe bollocking. No fly's on me. Our close proximity to Wick meant that we received frequent visits from Bill and we were pretty used to his presence in Thurso.

There had been no indications that this visit was likely to be different from any other until the Inspector came out of his office and instructed me to go and fetch Joyce. I wasn't told why they wanted her but I did have a sneaking suspicion that a summons from the boss was unlikely to be good news. Joyce lived with her aunt in Towerhill road and when I arrived there and told her that the boss wanted to see her but I didn't have any idea why, she immediately surmised that she was about to be transferred. I seriously hoped that she was wrong and I hovered about in the station to see what was happening. When Joyce eventually emerged from the Inspectors office she was clearly upset and when I asked her what was wrong she told me that she was being transferred to Wick.

She was devastated and showing it, I was devastated and trying my best not to show it. I was happy working in Thurso and even happier knowing that Joyce was there, and who knows maybe I would have gotten round to declaring my feelings sometime.

That was much less likely now so I made up my mind right then to make it my business to get myself transferred to Wick.

The police frequently find themselves involved in searches for missing persons and over the years I have been involved in quite a few. An elderly man of about 85 years of age had gone missing from his home in the village of Dunbeath when he failed to return from his afternoon walk. Receipt of this information immediately sparked a full scale search and I amongst many others found myself out on the hill inadequately equipped for the conditions and it was looking like a long night. Police, Coastguard and local volunteers were strung out across the hill carrying out a grid search of the area and as the evening progressed it was beginning to look like we would not be successful and none of us were giving much for the old fellows chances. As darkness fell the search was called off until daylight at about 5 o'clock the next morning. We were all in position as instructed the next morning and by this time I believe we were all of the opinion that we were looking for a corpse.

The news of the old fellow's loss had by now spread and as a consequence the amount of searchers had substantially increased allowing us to carry out much wider sweeps of the massive area we had to cover. A couple of hours and several sweeps of the terrain later saw the arrival of the R.A.F. Search and Rescue helicopter and we were called in to take a short break and a snack. A number of members of the R.A.F. mountain rescue team were also in attendance and strung themselves out to begin searching from where we had left off. As we sat in small groups drinking our coffee and eating sausage rolls the conversation inevitably got round to whether or not we were likely to find the old guy alive. Given the cold night it had been and the age of our missing person the general consensus, pretty much across the board was that he would have been unlikely to have survived the night.

The pilot of the helicopter had very quickly been briefed on the situation and we watched him lift off and very quickly disappear over the hill in the distance. Within a couple of minutes, and certainly no more time than it would have taken him to land and take off again, he was back, and landed nearby us. Out of the helicopter door, looking a sight fresher than any of us young guys, came the old fellow. He was waving like a Hollywood star on the red carpet at the Oscars and we all responded by clapping and cheering his arrival, he looked as if he was revelling in every moment of the attention.

How, at his age, had he managed to survive? A big part of his survival was clear for all of us to see, he was bulging all over. He had insulated himself using sheep's wool which he had gathered from the hill and from fences and stuffed the wool inside his jacket and trousers. This was clearly enough to maintain his body warmth and he looked as if he had spent a more comfortable night than many of his would be rescuers. He had also been a gamekeeper for all of his working life and even at 85 was as hardy as they came, not only that, he was at home on the hill and he knew it like the back of his hand. In this case we saw a happy conclusion to our search and I was going to witness a few more happy conclusions over the years but unfortunately considerably more not so happy.

The Police, and I know this may sound a bit of a contradiction given my previous comments about building new police stations, were always very careful with budgets.

Just to put the record straight, building police stations came under the heading of Capital spending and had no effect on our operational budget. When it came to spending money on equipment I always felt that the police operated a very much Scrooge mentality and that exists even today. I don't suppose that can be a bad thing and I am sure that any tax payer reading this is bound to agree. Absolutely nothing was bought without showing a good operational reason for supporting the purchase which over the years very much placed us in the position of being the poor relation amongst all of our partnership agencies. Just occasionally however this reluctance to spend money would be taken a little too far.

Each command area budget is broken down into various headings, each of which is allocated a cost. For example Wages, Uniform, Overtime, equipment and lots of others right down to how many miles each of our vehicles travelled in any given year and associated petrol costs was religiously scrutinised. A memorandum was circulated to the Sergeants and all staff regarding a projected over spend in respect of our mileage allowance and as a consequence appropriate steps had to be taken in order to bring it back on target. We were now restricted to a maximum mileage allowance of eleven miles per shift. The memorandum almost inevitably concluded with dire threats of reprisal and woe betide anyone who exceeded the allocated allowance.

Eleven miles, it had to be a joke didn't it, we did more than that just doing one circuit of the more remotely located properties on the night shift, which I may add we were expected to do twice a night. What about the nightly mail runs between Wick and Thurso, that ran away with twenty-two miles every return trip and we couldn't rely on the Post Office as we had to get court reports and other urgent communications through on a daily basis. Court attendances, prisoner escorts, emergency calls and countless other reasons made it impossible for us to comply but we were forced to try our best. As I have said before, "It is an ill wind that blows little good!" and that's exactly how it fell for me.

Every night of the night shift, because I was travelling daily from Wick to Thurso, Donald Mackay would let me finish at 7.30 am in order to deliver our mail to Wick police station. This situation suited me down to the ground as it got me home to bed slightly earlier and it suited the police because it saved twenty-two miles a night and occasionally more when I would pick up return mail on recommencing duty.

This arrangement brought me an even greater benefit because every morning when I arrived at Wick, Joyce would be starting her early shift. The first morning I walked into Wick police station and was speaking to the duty sergeant Kenny Mackintosh who I had never met before, our conversation was interrupted by a loud shout of "Robert!" and Joyce appeared at speed from the control room and quite literally wrapped herself around me. I was most definitely enjoying the moment while at the same time trying to appear indifferent as if this was the most natural thing in the world, while Kenny, clearly taken aback uttered the age old police phrase, "What's going on here."

No surprise to me, Joyce had already managed to endear herself to everyone in the station, including all the bosses and Kenny had already formed the opinion that there was more to our relationship than the friendship we both claimed. I only wished. I got a great reception every morning that Joyce was there although maybe not as demonstrative as the first one but it certainly strengthened my resolve for that transfer.

It wasn't too long after, that an informal interview with Bill Mackay secured for me exactly what I wanted, a transfer to Wick and the beginning of my campaign to win Joyce round.

After all, I was on home ground and Joyce, I had concluded, was vulnerable.

CHAPTER 8

WICK

How lucky was I, back in my hometown of Wick, living at home, no travelling expense and best of all, although not working on the same shift, seeing Joyce more frequently.

Life was good.

I found myself on shift with, of all people Kenny Mackintosh, Kenny was a great guy and I must say possibly the smartest policeman I ever worked with. Kenny, in uniform, looked like a tailors dummy but much more animated with an incredible personality. Kenny, in casual clothing, glittered. Kenny, in a boiler suit looked better than I did in my best suit. You wanted to hate him but you just couldn't. Other than Kenny I was working with John Campbell and a transferee from Fife Constabulary, John Grierson. His full name was Alexander John Grierson and I took to calling him A.J, and we were to become firm friends until this very day.

I had worked a backshift and my first week of night shift found AJ on leave, which meant I was on duty with Kenny and John Campbell. Just after midnight Kenny and John set of to carry out a motorised patrol and I buckled myself up to walk the night beat property. Because it was dark it was also an opportunity to walk Joyce home to her flat which was on my route and she was more than glad of the company. A quick cup of coffee with Joyce saw me back out walking the areas of Upper and Lower Pulteneytown and back to the station about three hours later to have my meal break. Kenny and John arrived back for their break and then continued their motor patrol while I walked the town centre night beat property. Completing this duty I then set about checking the Wick night beat property and found myself returning to the station just in time to book off.

The second night was the same, as was the third and fourth and I was rapidly getting seriously pissed off at what I thought was the unfairness of the situation. Here I was walking the property in all weathers while my two colleagues were driving about in a police car, and as far as I could see, doing bugger all constructive. The only consolation I had, but it was a big consolation, I was having a cup of coffee with Joyce every night. I decided I had to do something about it and the only course of action was to confront Kenny with what I believed to be a genuine grievance. I hadn't taken this decision lightly as a Constable of my short service daring to question a Sergeant was pretty much unheard of. Bolstered by Joyce's support who had assured me that Kenny would listen to what I had to say I decided to take the plunge. It was meal break and we were all in the station when I asked Kenny if I could have a word with him.

Kenny quite naturally agreed and we went into the Sergeants office where we could speak privately. How would I start the conversation, Kenny gave me an opening by asking if anything was wrong and I said "yes." I outlined my concerns and emphasised what I believed to be the unfairness of the situation and Kenny listened without interruption. When I had finished having my say Kenny looked up at me and I fully expected to get a severe blasting and put in my place, but at least I would have gotten it off my chest. Instead, Kenny, as always an absolute gentleman said "You are absolutely right, all I can do is apologise, and assure you it will never happen again." What a man, he was an absolute gem and every bit as good as his word as I knew he would be.

It was 1978, I was a fully fledged Constable having successfully completed my probationary period and I was expected to behave like one. AJ and I had started an early shift when I spotted in the Station Log Book a report of a smash and grab from the local Woolworth's store. This report had just come in and we were sent to investigate. A side plate glass display window had been smashed and a number of small portable radios removed from the most easily accessible shelves. We didn't have much to go on, in fact nothing, so we had to make our own luck. Speaking to some local taxi drivers who were inevitably on the go at all odd hours, I came up with a few possible names but one that stood out like a Belisha beacon. I was fairly convinced that this was most likely to be my man and decided to give him a call.

Other than a gut instinct I had little to go on and Grierson wasn't slow in reminding me of the fact but he was willing to play along. We called at my suspects address and prior to entering I suggested to A J that he should let me do all the speaking, a suggestion which he was more than ready to agree to as he couldn't see how I expected to get anywhere with the enquiry. The door was answered by my suspect's mother and when I asked if he was at home she told me that he was still in bed and invited us in. Standing in the living room of my suspect's home I asked his mother if she would be good enough to tell her son that I wished to speak with him.

Being no stranger to her son's fast expanding abilities at becoming the subject of police enquiries she didn't ask any questions and went into a bedroom directly off the sitting room and I heard her say "The police are here to see you again." Now was the time for me to play my bluff and I wasn't sure that it was going to work. He emerged from the bedroom wearing a shirt and boxer shorts and responded to my presence with a reasonably cheery "Aye, Aye Robbie." As he was walking towards me I said "You know why I am here ***** go and get the radios." Without breaking step he immediately about turned and with a "Right you are Robbie," entered the bedroom, and almost immediately re emerged with half a dozen portable radios. I had cracked it again and best of all Grierson was flabbergasted, he just couldn't believe what he had just witnessed and if I am being entirely truthful I was having difficulty with just how easy it had been myself. To this day he continues to tell the story to whoever will listen.

Another day shift and only two of us on shift. A.J. was however in his element as we had just taken delivery of a brand new shiny motorbike and he was desperate to try it out. I personally, had never taken the slightest interest in them and couldn't quite understand what all the excitement was about. Anyhow it was just after lunchtime on a lovely summer's day and the town centre was very busy. A.J was somewhere in the rural area of the beat trying out the new toy and I had just returned to the station when a 999 call was received from the post office reporting that a young man had just smashed up the public telephone kiosk to the front of their building. Armed with a brief description I immediately left the station and as soon as I emerged onto the main street I could see and was able to identify the culprit standing with several others outside one of the local banks. Knowing the subject to be violent and suspecting, given his most recent action, that he most probably wasn't in the best frame of mind I radioed the office and asked for immediate assistance.

The group hanging about outside the bank was made up of a number of local neer do wells who spent most of their time here when they had run out of drinking money.

I couldn't afford to hang about waiting for A.J to return as I had no idea where he was and how long it would take him to return. I approached the group of about a dozen or so young men and was greeted with some mumbled "Aye, Aye Robbie's" to which I made a similar response. Some of these guys had been at school with me but I knew the whole group by name and it was no surprise to me that they had chosen the lifestyle they had. A few of the number would in years to come move away from this lifestyle, hold down a job and become respectable married men with families but the majority were either destined to serve prison terms or die young following a life of alcohol and drug abuse. Not really the sort of thing you expect to read about the idyllic existence of life in the far North of Scotland but that is part of the reality of the situation.

I now decided that it was time to speak to my suspect and once again approached the subject in as delicate a fashion as I could as I wasn't keen to prompt any trouble given how busy the street was with locals and tourists. I am sure that to any bystander it must have looked like a pleasant conversation between some young men and the local bobbie. I told my suspect about the nature of the report and he vehemently denied any involvement whist at the same time shouting and swearing at the top of his voice. I warned him to curb his language and quieten down but he was clearly having none of it. What made matters worse was he was now being egged on by the others who were taking a great delight in both his and my discomfort.

I knew that I had to bring the situation to a rapid close before it got worse and placed my hand on his shoulder and informed him that he was under arrest, followed by the classic line "I need you to accompany me to the police station." At this point he shouted "I'm ******* going nowhere," pushed me away with his left hand and at the same time took a wild swing at my head with his right fist. If it weren't for the initial push he would have landed a real haymaker on the side of my head but as it was I landed on my back in the middle of the pavement while my hat rolled into the middle of the road. Not the most dignified position to find yourself in. My suspect had by now taken to his heels and was running away up the main street cheered on his way by the hysterically laughing others. Calling for him to stop I rapidly took of after him and managed to close the gap quite quickly bringing the pursuit to a spectacular end with yet another first class rugby tackle. My prisoner was putting up quite a fight and the whole incident must have been very entertaining for locals and tourists alike but I could well have done without it.

After a short struggle I did manage to get him to some degree subdued and frog marched him down the road with one arm up his back and my free arm holding him across both shoulders. His friends immediately began to harangue me and accuse me of publicly assaulting their mate and they were going to see to it that I got my come uppance. I was in no mood to listen to their rantings and forcefully instructed one of their number to pick my hat up and place it on my head, which he immediately did. I then took a moment to tell them that if they wished to make a complaint that they should call at the police station and make it formal. I had clearly left them in no doubt that I wasn't about to take any shit from them.

As I began the remainder of the short journey to the police station the local C.I.D. car pulled up alongside me and Sandy Rosie got out and helped me handcuff and place the prisoner in the back of the vehicle. I was shattered and at the same time furious while being in no mood for the comment which was now made by Sandy's C.I.D colleague. "You can't arrest someone like that off the street." Bad enough to take these comments from Ned's on the street without having to listen to the same from your colleagues. "What would you know you weren't ******* there." Sandy could see that I was angry and turned to his colleague and said "Shut your ******* mouth."

I had rarely known Sandy to demonstrate his own anger quite as vocally as he was one of the most laid back, easy going guys I knew.

We returned to the police station and within a couple of minutes the public foyer was packed with the no hoper's from along the street, all of whom were claiming that I had assaulted their friend and insisting on making official statements. Every last one of them was spoken to and every last one gave fabricated statements which were careful to avoid the truth of the incident. To give the prisoner his due he wasn't making any complaint, he knew he was out of line and knew what he had done, he was guilty and wasn't about to make matters worse for himself. A complaint had been made against a police officer and it had to be investigated and to be honest it wasn't looking good for me. If you were to believe their story it was looking like this extremely aggressive police officer had approached them on the street and began to pick on a totally innocent member of their group before commencing to give him a severe thrashing. Nobody came forward to support my side of the story but to be fair they probably didn't imagine that they had to, from a bystanders point of view it would have looked fairly cut and dry. A couple of days later it was Sandy Rosie who came to my rescue. He had been at a local garage carrying out an enquiry when an innocent remark by one of the mechanics sparked his interest. "That was some battle on the street the other day." Sandy asked him to expand and it seemed that he and an apprentice who had been accompanying him had witnessed the whole incident. Their description of the event tinged with comments like "The bobbie got knocked to his arse" may not have been very flattering but more than sufficient to make a lie of the statements already given.

Sandy asked both mechanics if they would be willing to make a statement about the incident which they were more than willing to do and succeeded in putting an end to the complaint against me. It wasn't the first time and most certainly wouldn't be the last that I would find myself the subject of an unfounded discipline enquiry. It was to be another thing that I was to learn went with the territory.

Once again A.J and I were on day shift standing on the junction of Bridge Street and High Street, the town's main thoroughfare when we were approached by an off duty Joyce. I never tired of her company and was as usual delighted to see her. "Hello Boy's," there it was again and it never failed to give me shivers. "What do you think of my hair?" She had just had her hair done and I didn't like it. "Well Robert!" I decided to tell the truth and told her that I preferred her hair the way she normally wore it. This comment didn't go down to well and with a Harrumph she stalked away without further comment.

I had obviously succeeded in upsetting her, and worse, Grierson immediately surmised that I fancied her. How can you work that out from what basically amounted to an insult.

"You fancy her."

"No I don't."

"Yes, you do."

"I'm telling you, I don't, "

"And I'm telling you, you do."

It was beginning to sound like the lines you would expect to hear spoken in a pantomime.

"Okay, your right, I do."

"Well why don't you ask her out?"

"She would never go out with me."

"How would you know if you've never asked?"

No argument with that comment, how did I know?

Grierson now took it upon himself to act as matchmaker and between him and his wife Wilma, formulated a deception designed to quite literally entrap Joyce. I can't say that I undertook to involve myself in this situation without some degree of trepidation as I felt that it could bring a long term friendship to a rapid end. Grierson briefed me on the plan, I was to tell Joyce that because he and his wife were new to the area and didn't really know that many people, they hadn't had any real opportunity to socialise (blatant lie). There was a buffet dance due to be held in one of the local clubs which they would like to attend and it would be nice if they could go along with another couple. I wasn't sure, it sounded like a bad idea to me, but A.J had no intention of letting me of the hook and I was instructed to invite Joyce that very day when she came on duty at 4 O'clock. I needed to get Joyce on her own as I didn't want any of my colleagues to witness my embarrassment when she ripped me apart and told me that I was the last person she would ever consider going out with. For once I wasn't looking forward to a meeting with Joyce.

So it was I found myself maintaining observations on the rear door to the police station whilst trying to give the impression that I was engaged in completing the mileage record book in one of the vehicles. It was taking an age for Joyce to appear and I was getting cold feet. I just wasn't sure that I could go through with it. There she was it was time for me to make my play. "Joyce, can I get a word with you." Big smile, followed by an enquiring "Yes Robert!" I noticed that she was once again wearing her hair the way I liked it but I wasn't about to read anything into that. Head down, and avoiding eye contact as much as possible, I related the circumstances as instructed by Grierson, followed by "I wondered if you would like to come along?" "Yes Robert." Not quite the response I had expected, and I didn't know what to say next.

As non chalantly as I could possibly muster I said "OK I'll tell Grierson and I will buy the tickets." Joyce then walked away with a cheery "See you later." Woo Hoo, I was ecstatic, jumping the height of myself, Joyce was coming out on a date with me, I couldn't believe my luck.

Along came the night and I picked Joyce up at her flat and onward to Grierson's house where Joyce met Wilma for the first time. A quick cup of coffee and then it was off to the Dounreay Sports and Social Club, a well attended local dance venue which had first class live bands playing almost every weekend. Joyce, I have to say was wearing a very fetching two piece outfit which emphasised her gorgeous figure and I was to learn some time later had been bought specifically for the occasion. We were sitting having a few drinks when the compere announced that the buffet was now ready and everyone should help themselves. A.J and I being the gentlemen that we were suggested that we would fetch the food and the two ladies should remain seated, and let's not forget, I needed to impress. With two plates of food and a precariously placed trifle on top of each I made my way back to the table. Presenting Joyce with her share of the take, time seemed to move into slow motion as the trifle, I swear, appeared to take on a life of its own and tumbled from on top of the plate, splat, ending up dead centre in the middle of her lap. I wanted to die. A look of horror appeared on Wilma's face that came nowhere close to the same look on mine. Grierson on the other hand was having great difficulty in preventing himself from erupting into gales of laughter.

I had blown it, big time.

Apologising profusely and seeing the look of pure embarrassment on Joyce's face I couldn't help but think that I had failed to impress in spectacular fashion. Joyce, accompanied by Wilma, made their way to the toilet where she tidied up while I in the meantime was being called every stupid ******* under the sun by Grierson. I didn't need reminding, thank you very much but he was taking a perverted delight in my predicament. Joyce had fairly successfully removed the offending stain and I managed to recover a few Brownie points when I asked her to dance and was able to display a degree of ability at the pastime. Joyce loved dancing and I was happy to dance all night with her. Not the most successful first date in the history of first dates.

We were on a backshift and carrying out a routine motor patrol on the A9 South of Wick when we spotted a vehicle which wasn't showing any lights and was all over the road. Clearly this driver was either drunk or under the influence of some other substance but whatever the case he had to be stopped, he was an obvious danger to himself and other road users. Succeeding in pulling the vehicle over, Grierson and I although being no strangers to drunk drivers were shocked at just how drunk this guy was. He was lying over the steering wheel gibbering. The procedure was no different other than we had to have his vehicle removed from the road by a suspended tow as it was in far too dangerous a condition to drive.

On completing our station procedure and obtaining two samples of blood for analysis we then set about examining the car. I had never in my service up till then, nor indeed any time thereafter seen a vehicle which had been driven on the road in such a condition. Every tyre was so bald that canvas was showing through on the tread and parts of the walls, the whole front of the vehicle was being held in place with twisted pieces of electrical wire, the lights didn't work, the brakes were almost non existent as was the handbrake, indicators didn't work, brake lights didn't work, it had no windscreen wipers and hopefully by now you are beginning to get the picture. This vehicle was a death trap and to add to the myriad of Construction and Use offences the driver didn't have a driving licence, insurance or excise licence for the car. I suppose it goes without saying that he didn't have an M.O.T. either.

I have only listed some of the long list of faults that this vehicle displayed and to say that we threw the book at this guy would have been an understatement. On releasing the driver from custody we informed him that the car could only be removed from the police station by means of a suspended tow and that we never expected to see it on the road again. The vehicle lay at the police station for about six weeks and during that time we used it for training purposes and asked young probationary officers to try and identify all the faults on it. The boot of the car had been jammed and we were unable to gain entry to it but when a young probationer with a background in car repair succeeded in getting it open, lo and behold it was full of stolen tools. This was the reason then that our accused had been in no hurry to return to the police station to remove his property. After preferring additional charges of theft to his already long list of offences the car was removed a few days later.

It couldn't have been very many weeks later but for some reason or another I was working a day shift with Joyce. We were walking the town centre area when I replied to an urgent radio message instructing us to return to the station in order to attend a serious road accident on the Causeway Mire. Although by this stage in my service I had attended countless dozens of road accidents I always felt a tinge of trepidation when I heard the word, SERIOUS. The truth is you never knew what situation you were about to encounter.

The Causeway Mire, now a continuation of the main A9 road, basically cuts a diagonal across the County of Caithness from Its East coast to that of the North and the town of Thurso. This was one of the rare instances that high speed driving displaying blue lights was easily justified. On arrival at the location and having negotiated the line of inevitably parked vehicles backed up in both directions I had real difficulty in registering what I was seeing. The very same vehicle which we had hoped we would never see again was partially located on the carriageway and part of a lay by with debris strewn in all directions. The car, I can only describe as being virtually disintegrated.

I ran to the nearest side of the vehicle and was stopped in my tracks by the body of an eight year old boy lying on his back and clearly dead. I didn't have to have any medical training to know that there was nothing I could do for this child. Joyce, who had been carrying out the necessary initial procedures and making the area reasonably safe for us to operate in arrived at my side and was equally stunned at what she saw. She told me that a second casualty was lying on the opposite side of the vehicle and that he, apparently the driver, appeared to be alive. I went to the other side of the car where, exactly as indicated by Joyce, I found the second casualty lying on his back in a drunken stupor. I can only imagine that the casualty, (The same person as we had previously stopped driving this vehicle.) had been so drunk, that he had been extremely relaxed when thrown from the car thus sparing him serious injury. As I leaned over him I could hear him mumbling some words I couldn't quite make out so I got down on my knees and said "What is it?" "Don't get the police, don't get the police."

I dare not put down on paper what my feelings were at that moment, but needless to say, they were a million miles away from what you would expect of an apparent professional. Of course I was upset, I wouldn't be a human being if I wasn't. As much as you know that you can't get personally involved you inevitably do, but I had a job to get on with.

What worth did the court place on this child's life? One year's imprisonment and a ten year driving ban! With time off for good behaviour he could serve as little as six months and petition the court for restoration of his driving licence after five years. I had long since learned that I couldn't afford to dwell on the past, and although that is probably exactly what I am doing as I write, what I did know, was that life had to go on. It would be quite easy to decide that you had enough and pack it in but the job did have lots of lighter moments and I did consider it a very worthwhile profession.

I was still maintaining my campaign to win Joyce over but by now treading ever so wearily given the tragic events of the first date. I had allowed quite a lapse of time before I dared ask her out again in the hope that the bad memories had faded into the past and she might be willing to give me a second chance. Another Grierson instigated plan was put into action and involved a nice intimate meal at his home. Once again, to my surprise, Joyce agreed and we enjoyed a pleasant evening in each other's company. On walking her home I very much dawdled to extend our time together and when we reached her flat, rather than wanting to invite me in for a coffee, I think she felt obliged to invite me in.

Detecting what I felt was a degree of reluctance and although I was desperate to spend as much time as possible with her, I politely declined, making the excuse that I was on duty the following morning. A number of dates and refused invitations to coffee later, (I was playing hard to get.) I had eventually decided to take the bull by the horns and tell her exactly how I felt about her. Let's face it! I had to tell her sometime. I suppose the catalyst had to be on Valentine's Day when I had secretly sent her a large bunch of Carnations and she received no less than a further four bunches of Roses. Why hadn't I sent Roses? Quite simply, the Florist had run out! I knew then that I had more than one rival for her affections and if I didn't do something about it I was going to lose her. I was not about to let that happen and if I was going down, I was going down fighting.

Surprise, surprise, she felt exactly the same way about me and was just about giving up hope of my ever declaring my feelings. To put this Mills and Boon romance to bed, we married on the 26th of January 1979, in the midst of a blizzard, and I was the cat who had seriously got the cream.

I suppose I should mention my very good friend John Lawrence who served as my Best Man on the day. John was a serving officer with Grampian police and an ex soldier. When I told him that I was getting married, along with his wife June, they travelled up from their home in Forre's to meet Joyce for the first time. We had arranged to meet at the Queen's Hotel in Wick and John had immediately formed an impression about Joyce which was well wide of the mark. Both John and I had roughly the same service, about three and a half years and I suppose by now, both considered ourselves reasonably experienced police officers. As we stood at the bar fetching some drinks, John, expressing his opinion of Joyce, turned to me and said, "Very nice, but aren't you doing a bit of cradle snatching?" Joyce then, and to this day, doesn't look anything like her age and easily passes for much younger.

I realized where this was heading and was quite happy to have a laugh at his expense.

As we sat down with the girls, John directed his conversation to Joyce and began to talk about the police service. "So, do you think you will like the police Joyce?" I would have to say that this question was delivered in an ever so slightly condescending tone. "Oh yes." "And what service do you have now?" "Eight years."

John's mouth fell open and you could have knocked him over with a feather. June and I erupted into gales of laughter as she had obviously gleaned much more information from Joyce when they had been sitting alone together. June leaned over to John and said "That will teach you." It was a great ice breaker and we all got on like a house on fire.

Just to finish on this subject, there had been quite a few mumblings to the effect of why she was marrying me as no doubt she could have done considerably better. I will freely admit that I was in agreement with this thinking and there was nobody more surprised than me when she turned up at the church. Two theories spring to mind. She married me for my money! I still didn't have any. She had done something terrible in a former life and I was her penance. That's the one I am inclined to run with.

CHAPTER 9

C.I.D.

The power's that be had decided to place me in the Criminal Investigation Department for a period of six months. I was to be trained up in photography and scenes of crime examination in order that I could fulfil that role in event of staff shortage. Wick only had one full time Detective Constable and a Detective Sergeant at that time and their workload was quite considerable. I was delighted and very much looking forward to the experience and Joyce had decided that I needed a new wardrobe.

So it was that I was dragged into the men's department of Fred Shearer's Drapery store on the Cliff Road in Wick. I wasn't permitted any input into what I was going to be wearing and all decisions were made by Joyce and Raymond, the store manager. Having been side lined allowed me time to browse and there, in a rack of what must have amounted to about a hundred casual jackets I spotted an absolute monster. As far as I was concerned this was the jacket of many colours, stood out like a sore thumb and couldn't begin to imagine what sort of idiot would wear it. I was destined to be that idiot! Loaded down with shirts and matching ties, co-ordinated trousers and that jacket I left the shop dreading the laughing stock I was about to become. Luckily, I had got that one seriously wrong and when Kenny Mackintosh commented on how smart the jacket was, I knew that Joyce had got it absolutely right. I never again questioned my wife's taste in anything, other than me.

The C.I.D. at that time was staffed by Sandy Rosie and Detective Sergeant Tommy Nairn. Sandy was a local man with incredible knowledge of his craft and the ability to get on with absolutely everybody. I often wondered how the department would operate without him when he eventually retired but it didn't take me too long to discover that there is no such thing as an indispensable man. Tommy, on the other hand, hailed from Inverness, and if there is such a thing as a stereo typical policeman, it certainly wasn't Tommy.

Tommy told tall tales, and more often than not placed himself in the role of the hero and expected us to believe everything he said, which we didn't. On the rare occasion however, something would happen which would cause us to re-evaluate our opinion to disbelieving only 90% of his stories and reserving judgement on the remaining 10%.

I was dealing with a particularly tragic sudden death. A German tourist of about 35 years of age had been holidaying with his wife and two young daughters, camping at John O'Groats. When his wife had awoken in the morning she found her husband dead in his sleeping bag. As is not unusual in many of these cases, there had been no indication of illness and the man had made no mention of feeling unwell. These circumstances always dictate the requirement for a post mortem examination and the need for the police to take possession of the remains. The local policeman at Mey was dealing with the practicalities of the enquiry while I was trying to convey, as best I could, the procedure, to a grieving wife. This poor woman had no English whatsoever and I was obliged to converse with her through her ten year old daughter who had been learning English at primary school. I was having considerable difficulty in conversing with the woman when I became aware of someone standing behind me. I didn't turn around at that point and after about a minute a voice cut in to the conversation in what to me appeared to be fluent German. This was Tommy. He took over, and very quickly the situation had been fully explained and arrangements made to transport the family home.

About two months prior to this incident, Tommy had arrived in the office with a "Teach yourself German." Kit. A tape recorder, tapes of German language and headphones designed to be worn whilst asleep were all part of Tommy's plan to learn the language. Sandy and I were sceptical to say the least but on this occasion I was more than happy to have been proved wrong. I really don't know if this meant that Tommy was particularly clever or just vulnerable to suggestion.

I was working a late turn and Joyce was working a 4pm until midnight shift, and was out of the office engaged on some enquiry. I was alone, in the front office, when the public counter buzzer sounded. On attending the counter I was met with what I initially assumed to be a couple of waif's and stray's, and was more than surprised when the more confident of the pair introduced himself, in a broad Glaswegian accent, with the words, "We ur the noo Polis." I can't say that my immediate impression of this pair was good, and if anything, particularly un kind, as I thought to myself, "My God, what are we employing?" I invited them in and announced the arrival of Constable's Norman Kinnaird and David Murray to the duty sergeant.

Robert Gunn, the duty sergeant, who we had christened "Robert,Robert," in order to avoid any confusion between him and I, welcomed the new arrivals and informed them of the arrangements that had been made for accommodation etc. I have to say, the similarities between Robert and I were striking. He was about 6'3" tall to my 5'10". He was tall and slim while I was little and fat, and to cap it off he was about 20 years older than me. I don't know which one of us should have been the most insulted.

Anyhow, I was tasked to transport Norman Kinnaird to Thurso whilst David Murray remained behind in Wick, where he was to be stationed. On my return to Wick, some hours later, I was met by a much displeased Joyce who was rather unhappy with our brand new colleague. "That new fellow!" "Yes! what about him?" "I don't like him." "Why?" "When I came back to the office and met him, I asked if he knew where he was staying, and when he said no, I said, hasn't Robert told you where you are staying. He said, Robert? Ah! the wee fat fella wi the moustache." "What did you say?" "I told him that you weren't fat, you were cuddly, and my husband!" Hard to believe, but David was to be the first of many waif's that Joyce would mother over the years.

There most definitely was a rift that existed between uniform staff and C.I.D. The uniformed officers considered detective's to be somewhat elitist whilst they in turn, had a less than flattering opinion of their uniformed counterparts. I could never accuse Sandy Rosie of having been guilty of that attitude, but immediately I entered

the department, my uniformed colleagues tarred me with the same brush. I was very

much in no man's land. I wasn't a detective, and I wasn't one of them.

I would have to describe Sandy as the nearest thing to a Canadian Mounty I had

ever encountered, he always got his man, no matter what it took. We had received

a number of reports of housebreaking, to of all places, the local undertaker's. I

suspect that Sandy viewed this as a personal affront, as it had been going on for

some time and we hadn't managed to put a stop to it. What sort of person break's

in to an undertaker's, and why? We hadn't got a clue, and let's face it, where is the

art of detection, without clue's? Unknown to Tommy or I, Sandy had decided to

take the bull by the horns, and every night, for a number of weeks, no matter what

shift he was working, secreted himself, hidden amongst coffin's, in the undertaker's

shop.

Night after night Sandy lay in wait and it was beginning to look like he was wasting

his time when he spotted a torch beam shining through the workshop window. This

had to be it! Sandy hunched down amongst a stack of semi prepared coffins and

from the dark, watched the progress of the housebreaker. Sandy allowed his man to

crawl in through a service hatch from the outer yard and get well in to the premises

before he pounced. Rising quickly from the midst of the coffins, Sandy called out,

"Stay where you are!" The housebreaker, seeing Sandy appear from amongst the coffins must have thought that he was seeing a corpse rise from the dead and promptly screamed, and fainted. I probably would have reacted in exactly the same fashion, but then again, I wouldn't have been breaking in to an undertaker's, not for a pension of pot lids.

The post of Detective Inspector had been discontinued for some years in Wick and was now about to be re-instated with a new appointee to the role. As I was the only plain clothes officer on duty the day of his and his family's arrival, I was tasked to pick them up at the airport and transport them to their hotel. I knew that the new man was a Shetlander but for some reason, I had not been furnished with a name on the note that Tommy had left for me. I was particularly delighted when John Ratter, the sergeant who had tried to lift my spirits some years earlier, stepped off the aircraft. John was a new arrival to the area and I did everything I could to make their transition to living in Wick, and setting up their new home, as trouble free as I could. I like to think that John may have been as pleased to see me as I was to see him.

John, I discovered, was very much a hands on sort of guy and had decided that he would work shifts along with the rest of us. I would have to say that he was one of the new breed of senior officers, and anyhow, being a Shetlander, it was no surprise to me that he was not about to let promotion to senior ranks change who he was. With only 12 years police service, to be promoted to the rank of Inspector, although not unheard of, was still pretty rare. I also found him a real breath of fresh air in his dealings with other senior officers, some of whom were inclined to interfere with often delicate enquiries and did, on the odd occasion, cost us a detection, because of an insistence that we made an arrest before we were properly prepared. I never knew John to roll over for anybody and frequently witnessed raised voices when John would be telling it like it was.

Again, I was on an early turn alone when, as I had come to expect, as local businesses were opening to start the day's trade, we received the report of another break in. This time the perpetrators had gone to the rear of one of the local Café's and ice cream shop where they had broken into a number of parked ice cream van's, removed the cash float from each and made of with a considerable amount of cigarettes and tobacco. A number of factors suggested to me that the thief's, rather than having made away with their ill gotten gains, were more likely to have hidden them somewhere with the intention to return later and pick them up. You may ask how I had come to that conclusion. First of all, we were heading well into the summer and it wasn't falling dark before 10pm at night and was broad daylight again by 3am in the morning. The area was frequently busy until well after midnight and the amount of property they had stolen was likely to have needed a vehicle to carry it away, and I was fairly confident that would have been spotted. That was my logic and I was convinced I was right.

I had done everything I could at the locus of the incident and obtained all the necessary information I required to complete a report, but before I returned to the station I had every intention of testing my own theory. Being a local, I had a very good knowledge of the area and began a systematic search of what I surmised to be the most likely hiding spots. About two hours into this process I was beginning to lose confidence in my theory and began to make my way back to the station checking likely hiding places en route. I do believe I had given up and was making what was likely to have been my last scan of the area. I walked into a row of long since ruined dwelling house's and made my way through the remnants of a couple of rooms, when there, stacked neatly in front of me, was hundreds of packs of cigarettes and loose tobacco. I can't describe the feeling of having gotten it right, I was ecstatic, I had found the swag and now all I had to do was put the icing on the cake and lock up the bad guy's. I was on a roll and I was confident I was going to get them.

I now had to set up a watch and remain on duty in order to carry it out. Any overtime has to be authorised and I contacted John to apprise him of the situation and within minutes he joined me at the station. The uniform duty sergeant was made aware of our intention and instructed to pass the information on to the incoming sergeant should the watch be more protracted than we anticipated. That was going to prove to be a real understatement! As surreptitiously as possible we ensconced ourselves behind a ruined wall which allowed us an excellent view, and settled down for an unexpectedly long wait.

We had been waiting for getting on for six hours, in the most uncomfortable of positions. It was cold, darkness was beginning to fall and we had decided to give it another half hour or so before we would give up and pass the job onto another team of officers. Even though it had already been a long day, I wasn't too keen on this idea as I felt very strongly that this was my capture and I wanted to stick it out. Just then we were alerted by the sound of footsteps and people conversing in hushed tones. Shrinking as far back as we could behind a large fallen beam, we witnessed the arrival of two well known local tinkers. A more unlikely pairing would have been difficult to imagine. Dishevelled, dirty and smelly would be a fairly accurate, general description of many of that ilk then resident in Wick, and remains very much true to this day. They were both in their mid twenties, neither of them capable of holding down any form of job, and content to live on the generosity of the welfare state for the rest of their lives. Back then they would have been universally described as "Waster's" whilst in today's politically correct climate we are obliged to use the term underprivileged, or describe this pair as socially excluded. I still think that the term "Waster's" paints a more accurate description of this sort of blood sucker. I must now apologise for that little rant but some things can get right up my nose and put me off on one. So please believe me when I say sorry and back to the story.

The first of the two was tall, skinny and even from a man's point of view, pretty ugly, whilst the second member of the partnership was particularly stunted with the bandiest legs you ever saw in your life and every bit as ugly as the first guy. This pair undoubtedly stood out in a crowd. The reaction of the smaller of the two, on seeing the array of ill gotten gains, pretty much convinced John and I, that he had not been party to the initial break in. "My God! Where did you get all of this?" His accomplice replied "Hdoom shne wiv sleek." Or something equally unintelligible, as they both began to fill their pockets. Now, was our moment to pounce, "Police, stay where you are, you are both under arrest." John and I had prepared ourselves for a bit of a struggle, but what happened next left us both surprised, to say the least. On being taken unaware by our appearance, both bad lads performed what I can only describe as a comedic leap into the air, followed by the smaller of the two leaping onto the taller and begin to pummel him with his fists about the head and body. "Himdak, fartle, eek, shneedle," the taller of the two was screaming, as he frantically tried to defend himself against this unexpected onslaught. It was Gollam, from Lord of the Rings, but at least you could understand Gollam. We now intervened to pull the two protagonists apart and radioed the station to send a car around to pick us up and remove the evidence.

At no point did we anticipate a problem with the small member of this team and he was more than happy to sing like a bird, but this bird really couldn't tell us that much that would help us with the rest of the enquiry. At the end of the day, he was guilty of receiving stolen goods and nothing else. Tall, skinny, smelly, ugly guy, on the other hand, we knew, had all the information we required. What we did know for certain was that he was far too stupid to have carried out the break in, on his own. He was most definitely not, in our opinion, the brains behind the operation. So, he had to be interviewed and that was down to me.

"What is your name?"

"Nimid Mitshee."

I already knew what his name was but I had to go through the procedure.

"What is your date of birth?"

"Yen, widen nireen sifny vore."

I already knew that as well, in fact, there was very little I didn't know about him as I had dealt with him on numerous occasions over the years. A fifteen minute statement from anyone else, equated to about an hour and a half with Nimid. Interpretation was the problem and perseverance was the answer. I now knew that "Under Mitshee" led the raid, and even more of the swag was "Braid un im's faidurs beck grudin." Time to arrest and lock up "Under Mitshee." "Under" was an entirely different ball game, here was a guy considerably more street wise. He would have difficulty writing his own name but he had been locked up so often he knew exactly how the game was played. "Under" wasn't about to give anything away, not even when I told him that I was going to pick up the rest of the stolen goods which I knew was "Braid un im's faidurs beck grudin."

Armed with a search warrant, John Ratter, four uniformed officers and I arrived at "Under's faidurs" home, where, after gaining entry, we made him aware of our reason for being there and outlined our intentions. Throughout the explanation the householder did not move from his position, fully stretched out on a sofa, viewing a television set which was lying on it's side. I really thought that this was rather selfish, as the other members of the household who chose to seat themselves in a traditional fashion, upright in chairs, looked to me to be adopting a very uncomfortable leaning position. Neither could I help but notice another male member of the family who was engaged in washing his hair in the kitchen sink, whilst at the same time paying particular attention to what was going on in the sitting room through the wide open kitchen door. Constantly nodding and smiling he moved from the kitchen, acknowledging each one of us individually, and moved to the sitting room window where he grabbed hold of the curtain and spent some time rubbing his hair dry.

A number of hours later we had completed a search of the house, and after a few false starts, had succeeded in unearthing a tool box, stuffed full with more tobacco and cigarettes, from where it had been buried in the back garden. A final interview with a previously arrogant, non cooperative, "Under Mitshee," found him attempting to gain favour by singing like a bird in order to cushion the final reckoning in court. This event was not going to be my last encounter with "Under Mitshee," and "Nimid" was destined to cross my path on countless occasions, equally outrageous.

Murder, I am pleased to say, is still a rare occurrence in the Highlands but they do happen. Recent years, unfortunately, have seen some particularly violent cases, which from the word go, achieved the pre-meditated intention of taking an innocent's life. The reason I make this point is that many murders are almost inevitably not intended as such and are an end consequence of an assault gone horribly wrong. Attempted Murder, on the other hand, was an incident that you were more likely to find yourself involved in, and was a charge, generally dictated by the circumstances of an assault being so violent that the potential for the victim to have lost his, or her life, was pretty high. I have found myself to some greater or lesser degree, involved with both throughout my service.

I was off duty at home, when I received a phone call to turn out for duty as a C.I.D. officer was required to carry out an enquiry. I attended at the station and was informed that a particularly violent attempted murder had occurred a short time previously at the American naval base at Forss near Thurso. John Ratter and other detective officers were already in attendance and the victim had been transported by ambulance to the Bignold hospital at Wick. John had requested that I be instructed to attend there, ascertain the condition of the victim and if possible, obtain a statement from him. I already knew that this incident had involved the use of a firearm and consequently didn't anticipate much hope of being allowed an interview. As it turned out, by the time I arrived, medical staff had already stabilized the victim and made him as comfortable as possible prior to transfer to Aberdeen, and even more surprisingly were happy to allow me an interview.

The young American sailor was located in a private room and when I entered I noticed that he was heavily bandaged, still showing signs of dried and congealed blood and numerous small wounds on the exposed parts of his body that I could see. All the indications were that he had suffered an extremely traumatic incident. This having been said, he appeared to be quite comfortable and surprisingly alert. I introduced myself, explained the purpose of my visit and set about obtaining a lengthy statement.

The gist of the story was that this young man had been in the area of the base known as the main deck, and was engaged in making a telephone call home when his attention was drawn to another serviceman entering the deck via a doorway some several yards distant from him. Although he knew who the other sailor was, he claimed never to have had any social interaction with him, and as far as he was concerned, he was just another guy on the base. "I couldn't help but notice that he was carrying a blanket, and I thought that was strange!" he told me. Continuing with his telephone conversation he became aware that the other guy was standing about, and in his opinion, appeared to be somewhat agitated. "I don't know why, but he was beginning to make me nervous, and when I turned round to look at him, all I saw was two barrels of a shotgun poking out from underneath the blanket, pointing directly at me." I won't say, I can't imagine what he felt at that moment, because I believe that I could, having found myself in a not to dissimilar situation during my time in Shetland, but that is another story. Suffice it to say that I had no problem in believing him when he told me that he was absolutely terrified. The difference between the situation that I had found myself in, and this one was, that this guy actually pulled the trigger, not once but twice.

Ironically, it would seem, that the impact of the first shot was to be responsible for saving his life. The first shot succeeded in striking the victim in his right side and right arm removing considerable amounts of flesh, whilst at the same time, the force of the blow spun him around and sent him flying through the air. The split second between the first and second shots meant, that instead of the second shot striking the victim squarely in the chest, the pellets struck the lower and upper parts of his back and neck. The majority of the ammunition was clearly spent above the victim's airborne body. How lucky was he! I never knew the outcome of this case as the attacker, once our enquiries had been completed, was taken back to the United States to be tried and sentenced. The attack had occurred on American soil.

Another little aside, however! Sandy Rosie who had been one of the officers initially attending this incident was in the process of noting a statement from one of several witnesses. This witness, a Chief Petty Officer who had arrived on the scene mere seconds after the shooting, told Sandy that he had taken the shotgun and put it in the lady's Head. Sandy hadn't got a clue what he meant and coincidentally, at that very point an American female officer attended at the deck. This lady sported a rather large frizzy perm and on seeing her Sandy's train of attention was interrupted by the thought, "Yes, it's big, but surely you couldn't hide a gun in it!" What Sandy didn't know was that the term Head, in both the British and American navy, means toilet.

Although there are many stories I could relate about my, what was to become frequent sojourns, into the department, I intend to finish this chapter with a story which I refer to as Tommy's demise.

As many as Tommy's faults may have been, and let's face it, we all have them, he was a seriously nice fellow and would go out of his way to help you if he could. Just occasionally Tommy would take on a little more than he could handle and although Sandy and I knew that this trait would lead to his eventual downfall, we didn't expect it in the form in which it finally arrived. Senior officers from the Chief Constable down to Superintendent Rank met on a quarterly basis for a full day's meeting to discuss managerial force matters. These meetings, owing to the geographical nature of the Highlands, were held at various locations throughout the force area and in this instance the venue was set for the Queens Hotel in Wick. Infrequently, as was the case, you would find that this event was also used to acknowledge a retiring officer and would be followed by a meal and presentation, also attended by the officer's spouses. Where this was the case, it had been normal practice to have a photographer from headquarters in Inverness attend to take the official photographs. Tommy was, without question, a very good photographer. When he was sober!

Bill Mackay, who I have already mentioned, was our Chief Superintendent at that time, and also as I have said, a fairly easy going man. Bill had suggested to the Chief Constable that there would be no need for a photographer to be dispatched from Inverness on this occasion as we had a man in situ who was more than capable of doing the job. Getting this right was obviously very important to Bill and Tommy had reassured him that he wouldn't let him down. Sandy and I were already anticipating a tragedy as we knew something that Bill obviously didn't. Tommy was attending a wedding that very same day and as he wasn't due to arrive at the Queens Hotel until eight o'clock that same evening, it was fairly safe to assume that he was likely to be considerably the worse for wear. How right did we get that one!

Who was the unfortunate duty back shift officer that evening? OK, so you've guessed, it was me, and Sandy as normally sympathetic as he was, wasted no time in letting me know how glad he was that he wasn't on duty. Between us we had pretty much predicted the scenario. Just before 8, as instructed, I arrived at the Mercury Motor Inn where I picked up, not a drunk Tommy, but a steaming drunk Tommy. I spent some time practically pleading with him not to go, and told him that I was more than happy to do the job for him. Although I wasn't nearly as good a photographer as Tommy, I was fairly confident that I could make a reasonable job of it. I would offer some plausible excuse for his non attendance and as long as I took a reasonable photograph, problem solved. Tommy would have done the same for me but he wasn't having any of it. He was doing the job, come hell or high water.

We were met by Bill Mackay at the front entrance to the hotel. "Now you won't let me down Tommy." "No problem sir, I'll just take a few casual shots of the company before the presentations, and then I'll arrange the set up for the formal shots." Well, he seemed confident enough. I was handed a slave flash unit and instructed by Tommy in its use. Forty or fifty photographs and several drinks later, (Coke for me) I was transporting Tommy back to the wedding.

Monday morning, I was in the office along with Sandy discussing the events of the previous Friday night. Sandy, "How drunk was he?" Me, "Pished!" Our conversation was interrupted by the sound of an obviously agitated Tommy making his way up the stairs, and on appearing through the office door we could see, showing obvious signs of distress.

"What's wrong Tommy?" asked Sandy.

"The Photo's! Not one of them came out, it must have been the slave flash."

"You can **** right off Tommy, there was nothing wrong with the flash," I responded. At this point Tommy produced two packs of photographs not one of which was in focus. Neither Sandy, or I could believe that Tommy could have made such a simple mistake, but the evidence was clear, which was more than could be said for the photographs.

"What am I going to do? The boss will go of his head, what am I going to tell him?"

"You will just have to tell him the truth, as a matter of fact I would go along to his office right now and get it over with," offered Sandy.

I really don't believe that there can be such a thing as good advice in a situation like that, there's just advice, and Tommy chose to take it. Bill Mackay's office was along a long corridor and one flight higher than where we were located but we heard every word. Not many weeks later Tommy was a uniformed Sergeant pounding the beat in Lerwick, in the Shetland Islands. I don't know if Tommy deserved that fate but he certainly didn't deserve the fate that befell him just a few short years later, when he passed away, still a reasonably young man. Tommy must have been really unlucky, as he checked out, almost unbelievably, as a result of an

illness almost unheard of in this day and age, "Tuberculosis!" I don't know if I
would believe that story if Tommy was telling it!

CHAPTER 10

BACK ON THE BEAT

It was the final week of my six month secondment to C.I.D. and I was about to find
myself prematurely back in uniform. I was at home when a television news flash
announced that an aircraft had crashed on take off at Sumburgh Airport, in

Shetland. The information at that time was fairly sketchy and although it was clear that a number of passengers had survived the crash, an undisclosed figure had yet to be accounted for. This was clearly a major incident!

It wasn't long before my telephone was ringing and I was instructed to make myself available early the following morning, in uniform, to fly to Shetland on a chartered aircraft. The same call was going out all over the force and nobody had the slightest idea how long we would be there for. It was generally accepted that whilst working as a Detective officer you might allow your hair to grow a little longer than normal, and I was no exception to that rule. I didn't have time to have it cut to an acceptable uniform wearing length, but given the scale of things, it really was small potatoes and I didn't imagine that it would attract any comment. Anyhow, there I was the following morning boarding an Air Ecosse Banderante aircraft, en route to Shetland. Immediately on landing at Sumburgh we were ushered to a large portacabin where we were met by Pat Douglas, by now, a fully promoted Inspector. Pat was under considerable pressure as up to this point, the control of the whole incident was pretty much squarely on his shoulders. It was obvious that he hadn't had any sleep, he was unshaven and bleary eyed but clearly still had his finger directly on the pulse. We were given a quick but fairly comprehensive briefing of the situation right up to that point and then dispatched directly to the scene by waiting mini bus.

Sumburgh Airport had moved on leaps and bounds since I had last been there and millions of pounds of construction work was ongoing at that time. As a direct result of the growing oil industry Sumburgh was fast becoming one of the busiest airports in the UK.

The minibus dropped us off at a construction workers camp and we were told that our luggage would be delivered later, but right now we were needed on the runway. We were led some few hundred yards when over the hump of a small hill, the runway came into view. As well as Pat Douglas had briefed us, and as many diagrams as we would have cared to look at, could not have prepared us for the sight that we were now seeing. The end of the closed runway which jutted out into the sea was a hive of activity. Several groups of uniformed police officers, civilians in various garbs, technicians of one description or another, official photographers, divers and by their mode of dress, what I took to be medical staff, were all calmly busying themselves with the numerous tasks which surround pretty much any major incident involving multiple deaths. My eye's couldn't help but be drawn to the reason for all this activity and what I saw then, I hoped I would never see again.

A large "Dan Air" aeroplane appeared to be suspended in the sea, its tail fin rising high out of the water and no more than thirty or so feet from the shore. My memory may be playing tricks on me but I am fairly certain that I could see the full length of the aircraft with the possible exception of the flight deck, which was to some degree submerged under water. I could see a large crack which looked to me as if it ran all the way around the circumference of the fuselage about 15 0r 20 feet from the nose, and each time the tide ebbed, the plane opened up exposing part of the interior, and each time it flowed, the aircraft closed. The remaining metal which had not been cut through on impact was effectively acting as a hinge. The tail section and most of the fuselage appeared to be somehow anchored in position while the remainder of the nose was left feebly flapping. This to me, surreal sight was heightened by a frenzy of activity at the waters edge and a number of small boats bobbing about in close proximity to the crashed plane. Everyone there was intensely watching this constant opening and closing process and just occasionally a cry would go up when a body would float out of the exposed interior. Divers, already in the water, would then recover the body to one of the waiting boats and the remains were transported to a nearby small harbour. I can't imagine that any of us there weren't affected by what we saw but just as in every other situation we had a job to do.

Officers who had been on duty since the start of the incident were being given some brief respite to grab a bite to eat and a few hours of much needed sleep, while we, the new arrivals, were tasked with varying duties. A finger tip search of the runway and flanking grassed areas found me shoulder to shoulder, on my hands and knees with several colleagues, searching for any small item that may offer some clue as to how this tragedy had occurred. It was the end of July, a beautiful summer's day and it was going to be a long one.

As the light began to fade, probably about 10pm that night, fresh officers were drafted in to guard the location overnight. By that time, maybe ten of the seventeen people who had lost their lives in this accident had been recovered. We made our way back to where we had previously been dropped off and here we found our luggage unceremoniously dumped in a large heap in the middle of the roadway. How long it had been there God only knows but none of us were particularly happy about it. As my colleagues uplifted their cases, one by one they began to board a waiting minibus.

"Where are you lot going?" I asked. I don't recall who the wit was who responded, but I was less than happy with the reply. "We're not staying in that dump we've managed to get into the management accommodation. Enjoy yourselves boys." Of the twenty plus officers who had been barracked at this construction camp, three of us were left standing in the middle of the road with our mouths hanging open, John Wares, David Inglis and me. John, an officer of about twelve years service and senior to both David and I, after hurling considerable abuse in the direction of the fast diminishing minibus, then took control of the situation. Both David and I were happy to be led by John as I was already having visions of spending the night curled up between some portacabins using my suitcase as a pillow. John led us into one of only two large huts that was showing any illumination and it just happened to be the canteen. "Hello boys." It wasn't Joyce, but an equally welcome sight. "I was told to expect more of you lot, where are they?" We explained to this jolly lady cook exactly what had occurred and apologised profusely on behalf of our colleagues. "Not to worry boys, you will be ready for feeding." And what a feed! We were being treated like kings.

After consuming large beautifully cooked steaks with all the trimmings, a selection of sweets and drinking copious quantities of coffee, our new best friend then showed us to our accommodation. OK, it wasn't a five star hotel, but we each had a small, reasonably appointed room and shared a toilet and shower area. The whole block had been set aside for the police and only three of us were occupying it. "I will leave you to settle in boys and when you're ready, the bars open across the road." "The Bar!" Were we in heaven? A quick shower and change into civilian clothing later, we cautiously made our way into the bar which was absolutely heaving with hard working construction workers. They obviously knew who we were and any inhibitions we may have had about going into this place were quickly swept away on the tide of welcome we received. We weren't allowed to put our hands in our pockets as drink after drink was placed in front of us. As much as we insisted, we weren't allowed to reciprocate. "You boys are paying for nothing." I suspect that many of these hard men had some admiration for the job we were doing, and were doing what they could to make it that bit easier for us.

Early the following morning, I was in the toilet block having a shower and a shave when I was joined by David Inglis. John Wares arrived only moments later garbed as I remembered everyone to be during my first Week at the Scottish Police College. John, dressed in Paisley Print pyjamas, dressing gown, slippers and carrying a toilet bag, drew gales of laughter from David and me. I suppose we might have anticipated a slap for daring to show so much disrespect to a much senior colleague but John's only response was, "Well, you feel the cold when you get older." Many years later when John retired he made a comment which I loved, and learned for myself to be so true. "I loved working with the youngsters because it kept me young." Ageism, to my knowledge does not exist within the police service. Off now for an early breakfast which would easily have kept us satisfied for the whole day, given the quantities being heaped on our plates. Construction workers coming and going were greeting us like old pals and we were settling in nicely to this sort of treatment. By eight o'clock we had been joined by the rest of our colleagues. As it turned out they hadn't made the best choice in changing their accommodation arrangements. Without exception, they were complaining. The food was rubbish, they were sharing rooms, there was no hot water for their showers in the morning and the meagre breakfast they had been presented with wouldn't feed a sparrow. Served them right, was all I could say and we took exceptional delight in telling them how we had landed in absolute clover. It was now our turn to have abuse hurled at us but we were more than happy to take it.

The end of the runway was once again a hive of activity, and by now arrangements had been made to get heavy lifting equipment into position to remove the aircraft from the water. This was no quick fix and it couldn't be as simple as fixing a cable to the aircraft and dragging it from the water. Considerable care had to be employed in this process, not only because all of the victims had not yet been recovered but every effort had to be made to preserve evidence. The Civil Aviation Authority is the principal investigators in any incident of this type and their procedures are strictly observed. Throughout the whole of the procedure, rolls and rolls of film were used to record every aspect of the recovery, and photographic records would no doubt be utilised to precisely as possible reconstruct this aeroplanes last fatal moments, from the start of take off to the moment I was now witnessing.

Police officers were fulfilling several roles throughout the course of this incident, dealing with survivors, obtaining statements, recovering luggage, identifying owners, verifying identities of deceased and providing security at the crash location to name just a few of the dozens of jobs that needed to be done. I found myself, I would like to say, assisting with the photography but in reality I was carrying camera tripods and boxes of equipment for the real photographers. There was no shortage of jobs that needed doing and the morning was passing quickly.

It must have been approaching lunch time and even though I had indulged in a very large breakfast, my stomach was sending me signals to the effect that I craved further sustenance. I was a young growing lad after all and food of any description, then and to this day, maintains my good humour. I must have been sending out telepathic signals when I spotted a small van making its way, in my direction, along a dirt path. As the van approached I could see it was being driven by our best friend, the jolly lady cook. How had she made her way through the outer cordon? I suspect by claiming some official function and no small degree of bribery. "Lunch boys!" Trays of filled rolls, chocolate biscuits and large flasks of coffee were unloaded for the benefit of John Wares, David Inglis and me. There was enough to feed the 10,000 but her justification was that it would keep us going up until tea time. Our colleagues obviously considered our good fortune to be their good fortune also until we put them right. "Get yours from the management camp, this lot's for us." Cruel I know, but we were getting our own back and taking a great delight in rubbing their face's in it. I wouldn't want you to imagine that we maintained that position for too long, the truth is that nobody could in the face of the pleading and grovelling that we were being subjected to. In order to make them stew that little bit longer, the three of us decided to hold a meeting which was punctuated by loud sighs and considerable negative head shaking before terminating with much overacted nods of agreement. It was beginning to look like a scene from Oliver Twist when we returned to the waiting group of expectant faces. Off course we were always going to share it out, we just wanted to make them sweat.

Throughout the four day period that we were there our friendly cook never let us down, breakfast, lunch, tea time and late evening dinner. She treated us like kings, as I am sure she did every construction worker at the camp. They had landed a real gem and I'm pretty sure they knew it.

By now the aircraft had been removed from the water and more bodies had been recovered. The nose section and the open fuselage had been placed at the end of the runway secured in position, awaiting removal, I imagine to some waiting hangar. I had been tasked to maintain a guard on the fuselage section and restrict all but official access to it. I was standing directly to the front of the wide open, I suppose you would say cross sectioned fuselage, when I observed activity some considerable distance away on the beach. I could just make out what I took to be maybe a dozen or more people who I assumed were trying to get a view of the activity at the end of the runway. They weren't causing me a problem and they certainly weren't infringing anywhere near the cordoned off incident locus, therefore, I concluded, there was no issue. The following day I found myself emblazoned across the front pages of various national newspapers, framed directly in front of the fuselage, and their was no mistaking, it was me. As I have said, on the scale of things it was small potatoes, but I could see my long hair sticking out from the back of my hat and so could the rest of the country. There was no escaping those cameras, no matter how far away they were.

Pretty much all of the major activity was over at the end of the runway and by now it was a case of keeping the site secure and recovering the remaining victims. Three victims still remained outstanding and that final day that I was there two more were recovered. Only the pilot hadn't been found and everyone was willing the recovery of that one remaining body to bring the incident to a close. Absolutely everybody was hoping that he hadn't been washed out to sea, leaving a family with no remains to bury and no grave that they could visit. It was all very intense and it wasn't looking hopeful. The divers had been working countless hours and were by now operating a shift rota. It was beginning to fall dark and I was standing at the crash point speaking with the only present diver. He told me that he should really stop his search at this time but he wanted to give it one last go. He was determined to find the pilot and we were willing him to be successful. I watched the diver disappear under the waves and a few short minutes later I saw him surface and give me a thumb's up sign. I couldn't help myself, it was a very emotional moment, and I shouted "He's got him!" The responding cries of "Yes" and "Well done," has left me with the feeling that at that moment, all of our hopes and thousands of prayers had been answered.

Over the next few months, tales of heroism began to emerge from the aftermath of this tragedy. Stories surrounding survivor's attempts to save others, tributes being paid to the air crew and stories of some who had given up hope, prepared themselves for an unexpected death and then found that they were being dragged to safety by an unidentified fellow passenger. For those who survived and others who lost loved ones this event can only be a tragic memory. It is for me and I was only there after the tragedy had occurred, they lived through it and they still live with it.

Back on shift in Wick I now found myself working with Joyce, John Wares, the new boy David Murray, and a new Sergeant, Jack Dalton. I should point out that Joyce had very quickly given up her dislike of young Murray who only two days after his arrival in Caithness was taking up residence at my home because Joyce felt sorry for him. Jack Dalton was a Yorkshire man, who was to become a great pal but with no apology, I have to say, probably the most chauvinistic male I ever encountered in my life. His wife Joyce (different Joyce) must have been an angel, as I couldn't imagine any lesser being actually tolerating him. Both of them were extremely talented, Jack, in a very academic sense while Joyce was an extremely talented confectioner, baker and trained seamstress. Joyce went on to gain a private pilots licence, not that she ever had any intention of flying as a job but just to prove that she could. Jack's academic ability, H.N.C. in police studies and masters degree in the classics would see him quickly raised to the rank of Inspector, only to have his career cut short by medical retirement owing to a heart condition.

I found myself paired up with young Murray, who by now had several months service under his belt and I felt it safe to assume that he would be fairly well versed in police procedures. Another one I had got seriously wrong, he hadn't got a clue.

This boy was a challenge, both Joyce and John Wares had been doing all the work, carrying out enquiries, obtaining statements, writing reports and having David sign his name to them as reporting officer. A fairly common procedure for the first month or so as a probationer is training but after that you expect to see some progress. I realized my mistake in the very first minor incident we attended together. I had told David that he should take the lead and I would only interfere if I saw that he was having difficulty. About two minutes into the incident he was floundering and I was obliged to step in and take over. After the event I quizzed David on what training he had received up to that point only to find that he had been totally cosseted and quite literally living the life of Reilly. I left him in no doubt that things were now about to change and I expected him to pull his weight. A couple of months of intense training, serious bollockings and made to rewrite reports again and again saw David come on leaps and bounds and become a reasonably competent police officer. David would figure quite heavily in my life over the next number of years and remains one of my very best friends to this day. I will come back to him later.

Jack Dalton and I were on a back shift (4pm-12pm) and had been out carrying out some enquiry. We were on our way back to the station and just in the process of turning onto one of the two bridges which span Wick River when we were flagged down by a group of youngsters. "There's a dead body floating in the river," they were shouting. It was winter, it was early evening, it was dark and it was extremely cold. These youngsters were quite frantic and hurrying us to a point where a group of their friends were standing, intently peering over the bridge parapet. The water level was high and the river itself was flowing fairly fast, carrying with it large chunks of packed snow which had broken free of the river bank much further up. As I peered into the darkness, made worse by the black effect of the water, I was having considerable difficulty in distinguishing any particular shape or outline. Jack was faring no better than me and the youngsters were continuing to frantically gesture in the direction of the bank. "Look! Look there," they were saying. Finally I was able to distinguish some tangled tree branches in amongst which I could see the carcase of a dead sheep. My initial reaction was that these kid's had carried out a successful wind up until Jack said, "No, look, there's a body there too!" Right enough, it did look like a body floating face down and tangled in among the floating branches. We ran across the bridge and made our way along the side of a workshop negotiating piles of discarded metal, engine parts and years of accumulated industrial waste, which eventually allowed us access to the river bank.

Standing on the embankment we were able to confirm that there was indeed a body floating in among the trees some ten feet or so from the bank. I had already concluded that were it not for the presence of the mass of tree branches somehow anchored to the river bed, the remains would probably have long since been washed out to sea and possibly never recovered.

Without a moment's hesitation Jack leapt into the water while at the same time shouting to me, "Quick, he may still be alive." I obviously had a much greater self preservation instinct than Jack, and in the split second it took me to make my decision several thoughts occurred to me. The water was bitterly cold, I had no doubt that the body was a long time dead and wasn't going anywhere in a hurry, several onlookers had gathered on the bridge watching our every move and I was wearing brand new Doc Martin boots. "Oh Well," in as heroic a fashion as I could muster I too leapt into the water. I can assure you that although I had given this action considerably more thought than Jack obviously had, the time difference in our hitting the water would have been totally indiscernible to the gathering crowd. The initial shock of hitting the freezing cold water and a frantic struggle to maintain my balance on the uneven river bed succeeded in dislodging my brand new, rare as hen's teeth, Gannex Police hat, which I last saw floating out to sea under the bridge span. By the time we had waded out to where we could grab hold of the body the freezing cold water had reached waist level and the family jewels were by now in considerable distress.

Other than a short radio message back to the station to tell them that we were investigating the possible sighting of a body in the water we had been out of radio contact for quite a period and weren't at this point expecting any early assistance. A short numbing struggle to disentangle the body saw us dragging it ashore to a nearby slipway where we stood soaking wet and freezing. My serge trousers weren't so much drying on me as freezing into a solid block, and anyone other than those who had witnessed the incident who may have seen me walking back to the police vehicle could be forgiven for assuming that I had suffered an embarrassing accident.

Assistance from the station arrived just a short time later and Jack and I managed to take a short break to get ourselves dried off and rub some life back into frozen limbs. We then began the task of identifying our deceased, which unusually, took us some considerable time. The picture that we did eventually manage to build up was of a young man with a fairly serious drink problem, who while heavily intoxicated had accidentally fallen into the river and was too drunk to save himself. It really did turn out to be that simple and straight forward, and from the beginning of my police service to its end I would learn time and again that the demon drink was responsible for countless tragedies.

David Fraser was a new man, and what you would call a late starter having been a serving soldier for a number of years before moving into the Lighthouse Service and then on to the Police. David was about four or five years older than me at the time he joined. Now you may consider what I have just said as rather ridiculous as the laws of time remain reasonably constant and it is safe for you to assume that he remains four or five years older than me as I write. To clarify this matter what I will say is that age catches up on some of us much quicker than it does others. I am not saying that he looked like a schoolboy but if you happened to be the manager of licensed premises you would most certainly have questioned his legal rights to be drinking alcohol. A well known saying to the effect that "You know you are getting older when the policemen start looking younger," as far as I was concerned, was invented for David Fraser. He made me feel ancient, and I was only twenty four. The picture of Dorian Grey and Peter Pan both fit him nicely even to this day.

I was on duty with David and we had been instructed to enforce a number of outstanding arrest warrants for non payment of fines imposed by the court. The normal practice in these cases is to make the subject aware of the warrants existence and where they are unable to make the payment, place them under arrest for a later appearance in court. Almost inevitably it would be a list of the usual suspects and you knew that you were pretty much wasting your time. It came as no surprise to me that there amongst the list of names was none other than "Nimid Mitshee."

I had already had several encounters with Nimid but this was to be David's first and as such, I feel it worthy of recounting. Nimid was at that time most ironically and I feel rather appropriately living directly next door to the Social Security Office. I had tried to give David a brief outline of this character and warned him to prepare to be shocked although you could never anticipate in what manner the shock may manifest itself. The front door was answered by the father of the house who on seeing me immediately moved into grovelling mode and promoted me to the rank of Sergeant. I knew that by the time I left the house I would have reached the dizzying heights of Inspector. It was a fairly normal mode of greeting and farewell and one thing I will say is that you never left with a heavy heart. "How can I help you sergeant." "Is Nimid in?" "He's in his bed, come in." We were led along a long unlit corridor and up two short flights of stairs making no inconsiderable noise on the uncovered wooden flooring and stairway. The first landing served only to provide a toilet, and how did I know it was a toilet? It had no door on it and it stank to high heaven! Not only did it not have a door, it didn't have a toilet seat on the toilet either but that didn't matter because the toilet pan was pretty much in half and what was left of it was lipping with human excrement.

I really don't know what David was thinking at this point as I was having considerable difficulty in maintaining my professional calm and holding on to my stomach content. It certainly had to be an eye opener. Another two or three steps took us to the first landing where we were led along yet another corridor and directed to one of several rooms, none of which had a door. I will just take a moment to explain the missing doors which was fairly common in many of these households. Wooden interior doors were quite simply a cheap form of fuel for the open fire. You really wouldn't need to be a shy type living in one of these houses. Anyhow, in we went and there lying on an old iron bedstead heaped with blankets and obviously recovering from a night of indulgence on cheap wine, lay Nimid Mitshee. "Wake up Nimid, It's the police. I've got a warrant for your arrest." It was taking me all my time to stop myself from gagging as the smell in the room was quite overpowering but over the years you do manage to develop the ability to breath through your mouth rather than your nose. "Wha? A din notin!" "It's for not paying a fine." "Wha fin?" "It doesn't matter what fine, your coming with me." Undecipherable mumblings as he rose from the bed was followed by, "Yum nidan a pee." As unreasonable as some people may consider me to be I was not about to deny any man the opportunity to carry out his toilet although I was at a loss as to where.

It was only as Nimid bent over that I saw a row of cooking pot handles sticking out from under the bed. He pulled out the first pot which I could see was lipping with urine and with some disappointed mumbling shoved it back into position under the bed. The same process and similar result was carried out with a further four pots before Nimid was forced to further improvise his toilet needs. I can't say I expected it and I know David didn't expect it when Nimid quite casually ambled to the window, opened it and sent a stream of urine arcing to the garden below. All I can say is, thank god that there were no keen gardener's in the immediate vicinity at that particular moment.

Oh well, live and let live is what I say and did people really live like that, the short answer is yes, and they still do.

On a more personal note I had been married to my dream woman for a couple of years by now and Joyce in particular, was very keen to procreate and continue the line of Sutherland's. I was more than happy to participate in this exercise and was doing my level best to oblige her in this ambition. Up until now Joyce's maternal cravings had been more than adequately served by my countless and ever increasing band of nieces and nephews. It was quite literally a case of finished with that one for today get a new one for tomorrow. We both knew that this state of affairs could only be a temporary situation and the only way to fulfil her craving was to have one of our own. I would have to say that I initially found the mechanics of this operation quite delightful but as they say, "too much of a good thing!" Joyce is not the most patient of people and she was becoming rapidly frustrated with our lack of success and I was becoming thinner and exhausted. What to do?

Joyce decided it was time to take the bull by the horns and convinced me that we needed to speak to our doctor just in case one of us had a problem. I can't say that I was very taken with this idea as I felt that this could well be mistaken for a lack of sexual prowess on my part. If it was what Joyce wanted I would give in and comply but I didn't have to be happy about it. We were very secretive about this process, I would have to say at my insistence as I felt that should any of my sympathetic colleagues hear about it, it wouldn't be long before the nickname Snowie became Eunuch. It didn't take long for Joyce to be given a clean bill of health but it looked like there may be a problem with me. "Low sperm count."

What did he mean, "Low sperm count," he couldn't be talking about me, could he? What sort of stud was I? I have no intention of going in to how the medical authorities reached that conclusion; suffice it to say that it involved a very embarrassing process which I choose to forget. So, what happens now? Three days of tests at Edinburgh Royal Infirmary. I would have to get time off work, I would have to tell them why, they would be sniggering behind my back and pointing at me, no, they would be laughing in my face and making my life a misery. They would announce it to the whole world! "B*******." I was steeling myself for the worst and preparing to tell the bosses when Joyce said "Guess what, I'm pregnant!" What a relief, my manhood was no longer in doubt and I was going to be a daddy.

Our young friend, David Murray had been transferred to Stromness in the Orkney Islands and Joyce was quite upset at his leaving, which for the life of me I cant understand as he constantly took a delight in making my life miserable and ran with tales to Joyce on the odd occasion that I decided to put him in his place. It wasn't to be too long before Joyce adopted another waif in the form of Gordon Sim. The boss had taken me in to his office and told me that we were about to get a new probationer and I was being given the job of knocking him into line. I wasn't hearing good reports about this boy and by the time the interview had finished I was anticipating the arrival of some kind of child monster. If I were to be brutally frank I would have to say that he was one of my biggest challenges to date, but he kept me laughing.

Gordon was just nineteen and had been a police cadet for a couple of years during which time he had achieved the distinction of becoming infamous throughout the force. This boy just didn't know how to roll over or lie down and play dead. If he had an opinion, he voiced it and didn't worry who he upset and if his opinion caused an argument he inevitably won it. Maybe this was why the bosses were wary of him, they weren't used to having their decisions questioned and Gordon questioned everything. I couldn't help but admire a young fellow with so much grit and maybe this is a bit of cliché but he reminded me so much of myself. Just to enhance the image I am building of Gordon he was also extremely intelligent and adopted a total devil may care attitude. You couldn't help but like him and I always said that he would either get kicked out on his arse or go right to the top of the service. As I write he is currently Superintendent and Area Commander of a large district in Belfast serving with the Police Service of Northern Ireland.

I didn't get the opportunity to say it to him at the time so I would like to say now, thanks for travelling all the way back to the North of Scotland to attend my retirement party, I would have been really upset if he hadn't been there.

Just another footnote for the fishermen amongst you, yes, he is that Gordon Sim.

CHAPTER 11

SHETLAND AGAIN

Be warned this next one is a long story!

It was 1982 and I was once again to find myself back in Shetland. Sullom Voe oil terminal, the largest construction site in Europe between 1973 and 1982 was due to be opened by her majesty the Queen. Needless to say an event of this magnitude, particularly with the presence of Royalty was a major security headache for the police service. The plan was that we would begin travelling to Shetland on the Friday morning, fly up from Inverness, spend the night and be refreshed and ready for our security duties on the Saturday. It wasn't destined to work out like that and I was about to find myself involved in the weekend from hell.

We were picked up by bus at 6am and the poor guys from Thurso half an hour earlier. Joyce had anticipated a lengthy journey to Inverness and had the foresight to see me off with a large bag of sandwiches and other munchies to see me through the trip. She really did look after me, after all I was soon to be the father of her child and she wanted more. We left Wick with maybe a dozen officers on board and stopped at every point South to pick up more. By ten o'clock we were still some distance from Inverness and no opportunity to stop for a cup of coffee or a bite to eat. It somehow became common knowledge that I was the only person aboard in possession of any form of sustenance and a debate commenced about my obligement to share the booty. Foolish I know but I readily agreed and passed the bag of goodies around the bus. It wasn't quite the miracle of the loaves and fish's as I discovered when I was presented with an empty bag. Although Joyce had had the foresight to provide I hadn't had the foresight to take my own share out first. "B*******."

By 11o'clock we had arrived outside of police headquarters in Inverness and were looking forward to disembarking and enjoying a very welcome cup of coffee and bacon rolls in the canteen while we waited for the Inverness contingent to join us. Someone always has to spoil the moment and a senior officer boarded the bus and told us we couldn't get off as we were on a tight schedule and an aircraft was waiting for us to board at Inverness airport. Considerable vocal protests served us absolutely no purpose and we settled down with our misery and rumbling bellies. A full half hour we sat and waited before another twenty or so officers joined us. "Where the **** have you lot been." "We were waiting in the canteen for you lot to arrive." I needn't bore you with the response that piece of information was met with.

Not that I intend to tell this story hour by hour but by twelve o'clock we had arrived at Inverness airport and surely now we would be allowed to grab a quick snack at the terminal. No such luck, we had to board the aircraft immediately. More moans of protest and mutiny was already looming large on the horizon. Out on to the tarmac and there in front of me, last seen floating off the end of a runway in Shetland, the same type of Dan Air aeroplane. I wasn't getting to many good vibes about this sojourn, not in the least. Hustled on board and seated we now had an aircraft full of policemen of all ranks and the intention was to fly directly to Sumburgh Airport.

Two senior ranks standing at the front of the aircraft now carried out a head count which they were co-ordinating with a document held by one of them. No, that didn't seem to add up. Do it again, this time everybody answering to their name with an aye or here. No, didn't work that time either. Same process again, didn't work either. What was the problem? Were they doing something wrong or were they just stupid? Numerous moans and less than flattering anonymous jibes wasn't helping matters and these guys were beginning to get seriously frustrated but no less frustrated than those of us who had been on the go since the early hours of the morning. I don't think any of us were in the mood to be tolerant of yet more inefficiency.

A final shot at reaching an agreed tally met, I believe with the result they were looking for, or maybe it didn't and they just said it did rather than suffer further abuse. Sounds like the course of action I may have taken myself given their predicament. Finally the aircraft took off to much murmurs of approval and we began what I knew to be a reasonably short flight to Shetland.

I was seated in a window seat to the front of the aircraft to the port or left side and seated along side me was a recent shift colleague, Jim Fraser. The flight up to this point was certainly not unpleasant and I was passing the time reading and moaning with Jim about the poor organization to date and the fact that we were both looking forward to a decent meal and a relaxing evening. I was becoming aware that we seemed to be taking rather a long time to reach our destination but put it down to my being mistaken about flight times. Out of the corner of my eye I spotted another aeroplane which disappeared as quickly as it appeared and some five or ten minutes later re-appeared yet again. This aircraft appeared on a further two occasions before I brought it to Jim's attention and told him that I suspected that we may well be circling and were by now well beyond our arrival time.

Just at this time the pilot announced that we had indeed been circling, not Sumburgh airport as I suspected, but much further North in the island at the old wartime Scatsta airfield. Scatsta had been resurrected for use by oil related commercial aircraft but we had been expecting to land at Sumburgh in the South of the island. Sumburgh it seems had been closed due to fog and we had been re-directed here. It was now that the pilot dropped the bombshell. The aircraft ahead of us had already made two attempts at landing and had been forced to overshoot the runway due to fog conditions on the ground. Looking out of the window, not only could I see the other plane but I could now clearly see the runway below. What was the problem? I could see the runway! The pilot then explained that the other plane was going to have another shot at landing and then we were going to have a go. He then went on to outline the conditions that we might experience in event of an overshoot and finished with, in my opinion a somewhat ominous reassurance that we had nothing to be concerned about. Yeah, sure, whatever you say!

Not too long after I saw the other plane again and the pilot told us to fasten seat belts as it was now our turn. Three times the other plane had tried and failed and I felt that there had to be some message which we should have been taking cognisance of in that fact, but then again I'm no pilot. Down we went in a series of spirals and severely angled approaches which I can't say I was very happy with but this guy surely knew what he was doing. At least I comforted myself with that thought. Before I knew it the clear sky's that I had been looking at became a thick white fog and we were flying totally blind. I didn't like it as a matter of fact I didn't like it a lot! It seemed to take forever and the next I knew there was the runway and we were down. At least I thought we were down but it was just another serious Robert got that one wrong again. We hadn't got enough runway left and I was thrown back into my seat as the pilot piled on the power and climbed steeply away. I wasn't the only one to find that particular incident seriously scary and I was in no hurry to go through it again but the pilot obviously had other ideas. "Gentlemen, I am sorry to inform you that I was obliged to overshoot." Try telling us something we didn't know! "The steward will pass amongst you with complimentary refreshments while we await the opportunity to make a further attempt."

What made this guy think that he could buy us off with free booze. It did however seem to do the trick and a few drinks later the guys were raring to go again. I had spent the time examining the aircraft specifications which wasn't the wisest thing I could have done as I was now not only worried about another overshoot but the possibility that we may fall out of the sky through lack of fuel.

So there we were circling an airfield, drinking free booze and as far as I was concerned preparing to enter the jaws of hell once more. I know I've said it before but hey ho, what the hell, there is absolutely no point in worrying about something you have absolutely no control over. It may have crossed my mind to storm the flight deck and force the pilot to take us back to Inverness but if it did, it was only for a fleeting moment. I didn't want to be the only one worrying about the possibility of us falling out of the sky so I felt it necessary to share this concern with Jim so that we could worry in tandem. It made me feel a little better knowing that I had scared the shit out of him as well as myself.

A second attempt at landing met with exactly the same result, namely my swearing that I would never get on another aeroplane in my life and vowing to take the pilots life as soon as we did land. We sped back, not to Inverness but Aberdeen airport, by this time I am fairly certain flying on fresh air. The drink had been flowing freely on the way back and the heat that had been generated with fifty plus bodies in close proximity to each other for five hours was just adding to my discomfort. I couldn't wait to get off that plane. When we did land the pilot made another announcement. "Gentlemen, if you would kindly remain in your seats, the aircraft will be refuelled, the bar re-stocked and I intend to have another go at landing at Scatsta." This announcement was met with floods of protest and mutiny was most definitely on the cards. I could hear mumbled threats from other officers who were only voicing exactly what I was considering myself, getting off the aircraft and to hell with the consequences.

I certainly wasn't feeling suicidal at the time and I was most definitely not willing to go through that experience a third time. The situation was however retrieved a few short minutes later with a second announcement from the pilot. "Gentlemen, I am sorry to inform you that Scatsta has been closed due to fog. Would you please disembark the aircraft where a bus is waiting to uplift you on the runway." I wasn't sorry and I'm fairly certain not one of my fellow passengers was sorry either.

Sitting on the bus I felt considerably more secure than I had for a number of hours and I was able once again to concern myself with more mundane matters such as an extreme lack of food. I was starving and so was everybody else, surely they would take us somewhere for food. My stomach thought that my throat was cut but I knew that this was just me hallucinating. I still had faith in the job but my faith was going to be sorely tried throughout the coming weekend.

We were driven through the city and eventually arrived at the harbour where we parked near to the Shetland car and passenger ferry, St Clair. The ship, although indicating a long sea passage was a very welcome sight and I along with everybody else was looking forward to boarding her, getting something to eat and relaxing until we arrived in Shetland. The ship was not however the welcome sight to everyone that it was to me. Jack Dalton in particular was not looking forward to this sea journey. "I will be sick," he moaned in his broad Yorkshire dialect. "Don't be stupid Jack, you'll be fine," I offered by way of some comfort. "No I wont, I'll be sick, I know I will. You'll stay with me wont you." I would have been a real monster to have ignored his pathetic pleadings and I agreed that I would stay with him. "Do you promise?" I could see that Jack was going to be a problem.

It seemed that we were never being allowed to disembark from this bus and up until now we didn't know what was causing the delay. Our Superintendent, who already knew that he was leading a volatile bunch somewhat pissed off with circumstances to date announced the problem in as diplomatic a fashion as he could muster. It seems that the St Clair had been especially chartered for the event by BP and the crew were already receiving generous remuneration from the company for their services. The arrival of fifty additional passengers had been the catalyst to kick of a threatened strike and BP was currently in negotiation with the crew to get us aboard. I can't say that we were in sympathy with the crew's demands, as a matter of fact I think it safe to say that without exception we were by now thoroughly pissed off and any crew member foolish enough to get too close was liable to be ripped limb from limb.

The Superintendent returned after a short absence and after calling for quiet informed us in as light hearted a fashion as possible that everything had been sorted out. We were being allowed to board the ship but unfortunately there was no beds available and we weren't allowed to enter any of the restaurants or bars. As gently as he tried to break this piece of news I am fairly certain that he knew in his heart of hearts that it would not be well received. On reflection, I feel sorry for him now but at the time I was as vocal as everyone else in voicing my displeasure. Nobody was pulling any punches and a river of curses only occasionally punctuated with a proper word assailed his ears. I wouldn't be surprised if he actually feared for his own life at that point, and I would have to say with good reason, but my concern was already for the crew. Guess what, I was right to be concerned.

We were quite literally herded aboard and made to stand in line for ages while some crew members tried to identify a vacant room where our baggage was unceremoniously thrown in a huge pile. I wasn't being paranoid; I knew we were being treated very badly, I knew the boys were already thoroughly pissed off and I was confident that it would all end in tears. We were by now already at the stage where rank was being ignored, requests were no longer polite and respectful and demands were more vocal and quite frankly menacing. We were fast becoming a rabble rather than a disciplined body of police officers and even now many years later I understand why.

They began to throw us the occasional bone, a meal was being prepared in the crew canteen, Chicken Fricassee, I hate Chicken Fricassee but I shovelled it in my mouth as fast as I possibly could. This was by no stretch of the imagination fine dining as we all attacked this concoction as if we hadn't eaten in a week and it did succeed in putting us in better spirits. More good news, they had found sufficient rooms to sleep twelve of us. The Superintendent had bought a pack of playing cards as the only fair way of dishing out these beds that he could see was based on a game of chance. If you drew a face card you got a bed, it was as simple as that. I drew a face card and Jack didn't! I was now faced with a double quandary. Jack was once again pleading with me that I shouldn't leave him and I was now confronted by an unknown whinger who had been circulating amongst face card holders declaring a painful back problem which would prevent him from any sleep if he didn't have a bed. I must have mug stamped all over my forehead but in exchange for the complete pack of playing cards, I gave up my bed.

The restaurants and bars were fairly busy; everything was free at the expense of BP and we weren't allowed to go in. I don't consider myself to be a rule breaker or indeed any kind of mercenary but I had just had enough and dragging a pathetic Jack Dalton behind me I thought, "bugger it," and I walked straight in and sat down. Jack, although a supervisory rank, being encouraged to ignore orders by a junior rank, was in no condition to object. I had been dozing him with sea sickness tablets I had bought on board the ship and the medication instructions warned that they would cause drowsiness should the recommended doze of two every six hours be exceeded. After all, it was just a recommended doze and he was currently averaging two every two hours. It was working for me! "Oooooh, will you look at that sea." "For Christ sake Jack, were still in the harbour." "I'm going to be sick." "No your not, shut up." A steward approached and asked what I would like to drink and at the same time threw several packs of cigarettes on the table for any smokers. Recalling a further recommendation that alcohol should be avoided while taking the sea sickness tablets I ordered a drink for Jack as well.

The steward returned with two of everything I had ordered, as he put it, it would cut down on the number of trips he would have to make from the bar. By now several thirsty faces were peering through the bar doors mouthing the words "how did you get in there," and feeling somewhat rebellious, I beckoned them in. The bar was now getting fairly busy with police officers who had been forbidden to enter and I suppose it was too much to hope for that the crew wouldn't notice. It wasn't long before the boss appeared suggesting that we should leave and the reception he received was far from polite being told in no uncertain manner where he could stuff his suggestion. A negotiated settlement led to a special bar being set up in the crew canteen exclusively for our use. Now I am no Svengalli but I knew that this wasn't a good idea!

The bar was set up and a continuous flow of crates of beer, all forms of alcohol and cigarettes was being piled into the canteen and now I was seeing lots of happy faces. But for how long I wondered! Jack was still pleading with me not to leave him alone and we sat together in the reception area where I continued to ply him with sea sickness tablets. More good news! For some strange reason the crew had found sufficient cabin space to give us all a bed. I don't know where these cabins appeared from and could only make one of three assumptions. Either the cabins had initially being occupying a different dimension when we arrived, or the crew had hurriedly constructed them or they had been encouraged in their endeavour by threats from an increasingly drunken rabble of policemen. I think I would plump for option three. I was unable to participate in the drinking and crew baiting exercise that was being encouraged and growing steadily worse as copious amounts of alcohol was being consumed. In all honesty I was quite happy not to be part of it as I would have great difficulty in explaining the presence and indeed the reason for having a Yorkshire man quite literally wrapped around me. It really had gotten that bad and as much of a soft touch as I normally am I was having great difficulty in remaining sympathetic to Jack's plight. He was becoming a serious pain in the arse.

Several times I quietly suggested that we should go to bed but was met with "No, I don't feel too well," or "No, please don't leave me." The reason that I was making this suggestion quietly was that I didn't want anyone who might happen to overhear to get the wrong impression and anyhow I didn't find Jack at all attractive. Several times when I thought Jack was asleep I made some attempt to move but he was obviously tuned in to his immediate surroundings and would grab hold of me pleading, "Don't go, don't go!" Several hours later and considerably more tablets he was eventually zonked and I was able to sneak away to my cabin in the bowels of the ship. The cabin slept four and you couldn't have swung a cat in it but I found the bunk bed particularly welcoming and I was shattered. I was first awoken by one of my cabin mates returning in the company of a whole bottle of whisky which he nursed in the bunk above me drinking deep from its well every time the fancy took him.

My next disturbance was much more spectacular as the cabin door violently burst inwards and there framed in the doorway looking like death warmed up stood Jack Dalton. "You B******, you left me!" He was out for revenge but was clearly not in a fit state to take any as he began to slide down the door jam. I got out of bed and dragged him into the cabin where I quite forcefully told him to get undressed, get into bed and stop moaning. Mumbling to himself and continuing to claim that I had abandoned him, he was making heavy work of getting undressed as he was dancing round the cabin trying to get his trousers off. I was forced to carry that particular operation out for him and was only thankful that the other occupant of the cabin was sound asleep and didn't have to witness this awkward situation. "Get in your bed," I commanded and as he was bent over his bunk all I heard was, "Oh no, how do I get in?" It really was a simple operation but with Jack being in the state he was, clearly beyond him. Out of my bunk again and now I had to sort out his duvet and guide him into the bunk.

Peace at last, or so I thought. "I can't lie down, me head's spinning!" I now had to talk him through a tried and tested method of avoiding this sensation by lying down in stages, and with some considerable patience and soothing noises on my part succeeded in getting him comfortable for the night. I was just beginning to doze off when Jack rose upright in his bunk and shouted, "Oh no!" "What the F**** wrong now," I politely enquired. "I've got no numbers in me epaulettes." By now I was absolutely raging and realised that the only way I was going to get any sleep was by either smothering him with his pillow or take the less drastic action of putting the shoulder numbers in for him. I chose the latter and spent the next half hour sorting out his uniform while he slept soundly. It did cross my mind that I might just have been being taken for a mug.

That wasn't to be the last disturbance of the night, but suffice it to say that the following morning as we were all lined up ready to disembark at Sullom Voe, I noticed a number of crew members sporting black eyes or swollen lips and at least one of our officers who was showing signs of having been in the wars. It hadn't been the best of days or indeed nights but we had at least made it to Shetland in one piece.

A very quick briefing surrounding the day's events and our specific duties was finished off quite nicely with the final piece of bribery. The boss in Shetland had been apprised of the nightmare journey and the underhand way in which we had been treated. His apologies were genuine and so was his announcement that we would be paid straight through, which went a very long way to restoring our spirits.

It was now time to be deployed throughout the site and individually dropped off at numerous junctions due to be passed by the Queen and her entourage during the course of her tour. I was in eye contact with an officer to my left and Jack Dalton to my right, who was by now sufficiently recovered to offer me abuse and cause me to wonder why I hadn't left him to die. Each junction was rapidly beginning to fill with construction workers, the majority of whom seemed to be dripping in all kinds of gold jewellery and carrying extremely expensive camera equipment. I was beginning to feel slightly vulnerable, surrounded as I was by some two hundred or so of these guys, all of whom seemed to be jockeying for the best position to get their photograph of the Queen. "Will I get a good shot here?" What did I know about photography other than taking shots of dead bodies or scenes of crime! "Yes." "Are you sure?" No, off course I wasn't sure but I wasn't about to admit it. "Yes, you should get a good shot here!" We spent some considerable time waiting for the queen to arrive during the course of which they all played Bait the Bobby while I laughed nervously and complimented them on their razor sharp wit. As much as I may have been offended by some fairly cutting banter, I had to remind myself that I was still just a boy and these were men.

It wouldn't have been wise in these circumstances to offer any form of reprisal and it would have been pure suicide to threaten arrest. I just had to bite my tongue and take it. Had circumstances been reversed I would probably have been one of the worst offenders. I've said it before and I will say it again, "It goes with the territory." The Queen's arrival was signalled by the appearance of police motorcycle outriders followed by marked police vehicles, two buses and following unmarked cars. My charges now jockeyed for the best position while I tried my best to herd them back off the road. The front of the convoy almost flew past and it was now apparent that her Majesty had been seated on the bus with blacked out windows. Nobody got a photo and nobody even claimed to have seen her, they weren't happy bears and it was beginning to sound like it was my entire fault. Luckily the following bus stopped to pick me up and as I quickly boarded under a hail of abuse I took the opportunity to leave them with a thought. "Don't worry boys you may not have seen her but she would definitely have seen you." The abuse was rising to a crescendo as the bus door closed behind me and I turned to wave through the clear glass.

We were now following directly behind the royal carriage and picking up police officers as we went before regrouping at the site of the opening ceremony. This process coupled with, I imagine, a quick stop for the Queen to get a cup of tea, allowed all the previous onlookers to congregate for this next phase. As we arrived at the site I could see that it was thronged with some five or six thousand people. Disembarking at the same point designated for the Queens arrival I was more than aware of a low growl and numerous shouted abusive comments which greeted every officer as they stepped down from the bus. I don't believe for one second that there was any possibility of trouble from this good natured crowd but how many opportunities do you get to give the police a hard time.

I was greeted in the same fashion as every other officer although I am fairly confident that some of my previous charges recognised me and were possibly a little more vocal. As I stepped down from the bus I once again took a moment to stop and shouted out for all to hear, "OK boys, spread out and surround them." The ridiculousness of this comment obviously appealed to the crowd's sense of humour and was met with an approving roar of laughter. I can't imagine that the Queen's arrival was greeted with either abuse or laughter but more a sense of excitement and delight from these hard men.

The area where the Queen was due to arrive was roped off and corridored by police shoulder to shoulder. I found myself as one of only two officers controlling a roped off throng of several thousand excited onlookers. The distance between me and my nearest colleague must have been a good thirty or forty yards and I would have to admit that I had not realised the significance of that situation. During the short wait I was having a good natured conversation with a group of younger employees who were desperate to know if the Queen was likely to stop and speak to them. Obviously, just as was the case with the guys wanting to know where they would get the best photograph, I didn't know the answer. This group continued to press me with the same question until I was forced to make a prediction. "The Queen will definitely stop and speak to you," I told them. They had gotten the answer they were looking for, but not being happy with that, they now wanted to know if I was sure. "I am certain the Queen will stop and speak to you." Still not happy with this answer they now enquired "How do you know?"

I could see I was being pressed into revealing my police logic which, if I was correct, would have left me with an air of mystique if I didn't tell them. "I just know," was insufficient response for these young enquiring minds and I was forced to lay my logic bare. "Take a look around this crowd," I instructed them. "Yeah!" "Do you see any females?" I enquired. Now it dawned on them, the only female visible in the crowd was in this group and she was right at the front. "If the Queen spot's you she will definitely stop," I told the girl, and she was delighted as were her friends. I hoped I was right!

I was right, and the Queen stopped and spent a slightly longer time speaking to this young girl. I was delighted for these youngsters as no doubt they would relate this story for years. I now became aware that the crowd were beginning to surge forward and I was trying my best to hold them back, at the same time realising that all that was between her and them was me and a length of rope. I was fighting a losing battle and very quickly the rope was down and the Queen surrounded. I did the only thing I could think of doing under the circumstances and stepped forward and literally wrapped myself around her in a fairly pathetic attempt to offer her some protection. It was a very panicky moment and I hoped she didn't think I was trying to make a pass. It seemed an age, although I'm sure it was only a short time before I was joined by my nearest colleague who had forced his way through the crowd, and together, still pretty much wrapped around her we shouldered our way through the throng.   More officers arrived and the situation was now quickly controlled and I was able to mumble some apology as I stepped away.   This moment of heroism, with no thought for my own safety, had to be worth at least a medal, if not a knighthood. Didn't happen!

Another footnote I should add to this particular part of the story. A couple of months after the event I was sitting at home when a knock came to my door. On answering I was confronted by Murdo Macleod, a family friend for many years. "Hi Robbie, I've got something for you!" What could Murdo possibly have for me, I pondered as I invited him in. He was carrying a large envelope which was intriguing me as I gathered its content was what he was referring to. Murdo had been working at Sullom Voe and had been present when the crowd had surged forward. A keen photographer, he had recorded the whole incident and on later review spotted an excellent shot of me just seconds before the incident which he had enlarged and now presented me with. Thanks Murdo.

I don't know if I heard any explosion, at least I don't remember hearing any explosion. I may have heard a dull thud and if I did I most probably put it down to the sort of noise you might expect to hear on a large construction site and dismissed it as such. Needless to say I have no such recollection but let me assure you it did happen. Although we weren't informed at the time it would appear that the Irish Republican Army had planted a small bomb in one of the pumping houses and had it timed to go off during the opening ceremony. The subsequent enquiry which I will relate shortly brought the event into some sort of focus.

Anyhow, the opening ceremony completed we were now bussed down to Lerwick where we were once again dropped off at various points along the route of the Queen's tour of the town and then on to where the Royal Yacht Britannia was berthed. Another large crowd was gathered here and amongst them a number of protesters carrying placards and banners emblazoned with their cause. I don't recall what the protest was but I was disappointed with the shouts and jeers which greeted the Queen's arrival as vocalised by this minority group. As valid as their protest may have been I didn't feel that it was advancing their cause by booing the Queen. Unfortunately there are those who consider her a valid target for such actions but I am inclined to disagree. Her Majesty left the Shetland Islands to the accompanying sounds of genuine cheers of affection which more than adequately drowned out the dissenters

A quick change at Lerwick police station now saw us bussed back to Sulom Voe and a very welcome meal before once again boarding our Dan Air flight from Scatsta to Lossiemouth. I most definitely hadn't enjoyed the aborted landings in an attempt to get to Shetland but surely nothing could go wrong this time. It came as no surprise that the head count once again was causing a problem and I should have taken this as an initial sign that things were about to get much worse. We were no more than twenty or so minutes into our return flight when the pilot announced that our intended destination of Lossiemouth had been closed due to fog and that we were now being diverted to Aberdeen. I didn't like the sound of that and I much less liked the sound of his second announcement informing us that Aberdeen had been closed due to fog and that we were now being diverted to Glasgow. Our transport back North had been due to pick us up at Lossiemouth and we had no way of informing the bus driver of our predicament.

It couldn't get worse could it, and then, "Gentlemen I am sorry to inform you that Glasgow has been closed due to fog conditions." Christ! We were going to be up here all day, where now I wondered. I wasn't to be left in suspense much longer as the pilot announced, "Gentlemen, I am re-diverting to our original destination of Lossiemouth where they have the capability of landing us through instruments." Instruments, what the hell did he mean instruments, "Banjo's," "Guitars," "Combs with bits of paper," how were they meant to get us down out of the sky without killing us all? Yes you've guessed it I was seriously shitting myself once again.

It was getting on for one in the morning and out of the aircraft window all I could see was nothing. It was pitch black and the plane was totally silent as all conversation had been abruptly halted by the pilot's announcement that we should fasten seat belts as he was now commencing his approach. The silence on the plane I can best describe as eerie and was doing absolutely nothing to allay my feeling of impending disaster. As I surveyed my surroundings and the faces of my colleagues I once more asked myself if I was the only passenger who was inwardly terrified until I rested on the face of my friend Jack Dalton. Jack's eyes were bulging and his features were frozen in a Hammer House of Horror grimace which surprisingly, given the circumstances, caused me to inwardly chuckle as I was satisfied that he was shitting himself too. The aborted overshoots at Scatsta had been terrifying enough and I never imagined that I would go through a worse experience until now.

The approach seemed to last forever and consisted of very steep descents punctuated by the roaring of the engines as the pilot throttled back and throttled back before moving into tight spirals. I don't know how many times we moved between the one form of aerobatics and the other and quite frankly I had ceased to care as by now I was quite convinced that we were all doomed. Another glance in Jack's direction basically confirmed my worst fears as his eyes had by now taken on the dimensions of soup plates and I could only thank god that I didn't have a mirror in front of me to witness my own expression. The approach and subsequent landing I can only describe as a terrifying white knuckle ride which I would never want to repeat and just to emphasise how bad it was the silence of the experience was broken by a spontaneous burst of applause and cheering as the aircraft taxied to a halt. It wasn't just me and Jack, they had all been shitting themselves.

We still had a bus ride into Inverness and onward journey North to contend with but it was great to be on Terra Firma and concern ourselves once again with mundane matters such as food and where we would get some at that hour. A number of older colleagues suggested that it would be a good idea to buy some fish and chips, put five pounds each into a kitty, buy a huge quantity of alcohol and advance North getting steadily drunk. I needed food if not just to convince myself that I was alive then at least as a reassurance that I was still capable of digesting solids. We did manage to reach some form of compromise and it was decided that those of us who needed the break and wanted some real food went to a local Indian Restaurant whilst those more in need of alcoholic refreshment purchased the booze and got themselves some fish and chips. I had predicted the foolishness of the £5 contribution stumped up by my younger and more gullible colleagues towards the giant carry out. In the early eighties that sum of money would have bought you a full bottle of whisky but all it bought them was a can of beer and a single measure of spirits. The huge carry out was retained at the front of the bus and shared out amongst the older more hardened drinkers whilst the youngsters at the back were left moaning about the injustice of the situation but unwilling to challenge their older counterparts for a fair share of the booze. I was reminded of a pack of lions tearing a carcase to pieces while a group of jackals hung about on the periphery of the kill waiting to dart in to steal their share.

About 5am in the morning a half drunk, half sober bus load of policemen arrived back in the far North of mainland Scotland having in my opinion, just survived the week end from Hell.

CHAPTER 12

BOMB ENQUIRY

The weekend from hell was over and I was once again snug in the Lea of Bum Island wrapped around my gorgeous, pregnant wife who I had at times doubted I might ever see again. Joyce was delighted to have me home as we had already developed a habit of never being apart and tended to be, as I term it, joined at the hip, which continues to be the case to this day. I have to say that on the rare occasions that we have been apart it has been really great getting back together, the meaning of which I will leave to your imagination, if you can bear it.

All good things must come to an end and this was to be no exception. It seemed I was no sooner home than I was told to pack my bags again to return to Shetland on the Monday morning. I was to make up part of an enquiry team which had been put together to investigate the I.R.A. bombing for which they had already claimed responsibility. Three days they said, but once again, Joyce, employing considerably more foresight than I have ever been guilty of, decided to pack me enough clothes to do for a week. "You never know, you could be there for weeks, you know what their like!" Yes, I did know what they were like but I don't know if I ever learned the lesson. I took my long lingering leave of Joyce on the Monday morning and boarded an Air Ecosse Banderante flying from Wick to Sumburgh. I was in company with John Wares, Sandy Rosie and no less exalted a personage than the Chief Constable himself who had flown up from Inverness. The aircraft which had been chartered for the flight was full of police officers and I had by now come to the conclusion that I was never again likely to be comfortable in a plane loaded with nothing but policemen.

We landed in Shetland and were immediately bussed the 26 miles or so up to Lerwick police station where after dropping off our luggage continued on to the police station at Brae in the North of the island. It was on our arrival here that we learned the horrible truth. Our team of approximately 50 officers were tasked with interviewing some 5 to 6 thousand construction workers and that was likely to take about three weeks. Three weeks; how was I going to tell Joyce? How was I going to manage? Who was going to do my washing? Who was going to rub my back when I lay in bed at night? I couldn't identify any likely candidates for the job in my immediate company and was obliged to move into a considerable period of depression whilst wallowing in self pity. John Wares took the news even worse than I did, "We were told that we were only coming here for three days and I only packed enough to do me for that long." Rumblings of agreement were followed by official denial. "That is not the information we gave out." "Well that's the information we got, what are you going to do about it?" "Don't worry, arrangements will be made." No doubt, but what sort of arrangements I was asking myself.

The group was now designated specific roles, interview officers of which I was one, statement readers and follow up enquiry teams not to mention the various administration and logistical requirements of an enquiry of this magnitude. The officers already in situ had not been idle while awaiting our arrival and we were presented with lengthy questionnaires to put to each interviewee, which, as the enquiry progressed, would change to take account of the information we were obtaining.

No time was being wasted and those of us designated interview officers were split into teams of three and I, along with Stewart Williamson and Mark Duncan were tasked to interview a senior management group. All the stops had been pulled out to assist us in the enquiry and nothing appeared to be too much trouble. We were located in a fairly plush office and a secretary presented us with a list of all the senior, middle and lower management personnel we were to interview, and not only that, but also the order in which they would attend. They hadn't been letting the grass grow under their feet. Frequent visits of the tea lady laden with all manner of filled rolls, chocolate biscuits and other fattening goodies saw my diet of the previous three months totally blown out of the water.

The rumour mill had been doing the rounds and given that all of us were in plain clothes linked with the nature of the enquiry, 2 and 2 had been added up to 5 and every one of us were now Special Branch officers. As much as I denied any affiliation to this group I am pretty sure that nobody believed me and treated any denial on our part as dis-information. Let's face it, if you were going to relate the story in a pub to your mates what would sound better.

That first day, as every other day, we had worked on until ten in the evening before we were transported back to Lerwick where we were to be accommodated. A nice hotel where we could have a shower and relax for a couple of hours in the bar before bed was a most welcome thought. You already know before I say it that I had gotten that one seriously wrong as well. Our bus came to a halt on the Northern outskirts of Lerwick outside of what I can only describe as a second war German prisoner of war camp. Staney Hill hostel had been a construction workers camp consisting of wooden Nissan type accommodation huts surrounding a central kitchen and recreation block. That in itself wouldn't have been so bad if the place had been in recent use but as we learned it had been brought back into service purely for us.

Surprisingly neither the Chief Constable nor any of the other senior officers stayed there with us. Our luggage had already made its way there and it was now a case of finding a room. Well I suppose it was a room but I am fairly confident that no estate agent would dare to describe it as such. A single bed which must have been constructed in situ was complimented by a bedside table, small chest and single wardrobe which left just about enough room to turn around. The lap of luxury this most definitely was not. Just to add insult to injury the communal toilet and shower block had no hot water and the automatic washing machines located there had been un plumbed. We had no option but to make the best of a bad job. Nobody was happy and our unofficial shop steward John Wares was more than happy to voice our complaints. The following morning the best that we could manage was a cold water shave and basin wash down. It wasn't nice but at least we got a decent breakfast.

Back to the enquiry and surprisingly enough, even at this level of employee we were unearthing the occasional gem. What did become rapidly apparent, dependant on what part of the country the interviewee hailed from more or less dictated their lesser or indeed sometimes greater knowledge of I.R.A. activity and frequently no surprise that an I.R.A. cell was active in Sulom Voe. In these instances we would pursue the interview beyond the boundaries of the questionnaire and mark the statements for particular attention of the statement readers and follow up enquiry teams. In some instances it was apparent that the interviewee was less than keen to be interviewed and just occasionally there was also a very tangible sense of a deep rooted fear of reprisal. I have to admit that I was frequently shocked but before very long we were to learn that we were rattling the right cages.

I was lying in my sparse cell on my very uncomfortable bed engaged in wet dreams involving my wife when I was rudely awakened by a loud voice shouting "Who is in charge here?" As my room was nearest to the front access door I made it out into the corridor first closely followed by John Wares. This time the same question delivered at the same decibel level was directed at me. I was more than happy to indicate to my interrogator that John could more than adequately meet the criteria of being in charge. Given that John didn't deny or refuse this accolade all comments were now directed at him and that suited me down to the ground. The corridor was by now rapidly filling with partially clothed police officers many of whom were quite literally climbing over others to find out what all the noise was about.

John never really got excited or at least I never knew him to over react to anything and with his usual aplomb quietly enquired "What's wrong?" "The I.R.A. has threatened to blow up the enquiry team!" This rather dramatic statement served to quieten the gathered rabble quite effectively. "So what action do you propose we take?" asked John. The ensuing discussion terminated with a decision that we would be guarded by two armed officers who would remain alert and patrol the area of our accommodation throughout the remaining nights we were to be there. Prone to worry as I am about falling out of the sky and various other methods of falling to my death this, I am sure, was the first time I had real concerns about meeting death on an upward trajectory. I suppose I should have been re-assured with the presence of two armed guards posted for our protection but that really wasn't the case. I am fairly certain that I would have slept much more securely if I hadn't known both of them. Checking our transport each morning for concealed explosive devices did absolutely nothing for my sense of well being and I never quite understood why we stood about in a single bunch alongside the bus as this task was being carried out.

As I have said, Joyce had packed me enough clothes to do for five days and my case was becoming fairly smelly as my washing was beginning to mount up. As much as we complained any effort to rectify our domestic situation was extremely slow at manifesting itself. We had no hot water to shave and wash so we were provided with kettles. Kettles are all very well but there were no sockets to plug them into in the toilet block. Passing each other in the narrow corridors laden with toilet bags and steaming kettles, I know, would have caused the health and safety conscious of today's society to have a hairy fit. John Wares had also lobbied on our behalf to source some method of washing our clothes and with typical police efficiency we were provided with a huge supply of automatic washing powder. Nice you may say but hopefully you will recall that relevant piece of information surrounding the fact that the washing machines had been un-plumbed.

Have you ever tried to create lather with a combination of automatic washing powder and cold water? Just like a dead horse, it doesn't work. Every night found us washing out our underwear, socks and shirts in a scum infested basin and hanging them out to dry in a storeroom at the end of the corridor that John had criss crossed with string which acted as a washing line. No irons and no ironing boards meant that we picked a shirt off the line and put it directly on our backs in the hope that body heat would remove the worst of the creases. I will re-iterate however, we were well fed.

We had completed our task with the management group and now we found ourselves in less than salubrious surroundings interviewing the scaffolders. How many hundred scaffolders worked on that site I don't know but their seemed to be a never ending supply? Another tea lady made frequent appearances and this time the content of her trolley was even more inviting. Bacon rolls, sausage rolls, egg rolls or any combination of rolls in any quantity you desired was immediately available. I suspect we spent more time eating than we did interviewing. The scaffolders themselves were a fairly down to earth bunch with no heirs and graces but once again they never ceased to amaze me. As each one came in they seemed to be dripping with more gold than the previous one. Most of these guys had worked all over the world and obviously took the view that they should invest in gold that they could carry with them adorning various body parts.

Rings on every finger, heavy gold chains around their necks and wrists, ear rings, Rolex and Longines watches that was worth more than my annual wage. I did feel that it was more often than not considerably over done and possibly a little effeminate, not that I would have dared to voice that opinion or maybe I was just jealous. Interviewing these guys was no picnic as several seemed to take the view that Special Branch officers were underhand and out to get them. As often as I made the statement "I am not Special Branch," equalled the frequency with which I was called a liar. I had reached the stage where I was no longer denying or confirming, it was much easier that way. These were the hard men of the time but even several of them, when we got down to the nitty gritty were visibly shaking and refusing to say any more when pressed. I frequently felt quite bad about marking some of these men for further attention as they were genuinely afraid. "You don't know what it's like when you're in a pub and these guys come collecting money. You give it to them, not because you want to, because you're afraid of what might happen if you don't." No, I didn't know what it was like to live in such a climate of fear and I felt genuinely sorry for those who did.

Not being slow to take advantage of a situation we found our supply of interviewees drying up just before lunchtime. Making the assumption that we had exhausted our supply of scaffolders prematurely we were now wondering where our next port of call may be. "You haven't seen them all yet," we were informed. "Why where are they? We enquired. "They've gone on strike." Why had they gone on strike, what reason did they have for going on strike? It seems that the reason for this course of action was our aggressive interview technique. In truth I felt that we could not have been nicer and more considerate, we had been treating the whole enquiry as extremely sensitive from day one and we had not set out to alienate anyone. The truth of the matter was exposed the following morning when we learned that they had all taken the afternoon off to watch an international football match and our presence was used as a means to an end. These guys were working 12 and 14 hours a day, 7 days a week for a month and more at a time so who was I to deny them a bit of time off to wind down.

To say I was missing Joyce would be a total understatement. I had been taking every opportunity to phone home when I could find a public telephone. This was well before the days of mobile phones and the cost of making a call from a public kiosk was absolutely extortionate. She hadn't taken the news of my prolonged absence terribly well and it had actually reduced her to tears. I did wonder if these were tears of joy at the unexpected period of peace she was enjoying or as I prefer to believe, and gave me a strange sense of satisfaction, her need to be with me.

We were definitely causing waves amongst those who we were investigating as could be confirmed by the next threat that was received. The I.R.A. had now made a clear statement of their intent to assassinate the senior investigating officer. The gentleman who held that particular distinction was a Detective Superintendent from headquarters in Inverness and was not unusual of his time as being a little eccentric. As usual I thought he was absolutely ancient although no doubt much younger than I am as I write. I hate to imagine what view young police officers hold of me today, probably, Grumpy Old Man, and if that is indeed the case I stand on my right to have earned the title and wear it with pride. The Detective Superintendent most certainly stood out in a crowd as emphasised by his chosen mode of dress. Fore and aft cap and plus fours wasn't what you would have called the height of fashion even amongst the landed gentry of the time who had already moved on to wax jackets and flat caps, but that was how he chose to dress. I would love to think that he smoked a pipe but in truth I can't remember. I think you would say he was difficult to miss which would be a rather poor turn of phrase as the I.R.A. had threatened to shoot him.

So how did the movers and shakers decide to deal with this threat, well believe it or not some poor simple thing, at least I am obliged to believe he must have been a poor simple thing, volunteered to dress up as the Detective Superintendent. The bosses thought this was a great idea, as no doubt they would, and decided to run with it offering up this piece of cannon fodder as a target. What a total idiot! Not one single member of the investigating team held an opposing view. I tried to imagine being selfless enough to offer myself as a sacrifice. "Don't worry sir, I will dress up in your clothes and wander about the town in an effort to draw their fire. I will happily take the bullet for you." No; I thought not!

Needless to say the I.R.A. didn't assassinate the detective superintendent and there is even less point in saying that they didn't blow me up or I wouldn't have been able to write the story. We had managed to carry out the bulk of the interviews in record time and now that there were only a few follow up enquiries to round off the investigation we were at last allowed to go home. I can't say that I was sorry to see the end of that particular period but it was both a real experience and quite an eye opener. What had we achieved? Although I never saw any final conclusion of the enquiry I do know that we had carried out a major intelligence gathering exercise, identified an active I.R.A. terrorist cell present in Shetland and stirred up the leadership of that group to quite a degree. Had this been a serious attempt on the Queens life? I somehow doubt it. Had this been a show of the group's ability to carry out such an act had they chosen to do so? I think, probably!

Once again, and for a considerably lengthy period I was returning unscathed to

Joyce.

CHAPTER 13

UNLUCKY FOR SOME

I was back home and comfortable and once again back on shift. Although I was seconded to C.I.D. on a number of occasions I never really had any ambition to be a permanent member of that group. Officers like Sandy Rosie were great to work with, I learned lots from him but I had a real problem with senior officers constantly hounding you for results. Equally, I couldn't come to terms with being nice to the guys you really needed to be nasty with. It was a means to an end that frequently stuck in my throat. I was a natural C.I.D. officer I had been told but I don't believe that anybody is a natural anything, you have to work at it and develop a style the same way as I had to work at it to become a reasonably competent uniformed officer. I really felt that being a uniformed beat policeman was what I had joined for.

My oldest nephew, although I consider him to be more of a younger brother had already joined the job as a Police Cadet. Garry was my oldest brother's son and was only eight years younger than me. As far as my brother was concerned he was destined for great things as an officer in the Queens Own Highlanders testament to which was abundant. Letters from the Colonel of the Regiment looking forward to Garry joining the Mess, a list of his achievements during his time as an Army Cadet, Company Cadet, Battalion Cadet and the ultimate accolade as the top cadet in the United Kingdom. Little wonder then that his future appeared to be clearly mapped out. I suspect that I may have had something to do with his alternative chosen path as Garry developed, from my brother's point of view, a somewhat unhealthy interest in the police service. I wasn't guilty of encouraging him but I was definitely not about to discourage him and I believe that my brother laid the blame squarely at my door when he did join. As much of an achiever as Garry has been I always said he would never amount to anything and I remain firm in that belief as he sits at police headquarters in Inverness occupying the office of Deputy Chief Constable. At the time of his appointment to that post I believe he was the youngest in Scotland and the first from Northern Constabulary to achieve A.C.P.O.S. rank. I am certain that he could long since have occupied the post of Chief Constable in some force or another but that would mean him leaving the North of Scotland, a sacrifice to date, he is not prepared to make.

The only other thing that I will say about Garry is that he has always been somewhat prone to being involved in road accidents the most spectacular of which was his first. He had been driving home from Inverness and on the very final leg of his journey had succeeded in leaving the road and writing his car off. Although treated at the accident and emergency department of the local hospital it was a number of years later that it was discovered that he had actually broken his neck. He was very lucky to be alive but to every cloud there is a silver lining. On any given day you can predict the weather by the angle of his head.

Garry's dad, my brother Adam, by the way Garry is also Adam but called by his middle name apparently to differentiate between Snr and Jnr. I never really understood why his mother didn't think we could tell the difference between a thirty year old bald man and a bald baby. Anyhow my brother Adam who had been Company Commander of the Caithness Army Cadets phoned me up one day to tell me that the Wick Sea Cadet Unit was in a bad way and close to folding. Adam knew that I had been a Sea Cadet for years and suggested that I could maybe help them out. "What do you want me to do?" I asked him. "Just go along on their next parade night and see what you can do to help." I can't say that I was enamoured with the idea but it was always difficult to say no to Adam. I know he was my brother but he was a really nice guy. "OK, I'll go, but I'm not committing to anything." Famous last words. My shift colleague and very good friend Donald

Cameron was ex Royal Navy and as far as I was concerned, the ideal man to rope into this potential disaster. Donald, although older than me was my appointed probationer.

I was responsible for his training and wrote Monthly reports on his progress. Good or bad, it was down to me and I reminded him of this fact prior to making him aware of my proposal. Make use of your available tools is what I always say and in this case, the best tool available was bribery.

The police were always very good about anything which came under the heading Community Involvement and as long as what was termed, (Exigencies of duty permitting) you would be allowed to attend on duty evenings. You were however expected to commit on off duty evenings also. Donald and I attended our first meeting of the Sea Cadets which was held in a Crypt under one of the local churches on a Tuesday evening. One adult instructor, half a dozen boy horrors and surroundings akin to a fish storage cellar confirmed my brother's assessment of the situation. The adult instructor/commanding officer was delighted to see us and told me that he was expecting us as my brother had told him that he had sourced new instructors for him. I had told Adam that I wasn't committing to anything but he had obviously decided that he was in a position to commit me by proxy. The following Tuesday night Donald and I turned up and the commanding officer didn't. We never saw him again. How was that for being left holding the baby?

Our cadets were an extremely motley crew and more suited to being a bunch of pirates being chased by the Royal Navy than respected members of the Senior Service. Thomas Mackay, my senior cadet of the moment now a very well known and respected local newsagent, Philip Green, a senior officer in the Highlands and Islands Fire Service, Geordie Crawford, a Clerk of Works for the Local Authority, to name only a few. Let me say that the best I would have predicted for them at the time may have been lengthy jail sentences. We certainly had our work cut out for us but a recruiting drive which totally ignored minimum age limits coupled with an intense fund raising programme saw us able to purchase a hut which became our headquarters. The Wick Sea Cadet Unit was to become a total commitment which I had sworn I would never make.

Joyce was pregnant but even at nine months you would have had difficulty guessing that she was. Her doctor had projected the 13th of March as being the delivery date and it was beginning to look like he was going to be bang on. Sometime about six in the morning on the 12th of March Joyce woke up suffering minor labour pains. I moved immediately into expectant father mode and began to panic. Joyce reassured me that there was no immediate cause for concern and that she was more than able to attend a pre arranged appointment later that morning. Time for a calming cup of coffee which she thoroughly enjoyed while paying not the slightest bit of attention to my delicate mental state. Had this woman got the slightest clue of what I was going through and did she in fact care? "My God!" I wanted to scream, "I'm having a baby and you haven't a clue what I'm going through. How can you sit there drinking coffee?" Pregnant women are so inconsiderate.

We made it to the appointment at ten that morning when I was instructed to take Joyce directly to the Maternity Unit at the Dunbar Hospital in Thurso, some 21 miles away. We had come prepared with the pre packed suitcase in the boot of the car. What I wasn't prepared for was the fact that it had begun to snow while we were waiting in the hospital. This wasn't a light fall of snow, it was really quite a heavy fall of snow and by the time I was just a few miles into my journey we were in the middle of a blizzard. What was this thing we had with snow, we had married in the midst of a blizzard and now I was having visions of trying to deliver a baby in the back seat of my car in the middle of one. Given my state of mind at the time I could certainly have well done without this added complication. It was Joyce who pretty much saved the day when she spotted a snow plough travelling some distance ahead of us its rotating Orange lights just discernible through the almost White out conditions. "Thank God!" All I had to do was get as close into the back of this thing as I could and stay there until we reached Thurso. The plan didn't work out exactly as I had anticipated. We made it to Thurso, but only just. I had been travelling so close behind the snow plough that its big tyres had been throwing snow up into the engine compartment of my car and by the time I was negotiating the last final hill to the hospital, the engine was coughing and spluttering on two cylinders and barely able to make ten miles per hour. I was never as relieved as when I pulled up at the front door of the Dunbar Hospital.

The staff were very efficient at their jobs and very quickly had Joyce settled into a ward where after allowing me a few short minutes, shooed me off the premises with the instruction to return at visiting hours as nothing was likely to happen before then. They didn't understand my delicate state either, or maybe they did and that's why they wanted rid of me. I spent the hours waiting at Thurso police station where my old colleagues spent some time reassuring me with comments like, "We didn't know you had it in you," and "Are you sure you are the father." I was in no fit state to argue and just let them have their fun but at the same time remembering names and faces. I returned to the hospital at three along with a number of other expectant and newly created fathers.

Joyce was in a ward of four beds and was by now suffering fairly extreme labour pains for which she was blaming me. I was told that I should remain behind at the end of visiting hours when Joyce would be transferred to a delivery room. So this was it, the event was imminent. Eight hours later after much screaming, begging for a mixture of gas and air and pleading for Pethadine injections, none of which they would give me, the delivery was in full flow. (Pardon the Pun.) I don't care what they say about women doing all the work, it just isn't true. I went through every second of that pregnancy and I pushed just as hard as Joyce at the delivery. I was shattered, I was an emotional wreck, I was stressed out but I was blooming. During the course of the delivery I suffered frequent abuse from Joyce, "It's all your fault," "This wont be happening again, I can assure you," and several threats of castration. Eighteen minutes past midnight on the 13th of March, as predicted, we had a baby. "What is it?" I couldn't tell, there were so many strings about I couldn't be sure. "It's a boy, no it's a girl, no it's a boy." A somewhat frustrated nurse handed the newly born to Joyce with a dismissive, "It's a girl." So I had a daughter and I was over the moon. Joyce had somewhat surprisingly gotten over her previous rants and threats and was once again deeply in love with me. I will never understand women.

I had done something no other person on the face of the planet had done, I had made a baby and she was the most beautiful baby in the world. I was unique or at least that's how ecstatic I was at the time until I eventually had to accept that baby's are pretty much an everyday occurrence and you don't need any special qualifications to make one. I wrote a little ditty at the time to celebrate Lynsay Marie Inrig Sutherland's arrival.

> T'was on the thirteenth day of March
>
> This year of eighty two
>
> Having waited three long years
>
> At last, my dreams came true.

My darling wife presented to me

A bundle of pure joy

And in my haste, a natural mistake,

I thought she was a boy.

To finish with yet another aside. All through the period of the pregnancy countless people would make comments surrounding the imminent changes to our lifestyle once the baby had arrived. "You wont be able to have nights out when the baby comes." "You wont get very much sleep when the baby comes." "Things will be different when the baby comes." What was I, "stupid?" Probably, but I had at least worked out that life was going to be considerably different. I could never quite get my head around this phrase, "when the baby comes," surely there was only one method of arrival or had I got that wrong as well. I couldn't help but visualise a gentle tapping at my front door and when I answered I would encounter a baby with a suitcase. "Hi, I'm your new baby I just arrived by bus." "Nice to meet you, come in your mothers been expecting you. Joyce, the baby's come." There has to be potential in that for one of those comedy sketch programmes.

Donald and I had been very successful in building up the Sea Cadet unit and by now we had somewhere in the region of twenty or so teenage pains in the arse. I was one of them once and remain one as an adult, so I couldn't really complain. We had generated interest by creating as many activities as possible, sending boys away on courses and getting as much information into the local papers as we could.

This strategy paid off and we were beginning to have a good ships company that we could rely on not to let us down when it mattered. I won't go into detail regarding the times that it didn't matter, but suffice it to say I threatened murder on frequent occasions. For a number of years we made use of the old British Aluminium workers camp at Foyers in Invernesshire for a unit training week. The camp had been taken over by the police and maintained for the use of by youth groups. It was a great facility and the boys loved it. We had completed our annual week at Foyers and had been back about our normal business for a couple of months when we announced that Joyce was once again pregnant. It had taken quite some time for Joyce to achieve this state first time round but now that I had learned the technique there was no stopping me. I was quite the stud.

The information was made public very quickly and I found myself being challenged by one of my cadets on a Tuesday parade night. I was approached by a thirteen year old Geordie Crawford with, "Aye Aye Robbie I hear Joyce is pregnant again." "That's right Geordie." "When is she due?" "Doctor Say's 11th October." Clearly happy with the information Geordie walked away from me and got into an immediate huddle with a number of other cadets. I had no reason to be suspicious and assumed nothing more than enquiring young minds. I was only happy that sex education was not part of my remit and that sort of thing could be adequately dealt with at school. At the end of the evening activities I was once again approached by Geordie and I could not help but notice that he was being eagerly observed by the rest of the unit who were for once not rushing out of the door. "Em's, Robbie?" "Yes Geordie?" "Joyce is due on the 11th October, is that right?" "Yes, that's right, why?" "Well, me and the boy's have been working it out and that means that you and Joyce were at it when we were at Foyers." I couldn't deny it, it was true but how could I have anticipated being challenged on the point by a thirteen year old. "You dirty expletive, you've scarred our young minds."

Roars of laughter indicated that I had been perfectly set up and left rapidly reddening by a bunch of kid's. I frequently found myself on the receiving end of their sense of humour from being dumped in the river to seeing Joyce's underwear flying from the top of the flagpole but I can honestly say I enjoyed every minute of my time with them. When it came to any one of the several important inspections that we had they never let me down and I was frequently filled with a sense of pride at their achievements. I was extremely sad to leave them when I was transferred and I like to think that they were sorry to see me go.

The unit folded in 1991 but was resurrected in 2005 and I have to say much more effectively and ably led by one of my best cadets of the day, Mark Cormack. I am delighted to say on my recommendation and that of my fellow management committee member Thomas Mackay.

I have entitled this chapter Unlucky for some, and you may wonder up until now, why? I was on night shift and busy shaking hands with door handles and rattling windows, making sure that our ever vigilant business community had secured their livelihood against unwanted intruders. You may just detect a degree of sarcasm in those last couple of sentences as I had lost count of the number of times I had walked in through the front door of shops and even chemists. How could you expect them to know what an Intruder Alarm System was if they didn't know how to work a key? Anyhow, it was about one in the morning when I received a radio message from the station instructing my immediate return as the Chief Inspector wanted to see me. What the Hell was the Chief Inspector doing at the station at that hour of the morning? This was serious cause for concern, what had I done wrong? I couldn't think of any recent misdemeanours I may have committed but that didn't mean anything. A complaint could come at you from the most unexpected of directions. I worried myself sick on the return journey to the station and became even more concerned when I spotted the Superintendent and the Chief Superintendent. I know I had threatened to kill several of the cadets on numerous occasions but I had never actually killed any of them.

As far as I was aware they were all fit and well and sound asleep in their beds by that time of the morning. "The Chief Inspector is in his office waiting to see you," I was informed by the duty sergeant. I entered the Chief Inspectors office with extreme trepidation and he clearly read the very obvious signs of concern on my face. "Its all right Robert, take a seat, you only have to worry if I keep you standing. As you know there was a transfer panel meeting in Inverness today." No, I didn't. "Your name came up and it was decided to transfer you to Stromness in the Orkney Islands." It was a bit of a bombshell but I learned later that I had also been considered for a posting to Barra in the Western Isles and all that saved me, (Apologies to the Western Isles.) was a previous memo which I had submitted requesting a transfer to Orkney when I entered the firing line. Any policing for the remainder of that night was out of the question as all I could concern myself with from then on was how I was going to break the news to Joyce.

Joyce was sound asleep when I got home and Lynsay was snoozing happily alongside in her Moses basket. I suppose it was Sods law but they were both having a long lie that morning and I just didn't have the heart to wake them. I had decided that it would be better for Joyce to wake naturally and then I would break the news. I fell asleep. About three in the afternoon I was woken by a frantic Joyce in floods of tears. "Tell me it's not true, were not going to Orkney, are we?" "Who told you?" Our next door neighbour was also police and had told his wife who in turn told Joyce assuming that she already knew. "Yes, it's true." "Well I'm not going, you can go by yourself, I hate you." Roughly the reaction I had expected. Six weeks later I was en route to Stromness accompanied by a heavily pregnant Joyce and a by now toddling Lynsay.

To this day I keep photographs taken as we were ready to board the ferry all of which clearly show Joyce in considerable distress because she didn't want to go.

CHAPTER 14

ORKNEY

We arrived in Stromness where we were met by none other than David Murray who had transferred there about a year or so earlier. David had arranged a meal for us in the Stromness Hotel which was extremely welcome and this period also allowed our furniture remover to pick up some help to unload the wagon. I had visited Stromness on numerous occasions and Joyce at least once before when we had taken the cadets over for a training weekend. Neither of us ever imagined that we would one day be living there. Our carpets had already been laid by one of my Stromness colleagues, Stewart Irvine who had been a carpet fitter before he was a policeman. Although I knew of Stewart when he lived in Wick I had never really socialised with him and hadn't been able to form any opinion in respect of him. As a youngster you have best pals and as an adult it happens too. Stewart Irvine was to become my very best mate and remains so today. There, I have said it and I haven't been sick and in the event that he ever reads this can I just say, Joyce made me say it.

The whole operation of a removal, take it from me, can be very stressful and the presence of my sister Janet at this time was very much appreciated. Joyce was heavily pregnant and demanding while Lynsay was just demanding. It was a late night and the removal van still wasn't empty and the driver was keen to get away for a pint or two. We had been getting beds together and emptying boxes and everyone was shattered and needing some sleep. The removal man was nearly biting his tongue off and decided that he would leave with a reassurance that he would return in the morning with the remainder of our belongings. None of us slept very well that night disturbed as we were by the unfamiliar sounds of the twilight hours and kept waking with some new sound or another. Joyce was quite convinced that she had heard some strange noises about six that morning but couldn't place what it may have been.

We rose early and continued with the unpacking while awaiting the return of the removal van which was never appearing. Joyce was of the opinion that there were considerably more boxes lying in the garden than I had thrown out the previous evening but I was convinced that she was imagining things. By 10am and still no sign of our removal van I phoned the police station and David carried out a quick enquiry. A short phone call later and I was informed that the van had left on the early ferry that morning. I couldn't believe what had happened and on going out to the garden to check here was a considerable amount of our property quite literally dumped there. Boxes of clothing, fairly expensive wedding present China, Royal Doulton Figurines and Crystal all basically abandoned to the elements. Needless to say I wasn't a very happy bear and immediately contacted the removal company and informed them of the circumstances. Luckily, nothing had been damaged other than the removal van which the driver, in his haste to board the ferry, had driven directly into the still rising half deck causing thousands of pounds worth of damage.

I learned later that the driver had abandoned the removal van at the ferry terminal on the mainland and gone on a drinking binge. The whole event also cost him his job.

Stromness police station located on what is known as the West Mainland of the main island of Pomona was manned by yours truly, Stewart Irvine, Douglas Durrand and the Section Sergeant William Fea Muir. (A descendant I believe of the infamous pirate Fea.) The section also had responsibility for the islands of Flotta, (Oil Terminal) Switha, (Bird Sanctuary) Graemsay, the island of Hoy and several smaller uninhabited islets. The island of Hoy boasted its own police station at the village of Longhope manned by an old school chum, Jimmy Williamson. The circumstances in the West Mainland section were such that you more frequently worked alone than teamed up with a colleague.

This was fine and allowed for much broader police coverage than would have been the case if we were obliged to work in pairs, that was assuming that you knew where you were going, which I didn't. It always takes a bit of time to get used to a new area, working out the geography and getting to know the communities. This wasn't quite the case with the community as unlike the inhabitants of my home county who made it their business to find out as much as possible about you in an initial meeting as was physically possible, the Orcadian, I concluded was quite the opposite. Anything you wanted to know they were quite happy to relate and this was also the case if you didn't want to know. A more open people I have never met and I honestly believe they would have great difficulty in being underhand as I witnessed on the odd occasion when someone did try such an approach to my police enquiries. I never came across an Orcadian who had mastered the art of lying well. They were most definitely not cut out to be crooks.

Joyce, as I have said was heavily pregnant with our second child and unlike her first pregnancy which was barely noticeable, this time round there was no mistaking her maternal state. It was hard to believe that someone so petite could balloon to such proportions. I had been working a late turn from 5pm until 1am on the morning of, as predicted, 11th October and was due to recommence duty on what we called the quick changeover at 8am that same morning. Arriving home shortly after 1am Joyce informed me that she thought that she was ready to have the baby. I didn't panic nearly as much as I did first time round as by now I was very much the old hand at this sort of thing and immediately contacted the doctor. Dr Rae, the local physician of the day wasted no time and instructed me to take Joyce directly to the maternity unit at the Balfour hospital in Kirkwall. David Murray, although living in the single man hostel above the police station in Stromness was actually stationed in Kirkwall and I spoke to him when I telephoned to report that I would be unlikely to be on duty that morning. David said he would be in touch.

I arrived at the maternity unit sometime around 3am and was informed that their was a phone call waiting for me. I wondered what could possibly be wrong, was Lynsay all right? Was I being taken from the birth of my second child to attend some inconsequential domestic dispute? Nothing that important. "Hello." "Hi, Robert what did she have?" This was David Murray demonstrating his complete lack of knowledge surrounding the birthing process. "What do you mean, what did she have, we've just got here." "What, she hasn't had it yet! How long does it take?" " I don't know how long it takes, it could be ages yet." "Will she have it by eight o'clock?" Which just happened to be the time that David would be coming off duty. "I don't know. Maybe!" "OK, I'll check again then." Imagine being that stupid but then again he was only twenty years of age. Joyce was already in a side ward and being attended by a midwife.

This was going to be an entirely different experience from the first one and I was considerably less stressed. The midwife was pretty much in constant attendance and I am fairly certain that her presence curtailed Joyce with regard to unfounded allegations directed at me. The maternity unit was small enough to retain that personal touch and the staff went seriously out of their way to make both the expectant mother and the expectant father as comfortable as possible. A regular supply of tea and biscuits and loads of reassurance was the order of the day. I won't say I was relaxed but at least I wasn't climbing the walls and Joyce wasn't digging her lengthy talons into the back of my hand.

The maternity unit was totally self sufficient with its own dedicated kitchen and cleaning staff who arrived in about 6.30am each day. As was normal they would enquire of the night staff if there had been any new admittances and who they might be. The only information they were given that morning related to the arrival of a policeman's wife from Stromness. At 8am that morning I was in the delivery room of the Balfour hospital maternity unit awaiting our new arrival.

Shortly after 8am David Murray arrived at the hospital in full police uniform. I have to say that the staff could be forgiven for making the mistake that they did, after all they had been told that the new patient was a policeman's wife from Stromness and here was a policeman. Two and two was added up and became five. David was greeted with "Hello son, you will have had a long night." That was a fair statement and David just having ended his night shift was inclined to agree. "You will be needing your breakfast," the cook offered and David responded with, "That would be very nice, thank you." Very quickly, David was seated at a table and presented with a plate of sausage, bacon, egg and mushrooms accompanied by a rack of toast and a pot of tea. All the while being fussed over by a number of mothering hen's David could equally be forgiven for thinking that he should visit this place more frequently. "Is this your first?" the cook enquired. "First what?" responded David. "Your first baby!" David almost choked on his sausage and had little time to consider his reply. "It's not mine," he blurted out and then realising the implication of this statement did his best to put the shocked ladies minds at rest.

"It's my mate's wife that's in; I've just finished the night shift." The looks of shock on the faces of the kitchen staff were replaced with looks of realisation at their understandable mistake and a good laugh was had by all. It didn't stop David from enjoying my breakfast and knowing that it was meant to be my breakfast made it taste even better.

I was at that time heavily involved in the birthing process, as a matter of fact I felt that I was so involved and dressed for the occasion that I may well have delivered the child on my own. "What is it?" Joyce was demanding. Well, it was most definitely a baby. "What is it?" this time voiced with a considerable degree of impatience. Joyce had to understand that I was not about to make the same mistake as I had first time round and I was making sure. "What is it?" I do believe that if I hadn't responded on that occasion she may well have killed me with one of the many instruments of torture immediately available. Having discounted a number of strings and other bits I was now in a position to reply, "It's a boy!" Joyce was delighted, I was delighted and I do believe that the staff were delighted as they no doubt are at every birth. We were in a side ward when David Murray was ushered in and with considerable relish, related the story of the mistaken breakfast. This was the first time that David had seen a newly born baby and I keep a photograph of him holding the newly arrived Ben Inrig Sutherland where David wears a much bigger and broader smile than either me or Joyce.

Many years later I received a telephone call from David. "Guess where I am just now and guess what I am doing?" "I give in David, where are you and what are you doing?." "I am sitting eating my breakfast after my wife has just given birth to my daughter." I had threatened that when the time came I would be there to eat his breakfast and this was him gloating.

The early eighties was not a period during which police pay and conditions were at there best and any overtime worked was paid at time and one third. The situation in Stromness was such that we were constantly understaffed and the only way that we could offer a reasonable degree of cover was to work regular overtime, especially at weekends. The addition of David Murray to our strength did little to improve the situation and even if our numbers were doubled we would still have had great difficulty in providing anything like twenty four hour cover. The main station at Kirkwall boasted no less than sixteen officers, four uniformed sergeants, a detective sergeant and constable, Inspector and Chief Inspector, not to mention a community involvement officer and various civilian members of staff.

The balance was far from fair given that we dealt with approximately one third of the workload for the whole of the islands. The understanding was that officers from Kirkwall would deal with matters on the West Mainland which occurred out with our normal working hours, our earliest finishing time being 1am and latest 3am unless we were obliged to work late owing to an ongoing enquiry. To my knowledge it never worked that way and we were being constantly called out for the most trivial of matters. I would frequently find myself arriving home shortly after 1am when I would sit and have a cup of coffee with Joyce and never considered going to bed before 2am just in case I was called out. Sod's law pretty much dictated that my head would no sooner hit the pillow than the phone would ring and I would be on my way to some incident or another.

The best example of ridiculous call outs I can offer goes like this. I had just finished my late turn at 1am and was due to recommence duty at 9am the same morning. I was on that quick turn around I have already mentioned and as usual wasn't prepared to go to bed before 2am. Shortly after two the almost inevitable phone call had me out of bed and attending at an address in Stromness. The only information I had been given was that there was a problem and the complainer had sounded somewhat confused. I wouldn't claim that when attending incidents in the middle of the night that I was always at my best and most alert and I was rarely properly dressed for the occasion. I always made sure I was identifiable as a police officer although not the smartest one you were likely to encounter. I attended at a little storey and a half cottage and found the front door wide open, I could only assume to offer me admittance. It was dark outside and even darker inside as I peered into the house and called out in order to attract the attention of the householder.

Edging slowly into the house all the while calling out to attract attention my heart almost came to a sudden stop when I spotted an elderly lady, she must have been eighty if she was a day, standing at the bottom of the staircase beckoning to me. "It's the police, what's wrong?" She didn't answer and again I asked what was wrong. All she did was stand there crooking her finger directing me to move towards her. As many times as I asked equalled the amount of times I got no reply other than this continuing beckoning. I don't know if I was afraid but I was certainly concerned, for all I knew she had a large knife in the other hand just waiting for me to get close enough and before I knew it, it would be all over with me lying on the floor with blood gushing out of my open throat. As I got nearer she turned and began to make her way up the stairs constantly turning and continuing to beckon me to follow. I continued to ask what was wrong but never yet gained a response.

On reaching the top of the stairs she stopped and pointed to an open bedroom door and their lying on the floor, obviously having fallen out of bed, was an even older lady. "Thank goodness you're here I've fallen out of bed and I can't get back in." After ascertaining that she was all right and offering her any necessary medical attention I picked her up and deposited her back in her bed. I believe they were two spinster sisters; the first of whom I had encountered was both deaf and mute and unable to respond to my initial enquiries. The phone call to the emergency service had been made by the lady who had fallen out of bed. I returned home and reported in to Kirkwall updating them in respect of the incident. Surely now I would get some sleep.

Shortly after 5am, there was the phone going again. What was it this time I wondered? "Hi Robbie, sorry to bother you again!" "That's okay." (It wasn't really.) It seemed that some student or another was on his way home to Orkney and had lost his wallet. He had no money to pay for his ferry crossing from Scrabster and was currently at the police station in Inverness where they would advance him a sum of money providing that I could obtain that same amount from his parents in Stromness. Once again I had to get out of bed and head for this students address. The reception I got from his father while I stood at his front door was far from pleasant. "This is a ridiculous time of morning to be getting people out of their bed for something like this, I will be complaining to your superiors." His attitude, from my point of view was a major mistake and I wasted no time in telling him that this was my second time called from my bed, my family disturbed and I wasn't about to listen to any of his shit.

He either gave me the money or he didn't and I left him in no doubt that I really didn't care either way whether his son got home or not. Seeing the error of his ways he quickly handed over the money and apologised profusely for his attitude. I then contacted Kirkwall and updated them in respect of the matter. I may still manage a couple of hours.

It seemed like my head had barely touched the pillow when there was the phone ringing again. The Kirkwall officer on the other end of the phone bore the brunt of my displeasure and I suspect was prepared for it knowing that this was my third call out. Some idiot of a driver had locked himself out of his car while in the early morning ferry queue and no other vehicles could pass to board. Off I went once more to the rescue. Opening a car only took a few minutes but by now there was no point in even thinking about getting any sleep. I had to be on duty at 9am and it seemed like I had never been off duty.

I started this story by referring to these incidents as ridiculous call out's, let me tell you why. The first incident would have been more appropriately dealt with by the medical authorities and at that time there were at least 6 district nurses living in Stromness that I knew of. All of these nurses were likely to have had some local knowledge of the elderly ladies situation and would have been in a better position than I to assess her medical needs. The second incident could easily have been dealt with once I was due to come on duty at 9am.

The student had his rail ticket through to Thurso and could have called at the police station there and still have had plenty of time to make his ferry connection. His father wouldn't have been upset and I wouldn't have been annoyed. As far as the idiot locked out of his car goes, all that was required there was to call out one of the local garages, but that would have cost money and the police were free. The Scottish Police Federation recognised that these situations were common throughout the service and took steps to improve our lot. Call out's, out with a police officers normal rostered tour of duty would now be paid at a minimum of four hours at the appropriate enhanced rate. I now began to get a more frequent full night's sleep.

Up until now everything I have written has been absolutely true and accurate as far as my memory allows. I am not making this point because I am about to start telling lies but I am fairly certain that some of the stories I am about to relate, you will find much harder to believe than some of those that have gone before.

Our staffing level and shift system was such that I found myself working with only three of the other four officers in the station. I rarely found myself on duty with Douglas Durrand other than when we were crossing over or one or the other of us had agreed to work a shift for another colleague. This was also true of the others, for instance Stewart may not have worked with David Murray and Billy Muir may not have worked with Stewart. One of the rare occasions that I did find myself on duty with Douglas is a story which is deserving of its own title, hence;

GHENGIS HEN

Douglas and I found ourselves together on an early turn. I don't remember what the enquiry was but it must have been reasonably urgent to require the two of us to make our way to the island of Hoy. The local policeman was on annual leave and the enquiry could not wait for his return. We left Stromness on Stevie Mowat's small passenger ferry and after a brief call at the island of Graemsay we were dropped of at Hoy pier in the North of the island where we were met by a local Special Constable who frequently made his car available for our use when required.

We only had to cross the width of the island from Hoy pier forming part of the inner boundary of the famous Scapa Flow to Rackwick Bay overlooking the equally famous Pentland Firth and only a short walk to the Old Man of Hoy. Rackwick bay and its beach poetically known as the singing sands is a most spectacular sight and as far as I am concerned an absolute step back in time. A one time thriving fishing community has for a long time been all but deserted with the exception of two residents. The world famous composer, Peter Maxwell Davis lived there at the time as did the subject of our enquiry, a reclusive one time male nurse. If memory serves me correctly he had been on one of his rare shopping trips to Kirkwall when he had either witnessed or been the victim of a crime and an urgent statement was required.

His home like all the other uninhabited ones dotted about the valley was built of large stones from the beach and furnished most beautifully with his own handiwork fashioned from what he could scavenge from the beach. The approach to his little house by way of a steep hill, green in patches and other patches of golden sand was,

I would have to say a most satisfying walk. The less than urgent approach allowed me to appreciate the rustic beauty of the house itself and the spectacular views across the Pentland Firth. You would really need to go there to appreciate just how perfect it is.

Approaching the house I could see that it's resident was as self sufficient as you could expect, generating his electricity from a small windmill, water storage barrels, a stock of wood for burning and the whole picture framed by a boundary made up of differing colours of net and wood washed ashore. This makeshift fence also served the purpose of enclosing a number of marauding Hens. I was in the lead and opened the small gate allowing me into the enclosed space and the path leading to the house. As I approached the house I seemed to sense that Douglas wasn't following and when I turned around to see what was keeping him, here he was still standing on the outside of the gate. "Hurry up Dougie," I shouted. "I'm not going in there." "Why not?" I enquired. "That Hen is going to have me," he replied pointing out a particular Hen who, I would have to say, on reflection was puffing itself up considerably more than any of the several others wandering about in the enclosure.

What I didn't know and Dougie hadn't felt it necessary to tell me, was that he had a morbid fear of Hen's. I have a morbid fear of heights and I tell everyone who is willing to listen but I must admit I think I deal with it quite well by refusing to climb higher than the height of a pavement and not looking down. I get dizzy climbing a step ladder but it is a great excuse for not decorating. Suffering from an equally foolish fear did not however incline me to offer Dougie any sympathy and if anything I was really quite cruel. "For God's sake Dougie, it's only a Hen; it's not going to touch you." Dougie was still refusing to progress beyond the gate so now I stooped to name calling in order to get him through. "You great big calf, look at the size of you and scared of a little Hen, come on." Still Dougie was refusing to move and the situation was beginning to get ridiculous.

Considerably more name calling and a degree of coaxing and assurances from me that he would be all right saw Dougie quite literally slither through the gate and begin to walk sideways up the path all the while keeping his eyes on the threatening Hen. As I watched Dougie and at the same time watching the Hen I began to realise that he may well be right. The Hen had drawn as much of a bead on Dougie as Dougie had on the Hen and the Hen was strutting and puffing like a Cockerel. Even though I realised that things could possibly turn out quite nasty I couldn't help but see the ridiculousness of the situation and was having great difficulty in containing my amusement. It was like a scene out of High Noon and the only thing that was missing was the theme music.

The only question now was, is something going to happen or is nothing going to happen, who was going to be first to back down or was one of them going to go for their gun. Was Dougie going to make the first move or would it be the Hen? My money was on the Hen as Dougie appeared to have taken route where he stood. Before I could bless myself it happened amidst much flapping of clipped wings, clucking and screams. The Hen launched itself at Dougie quite literally wrapping itself around his thigh and Dougie took of down the path and through the gate with the Hen still attached. Feathers were flying everywhere, the Hen was clucking victory calls and Dougie was screaming at the top of his voice. I know I should have been concerned but you had to be there, I was doubled up laughing and that's how the house resident found me, attracted as he had been by the commotion. "What's wrong?" he enquired and all I could do was point down the hill at Dougie being pursued by a Hen. "That bloody Ghengis, he's nothing but trouble, it's time he was a Sunday roast."

It seems that Ghengis was a Hen with an identity crisis who actually thought he was a Cock. We did manage to get our enquiry completed and I enjoyed a lovely cup of tea and home baked cake which Dougie couldn't relish to the same degree as me as all he could concern himself with was managing to get away unscathed. Flanked by the householder and myself Dougie left the area of the fateful duel (Which he lost.) and it felt like we were escorting an assassin's target. As with my observation on not taking the I.R.A. bullet for the detective superintendent, neither was I prepared to take the Hen for Dougie.

Working with Stewart Irvine was an endless round of laughs and I do believe I never laughed so much in my life as we always seemed to be getting involved in hilarious incidents. If you didn't know Stewart you would imagine him to be humourless and a bit boring but nothing could be further from the truth. This little story was probably my first encounter with his outrageous sense of humour.

Stewart and I had been through in Kirkwall and were returning to Stromness. Stewart was driving and I was sitting in the passenger seat when our conversation, as it inevitably does, got round to sex. They say that men think about sex every six seconds which is probably about right when I manage to think about how often I manage to think about anything else. As a matter of fact I have written this book in six second bursts. I don't recall what particular route the conversation was taking or which particular sexual fantasy we were discussing but here's what happened. "Do you know what I like? Stewart enquired. "No!" "I like knee length, high heeled leather boots. I like fish net stockings and suspender belts. I like peep hole bra's." As Stewart was in the process of describing each item my imagination was beginning to form a not unpleasant picture of his wife Jennifer garbed as he was relating. "I like black knickers and those long silk black gloves.

I like those big bull whips." The image I had by now built up in my head was beginning to become quite outrageous. At this point Stewart leaned towards me and in a very conspiratorial tone said, "Do you know what I really like?" "No" I said. "Jennifer dressed the same." The image that I had built up was, in the blink of an eye, demolished and replaced with a similar version except this time it was Stewart. I was fighting between laughter and wanting to be sick. We couldn't carry on with any other conversation as both of us laughed all the way to the police station and I continued to laugh for days afterwards and still laugh today when I think about it.

This admission by Stewart of being a particularly perverted cross dresser, seen here in print, will I know scar his children's young minds for the rest of their lives

Orkney served up more than its fair share of tragedies ranging from the usual fatal road accidents to suicides and sudden deaths in its various forms. I was due to commence an early shift when sometime around 6am the phone went. A report had been received about a chimney fire in the town. My initial reaction to this information was somewhat sceptical as chimney fires were something that in my experience generally occurred during evenings and as a result of over fuelling and dirty flu's. It just seemed to be an unusual thing to be reported at that time of morning and I headed for the locus with some feeling of trepidation. The time it took me to drive to the police station, pick up the police vehicle and hand held radio pretty much ensured that the Fire Brigade would be at the fire before me. My initial instinct was to prove tragically true.

I have no intention of naming names although the whole event was reported in the local paper and in this case even made the nationals. One of the volunteer firemen who had entered the house wearing breathing apparatus was the son of the female victim. The reason that I mention this particular incident is that I saw something I had never experienced before and this would allow me to accurately assess an event only a few weeks later.

I was on a late turn commencing duty at 6pm and I hadn't been in the office very long before I received a call from Kirkwall police station. "Hi Robbie, we've had a report from a guy in Quoyloo saying that he hasn't seen his neighbour for a few days and he is a bit concerned." The report had come in a few hours earlier and the complainer was happy to wait until I came on duty to investigate. It was winter and the dark was falling early so by the time I had made my way the sixteen or seventeen miles to Quoyloo it was pitch black. I called at the complainer's address where I managed to get a brief background surrounding his concerns before he accompanied me to his neighbour's home on the hill overlooking his own.

As I drove up to the house I could see that it was of a type not uncommon in Orkney. A single storey dwelling the walls of which were formed from poured concrete with a flagstone roof. The house was in total darkness and I began by banging on the only entrance/exit doorway in an effort to attract some attention. It was at this point that the complainer said, "I forgot to mention that all the windows have been blacked out, which is a bit strange." Together we carried out a circuit of the house while I trained my torch on all of the windows. What I saw then was exactly what I had seen at the previous incident and was able to make some degree of an informed guess. It was only fair of me to tell the complainer what my suspicions were. "I don't believe that the windows have been blacked out. I think there has been a fire in this house which has burned itself out." I went on to explain that I now intended to force entry to the house and I anticipated that what I may encounter may not be very nice. I had to give him the option of staying with me or leaving as I felt it would not be fair to subject him to the potential horror I suspected I may find.

As often as a police officer may encounter horrific sights not normally seen by members of the public, for me it never became any easier and was best dealt with in the company of someone else rather than on your own. I won't say that I wasn't pleased when he made the decision to stay.

I had every reason to believe that I wasn't about to save anyone's life by frantically breaking my way into the house as whatever had gone on here was long since past. I now contacted Kirkwall police station, informed them of my suspicion and my intention to force entry to the house and requested that they stand by for my next transmission. Briefing my now partner as best I could about what we could expect to find and the potential dangers associated with our action I now prepared to shoulder the front door of the small porch. I put my full weight to what I considered to be a fairly flimsy door but it still took four or five tries to put it in.

The very small porch was showing no sign of damage but the smell assailing my nostrils was a fair indication that what I was looking for was contained behind a fairly substantial interior door. I realised that there was still a reasonable chance of a fire burning inside and knew that I had to take considerable care in opening the interior door. The Fire Brigade had been informed and were en route but I couldn't wait for their arrival. Instructing my partner to remain outside I hid myself as best I could behind the wall alongside the door and pushed the interior door open. The blast of heat released at this point was enough to take my breath away and I remained where I was for just a few seconds before I satisfied myself that it was safe to proceed. I didn't have to go very far as shining my torch into a pitch black sitting room I could see a naked male, totally black, lying outstretched on a sofa. My partner tried to force his way past me insisting that the male could still be alive and that his wife could be somewhere in the house also.

I was obliged to hold him back and forcefully explained, "He's dead and anyone else that may be in there is dead too." This was now a job for the Fire Brigade to go deeper into the house with breathing apparatus and a potential crime scene which I had to protect.

Once again I contacted Kirkwall and updated them on the situation requesting all the necessary equipment, lighting units and C.I.D. photography. A short wait later the Fire Brigade had arrived and my colleagues from Kirkwall. Detective Sergeant Willie Sutherland who I had known for several years attended and together, once we had the go ahead from the Fire Service, we began a search of the house. We didn't really know what we had here and consequently treated the matter as a suspicious death which required the presence of senior officers and the Procurator Fiscal. This was by no means the first time that I had encountered a death due to a house fire but it was most definitely the first and last time that I had encountered a death where the deceased was so determined to take his own life. I had read of various forms of death and suicides as illustrated in a very interesting book entitled Medical Jurisprudence and Toxicology and although I had dealt with most of them here was one I never expected to see as it was particularly rare.

Although I can't recall the technical name of the suicide I can relate the process. Some suicides may use more than one method to ensure their death such as taking an overdose of medication and hanging or taking pills and slashing their wrists or countless variations on numerous themes. Such methods of suicide are not uncommon but what we had here was multiple methods. The deceased, in this case had taken an overdose of pills along with alcohol, slashed his wrists and here is the unbelievable bit, taken an axe to his own head and set the place alight. The question we needed to answer was why.

The answer was particularly sad and tragic. This man who was in his late thirties early forties had run a successful business for a number of years somewhere in the South of England. He was married with a loving wife and family as was his business partner and they weren't only partners, they were friends and so were their families. The catalyst for the relationship we never found out but he began an affair with his partners wife and after some time both of them gave up their previous lives and ran away together to start a new life in Orkney. They set up home together on the island and began a little craft business which kept them adequately in their new life style. After a number of months the woman had realised that she had made a mistake and was secretly communicating with her husband who was desperate to have her back and so began a plan for their reconciliation.

As normal the victim left for his work on a Friday morning and was offered some plausible reason for his partner's non attendance that day. On his return home that same evening he was met with a lengthy dear John letter and the knowledge that his partner had long since left the island and was well on her way back to her husband. I can only begin to imagine his grief, he had given up his business, he had given up a loving wife and family and now he had lost the only thing he had left. I can only imagine that this was enough to disturb the balance of his mind and as far as he was concerned what option had he left.

Every year the Police on the island ran a charity event of some description to raise money for a needy cause. This particular year the Chief Inspector, fairly unreasonably I thought, decided that the Stromness section would be responsible for the fund raising. Kirkwall was teeming over with staff who could devote some time to such an undertaking whereas we were frequently struggling to keep up with our enquiries. Anyhow the dice was cast and it was down to Stewart Irvine, David Murray and I to arrange an event. We decided on a traditional Scottish Ceilidh and very quickly we had arranged a venue, a date and pretty much pulled all our local acts together. All we needed now was a compere and an audience. The best known character on the island at that time was the B.B.C. Scotland presenter, Howie Firth and he lived in Stromness. He was the obvious choice for compere and to run a Mr and Mrs competition. We now had to have tickets printed and most importantly get people to buy them. At two pounds a ticket we didn't consider them overpriced and set about our marketing strategy. "Do you want to buy a ticket for our Ceilidh?" "Bugger Off." "O.K." Just kidding, we very quickly sold some 200 tickets but I found myself a bit between a rock and a hard place.

Every time we managed to sell some tickets after listing the names of our acts I would be asked what I would be performing. In several instances we only managed to sell the tickets with an assurance that I would be performing some sort of entertainment. It was easy at the time to say that I would be doing something but as the event drew closer I didn't have a clue.

I don't know why so many people wanted to see me on a stage making a fool of myself, I could manage that quite adequately without going on a stage to do it. Maybe they wanted not so much to see me make a fool of myself as a Bobbie make a fool of himself but I didn't think they could be that cruel. To cut a long story short, the evening was a great success and we raised a considerable amount of money. David Murray and I performed a Yorkshire monologue entitled Capstick Comes Home sprinkled with some songs, a bit of my home grown poetry and loads of jokes. It went down a bomb and was to haunt me for the remainder of my time on the islands. I was quite literally bombarded with requests to do the never ending round of Ceilidhs and charity events but I will return later to my short career, treading the boards.

CHAPTER 15

ORKNEY PART 2

So many things happened in Orkney that I could probably write a book on it alone but by being selective I am hopeful that I can deal with some of the more outstanding points in two chapters.

Once again I was due to commence duty at 9am when I received that inevitable phone call from Kirkwall. "Hi Robbie, sorry to bother you but we've had a report of some guy acting strangely down at the ferry terminal." I quickly dressed, picked up the police car and headed for the terminal where I spoke to two well known P&O employees, Jim Stainger and Jim Carlyle. This guy pretty much stood out like a sore thumb and they had been keeping an eye on him for a while because of his strange behaviour. He was pretty much oblivious to everything that was going on around him and had failed to notice a gathering group of people observing his actions among which stood a uniformed policeman who had arrived in a fully marked police vehicle. He appeared to be picking up and stacking imaginary items and coiling non existent rope, at least that is what I would have concluded if he were a mime artist.

At no point did he stray any distance from the block of public toilets and I decided to have a look around the place before I approached this guy. He wasn't doing anything wrong and I concluded that he was no threat to himself or anyone else at that time. I was obliged to pass close by him and decided to acknowledge him in the passing to test his reaction. It was like I didn't exist, whatever this guy was seeing he certainly wasn't seeing me. I entered the public toilet and was stopped in my tracks by something close to a Chemist shop strewn about the floor. The place was covered in needles, syringes, phials of various drugs and any amount of related items. It was fairly obvious that either a Chemist shop or Doctors surgery had been screwed and my suspicious friend was likely to be responsible. All the indications were that a crime had been committed and the circumstances left me with no option but to arrest the obvious suspect. He was high as a kite and initially didn't understand a thing that was going on as he was totally lost in a world entirely of his own making.

I made arrangements to have the toilet secured, summoned assistance and returned with my prisoner to the police station. Within a short period Stewart Irvine had arrived and C.I.D. and a number of uniformed personnel. Very quickly we managed to establish that the local Doctors car had been broken into and ransacked of all it contained. My prisoner was beginning to return to the world of normal people and not surprisingly had little memory of the previous several hours leading up to his arrest. He was able to identify himself and told me that he had been living on the island for a few days visiting his brother and his friend. We now obtained a search warrant for the brother's address and set out mob handed to search the premises. None of us could have imagined what we were about to find and had we had twice the number of officers we could never have done a search real justice.

The brother and his friend occupied one massive room in a huge old mansion house which was teeming over with families of seventies type hippies who had moved to Orkney to escape the rat race. We were obliged to make the best of a bad job and split up into pairs with responsibility for specific areas. Various drug related items were beginning to turn up and we were running out of evidence bags, identification labels and security tags. Stewart Irvine volunteered himself to obtain a further stock of the necessary items and left the building.

Here comes the next particularly hard to believe part. My prisoner may well have stood out in a crowd but his brother was even more striking, so striking in fact that it was difficult for me to believe that these two were in fact brothers. He must have been 6'8" or so tall and so thin he could easily have hid himself behind a lamp standard. His hair was long, straight and black and hung easily half way down his back and his features were so sharp that if you stood too close you may well have cut yourself. For all the world here was Neil from the Young One's, except taller and thinner. We had split this room up into sections to be searched and I was dealing with the area occupied by Neil. I had explained the whole situation to him and he told me that his brother had a drugs problem and that he had warned him prior to his visit that he wasn't to get involved in anything. Hanging his head in his hands he said, "I should have known better."

He was also concerned that his brother's stupidity had brought this disruption to all his friends and it was likely to take him some time to make amends. I was about to begin my search and was aware that Neil was extremely nervous and jittery. My automatic assumption was that he was concerned that I was going to find more drugs and I decided to confront him with that suspicion. I put it to him that his demeanour suggested to me that something may be amiss and it would be much better if he just told me what the problem was. "You will just laugh at me," he said. "No I won't, why would I laugh at you?" "Well, you see, I am a Wizard."
I had come across a lot of different people during my time with the police, ranging from Ballerinas (Not that common in the North of Scotland) to various celebrities of the day but this was definitely the first time I had ever encountered a Wizard. I didn't laugh because this guy was so serious and had I laughed he would have been

devastated. He explained that were I to touch his various, dare I say, tools of the trade, he would have to spend considerable time cleansing everything and offering incantations to whomsoever these incantations were offered. Maybe I was a bit offended at the suggestion that I would in some way infect his things but rather than upset the guy any more than necessary I reached an agreement acceptable to both of us. I wanted to see everything and I would examine each item thoroughly but I wouldn't touch anything. He was over the moon and couldn't thank me enough.

A corner of the room had been screened off with a black satin sheet which he pulled to the side revealing what I can only describe as something resembling an Altar. Everything was entirely covered with black satin and I have to say that my initial reaction was to take a step back. On top of the Altar arrangement lay a Wizard's cloak. How did I know it was a Wizard's cloak, when he opened it up for my examination it was like everything else, made from black satin and as you may expect to find in a Disney cartoon decorated with half moon's and stars. Underneath the cloak there was two extremely thick and large books each of which was again covered with black satin. These, he explained were his spell books and I suppose what you would call his recipes for the various potions which he frequently mixed. Inside a large shelved cupboard I saw hundreds of items each of which was individually wrapped in black satin and together we painstakingly went through every item. I can't say I was so much interested as fascinated as he unwrapped each item and explained its purpose. I could see it was going to take an age to get through this stuff.

When involved in a search it is necessary to have any relevant find corroborated by one or more colleagues and consequently you would be taken away from your own task in order to fulfil this obligation. Dougie of Ghengis fame called for my assistance and I crossed to a large dresser where he was working. Here was four phials of Morphine which had to be recorded and bagged. The drawers in the dresser were lipping with all manner of random items most of which served no obvious purpose but might just come in handy for something at some time in the future. I think everybody has these sorts of drawers in their home so I suspect you will know exactly what I mean. I didn't expect to find a Wizard in the building and I most certainly didn't expect to see the next item that turned up in the drawer. Some ten or twelve instamatic photographs of two individuals in various sexual poses. Both of these males were I suppose what you would call, not well endowed, but extremely well endowed, so well endowed in fact as to make any other male viewing these photographs feel inadequate. I felt extremely inadequate.

If I were to say that these things were so huge that you could have flown a flag from them it would be an exaggeration, but only a slight one. I don't want to dwell on this for any length of time as I am beginning to feel inadequate as I write but I do need to describe one of these photographs, the reason for which I will reveal in due course. This particular shot was of a single totally naked male standing on a small hill. Other than a ridiculously huge item of manhood dangling between his legs he was standing, legs apart with both arms extended forward holding an extremely fierce looking bull whip.

By the time Stewart Irvine returned to the search we had already moved on to different areas of the house and had reached a particularly large entrance hall. This entrance hall, easily the equivalent of three or four good size sitting rooms was stacked with boxes, every one of which we had to go through. It was not a pleasing prospect. Again we had split up into various corners and begun the task of ploughing through this mountain of accumulated belongings which none of the residents had any apparent use for when Stewart arrived. "What do you want me to do boys?" Somebody directed him to an area as yet untouched and Stewart set about his task. About ten or fifteen minutes later I heard a surprised cry from Stewart, "What's this?" I stopped what I was doing as did everybody else to see what Stewart had discovered and when I turned around here was Stewart, standing legs apart with both arms extended in front of him clutching a large bull whip.

It was the exact pose; it was the exact bull whip except it was Stewart holding it this time. I was trying extremely hard not to laugh and may well have succeeded had the following conversation not taken place. "What do you use this for?" Stewart enquired and was answered with, "It's for training horses." That wouldn't have been so bad if Stewart could only have left it alone but he had to have the final word. In one of those knowing tones and being a little bit smart he replied, "Well, I hope you don't use it for any other purpose!" That was it, I couldn't help it, the image in the photograph was now in my mind replaced by Stewart and it was horrible and once again I wanted to be sick. Everybody erupted into hoots of laughter which Stewart mistakenly took to be a reaction to his apparently witty remark. We were rolling about and Stewart's next comment to the effect "It wasn't that funny," just made matters worse. It really was a shame when we later had to enlighten him about the real reason for the hilarity.

I can't really close on this story as, as was frequently the case, C.I.D. decided that this was a case for them to report and given that I was never required to appear in court I can only assume that my prisoner pled guilty. I never saw the wizard again either and yet another scar is added to Stewart's children's young minds.

Joyce really didn't want to go to Orkney but she settled in very quickly and totally immersed herself in the islands ancient and modern history. The fact that our son Ben was an Orcadian encouraged Joyce to learn as much about the place as she could. The fact that we were living there pretty much encouraged our very large family and circle of friends to take the opportunity to visit and we found ourselves taking bookings. "I can't take you that week but I can take you the following week end or for the full week the week after," became a very common telephone conversation in our house. I think we did more for the Orkney tourism industry and attracted more visitors than all of their advertising.

I was off course working shifts and couldn't commit much time to visitors but Joyce more than made up for my absence by acting as a first class tour guide. What she didn't know about Orkney wasn't worth knowing. She also took an interest in various evening classes and along with her friend Margaret Muir, (Billy Muir, the sergeant's wife.) attended Yoga classes, Keep fit classes and traditional Tapestry Weaving. I have to admit I liked the leotards and had I anything to do with it they would have been made compulsory dress for the weaving classes as well. Joyce's sojourn into the wider community made her a perfect target for the charity fundraisers who were running various forms of events for which a compere was required.

Rather than approach me, knowing full well that I would manufacture some excuse not to do the event, they would approach Joyce and she would pretty much guarantee my services. I would be told about it when I got home and was frequently obliged to make some alternative arrangement surrounding my shifts. I won't say that a lot of these things weren't good fun but they were becoming a fair commitment on my time between attending and preparation.

I was sitting at home one evening when Joyce answered the phone and I heard her say, "Yes Mr Mowat I will just let you speak to him, I am sure he will be able to help." Joyce had this terribly sexy telephone voice which I loved to listen to and not so many years ago a friend told me that he loved when he got her on the phone as he thought that her telephone manner was quite orgasmic. Anyhow I spoke to this guy who to my knowledge I had never met. "Mr Sutherland, I represent the Orkney Folk Festival and we would like to invite you to take part." I had heard of the Orkney Folk Festival but really didn't have much idea about how these things went. He outlined the dates and explained what was expected of me and I very quickly said that I couldn't do the event as I would be on duty. I didn't know whether I would be on duty on that date or not but it struck me as an easy out.

He wasn't taking no for an answer and the more I refused the more determined he became to convince me that I should do it. "We have heard great things about you and you have been recommended by quite a few people." So now he was resorting to flattery and as much as I enjoyed it, no matter how insincere, I wasn't about to give in. He was on the phone for what seemed like ages and the only way I was going to get any peace was to tell a blatant lie that would hopefully get him of my back. "All I can say is I will give it some thought and if I can do it I will give you a ring," I had absolutely no intention of ringing him back and as soon as I got off the phone I said to Joyce, "If that guy phones back tell him I'm not in." As far as I was concerned that was the end of it. Two weeks passed and then a third and I was fairly confident that I was off the hook when the phone rang. "Oh hello Mr Mowat, I'll just get him for you."

I was frantically miming to Joyce that I wasn't in and when that clearly wasn't going to work I began to mime the horrible death that awaited her when I got off the phone. "Hello Mr Mowat, I really should have called you back but I definitely can't do the festival, I'm on duty." My previous telephone experience with this guy had taught me that I had to get in first and take the legs from under him. I was beginning to feel quite smug and thought that I had made my point fairly well when he replied, "Oh! That's a bit unfortunate, you see we've printed the programmes." I hadn't committed to anything and I felt that it was a bit previous of his committee to print the programmes with my name on them. "But surely you can change the programmes," I enquired. "Well not really, it's quite a bit of work," he responded. "How many programmes have you printed?" I asked, expecting a reply of three or four hundred. "Ten thousand." I almost dropped the phone. Here I was thinking that this was just another one of the round of local Ceilidh's but this was obviously something much different and considerably bigger. I didn't know the first thing about folk festivals but I was learning fast.

The Orkney festival is one of the main events on the UK calendar and programmes are distributed throughout the country with an influx to the Orkney Islands of Folk Music fans. What could I do, I couldn't ask the guy to reprint ten thousand programmes so I said I would do it. I asked him to send me details of the acts so that I could prepare my material around them and create some links for the introductions. The event was a number of months away and I will return to it later in this epistle.

Once again I was on duty with Stewart Irvine when we received a report of a sudden death near to a little village called Dounby. Stewart and I set off to travel the ten or twelve miles to the locus expecting to deal with yet another straight forward sudden death. It has taken me years to realise that you should never expect anything to be straight forward and if it does just happen to turn out that way, then consider it a bonus. We arrived at what I can only describe as a ramshackle hut that had never seen a lick of paint in fifty years and I was extremely surprised to learn that it had in fact been inhabited.

We were met by a home help who explained that on her arrival that morning she had found the elderly male occupant still in bed and passed away. The old guy was approaching ninety years of age and had been living in as near squalor as you could imagine but that had been a personal choice dictated by his refusal to spend money. With the exception of his home help he had pretty much lived as a recluse for longer than anyone could remember. The home help didn't know much about him as he kept himself very much to himself and barely tolerated her presence in the house. The only thing that she could tell us surrounded what had become something of a local legend. He had apparently married some sixty years earlier and on the day of his wedding his bride was seen to run away from the house across the fields and back to her own home. They had by local account never spoken two words to each other since but it had occurred such a long time ago that nobody could confirm the truth or otherwise of the story. At least it was a possible starting point.

We had to go into Kirkwall to pick up a van and the necessary equipment to deal with a sudden death which meant we had to secure the house until our return. As we were about to leave the home help informed us that the deceased had a dog which was currently at her home and she couldn't keep it. We agreed to go with her to her house to pick the dog up and transfer it to the police kennels in Kirkwall. I should have guessed then that this event was going to be a comedy of errors from start to finish. The home help lived with her husband and family at a nearby croft and the approach to the house was such that we were obliged to leave the police car at the bottom of a short hill and rough track. As Stewart and I accompanied the lady up the hill she began to make general conversation, "You know it's a really wild dog." "What do you mean, wild dog?" I asked. "Well it bit my husband, it bit my son and it has bitten me."

I most definitely didn't like the sound of what I was hearing and I wasn't in any sort of mood to offer myself up as this animal's next meal. I felt that this was a job that Stewart could deal with more effectively, on his own! I very surreptitiously slowed down allowing Stewart and the home help to move well in front of me. Both of them were engrossed in conversation and consequently oblivious of my actions. When I felt that it was safe and I was unobserved I about turned and began a casual stroll back in the direction of the police car. I thought I had gotten away with it when I heard a roar from Stewart, "Sutherland, you B******!" This was the signal for me to take to my heels and make a bolt for the safety of the police vehicle closely pursued by Stewart hurling obscenities as he ran.

I just made it to the police car ahead of him and jumped in and locked all the doors just as he reached the drivers door which he was making futile attempts to wrench open while continuing to abuse my parentage at high decibels. Stewart was so engrossed in his intention to take my life that he had failed to see what I was seeing. The home help was standing at the top of the hill having considerable difficulty in believing what she was witnessing. I couldn't help but see the funny side of this incident and began to laugh hysterically as I rolled the drivers window down ever so slightly and told Stewart that he should go and fetch the dog. Amidst much threats of revenge Stewart stormed back up the hill and to this day I don't know how he explained our outrageous behaviour to the home help but I am fairly certain he would have couched his explanation around some claim of standard police procedures. After a short wait I saw Stewart and the home help emerge from the house and it should not have come as any surprise to see the Border Collie being led on a length of nylon rope by the lady. I remained seated in the police car while Stewart opened the hatch back and the home help put the dog in the back and secured it to the tailgate.

We had covered some half of the distance to Kirkwall with very little conversation and as I was driving I looked over at Stewart in the passenger seat. Stewart had pulled his seat as far forward as it could possibly go and he was quite literally perched on the front of the seat leaning forward with his nose not quite, but almost touching the windscreen. This seating position didn't only look strange but also extremely uncomfortable. I felt obliged to enquire, "Stewart, why are you sitting like that?" Stewart returned my stare and responded, "The same bloody reason you are," whilst gesturing towards the mad constantly growling dog which had been pulling so hard on its tether to get a bite at us that it had managed to stretch the nylon rope to such a degree that it was now just a hairs breadth away from taking a chunk out of either of us.

I was hoping that the animal might find Stewart that little bit more succulent and had I had the proper accoutrements on me at the time I would have both salted and peppered him to make sure of my own survival. We made it to Kirkwall police station in one piece and both of us couldn't get out of the car quick enough to be sure that we stayed in one piece. Now all we had to do was get the dog out of the car and neither of us were looking forward to that. I suggested that the dog should be allowed to keep the car and live out the rest of its days in it but nobody took that suggestion seriously. With considerable shouts of "Look out," and "Watch yourself," we eventually managed to get the mad beast out of the car and safely ensconced in the police kennels. I love dogs and personally have four of them but I was certainly glad to see the back of that one.

It was already falling dark and a fairly wild wind had managed to blow up by the time we were on the return journey to Dounby. We had left our police car in Kirkwall and picked up what I can only describe as a death trap of a Sherpa van which was difficult enough to keep on the road on a good day, never mind when it was blowing a gale. A local doctor had already attended and declared death to be due to natural causes but because the deceased had no obvious or known next of kin, we were obliged to take possession of the body. We arrived back at the wooden shack and set about our job. I can only describe the setting as eerie, it was dark, the wind was howling around the house and the few bushes in the area were literally bent double with the strength of the wind.

It seemed as if nature had decided to make our job as difficult as possible. We opened the double back doors of the van and I stepped in to pick up the head of the fibre glass coffin as Stewart took hold of the other end to assist me in carrying it out of the van. This was a slightly awkward process as you couldn't stand up and as I was about to step out of the van a fierce gust of wind caught the back door and slammed it viciously onto my right leg. I dropped the coffin and fell out of the van where I lay on the ground howling in pain. I was in so much pain I thought that I could possibly have broken my leg and Stewart was only disappointed that I hadn't. As I rolled about holding my leg and howling in agony Stewart just stood there bent double with laughter. Who needs enemies when you've got friends like that! "Get up, there's nothing wrong with you." "Jesus, I think my legs broken." "Your legs not broken, but it's no more than you deserve for leaving me with that dog." All I could think was that he was enjoying my pain and this was the beginning of his threatened revenge.

Stewart was not about to allow me any period of time for recovery and I very quickly found myself hobbling into the house, still in considerable pain, carrying the fibre glass coffin shell between us. It was pretty dark inside and the only illumination consisted of an uncovered light bulb in what you would have called the main sitting room. The house only consisted of a small single bedroom, the main sitting room and off it a small scullery. We made some space, laid the coffin down and Stewart was first to enter the bedroom.

There was no space to take the coffin into the bedroom which meant we would have to man handle the remains off the bed and carry the body through to the sitting room to put into the coffin. I don't care how many dead bodies I may have dealt with over the years but whoever you are I do believe that if you had the option you would go for the feet. Although I have had to do it many times I have a natural aversion to having the head of a corpse rolling around on my chest and consequently, where possible I would rather go for the feet. Stewart was at the feet and my brain was working out just how I might be able to reverse that situation. "That chair is in the way we will need to get rid of it," I suggested to Stewart.

Getting rid of the chair meant that Stewart would have to carry it out into the sitting room, at which point I would move up to the feet. I obviously hadn't worked out my strategy as well as I may have as all Stewart did was pick up the chair and hand it to me without changing position. Was he wise to my intention or was he quite innocent, I wasn't sure. What now, how could I get him to the head and me to the feet? "Stewart, the coffin is the wrong way round, we need to change it." This required that we both left the bedroom, I would go to the bottom of the coffin, Stewart at the top and when we turned it around I would walk back into the bedroom first and therefore find myself at the feet. This scam was bound to work. It started off as I intended, I was at the bottom and Stewart was at the top and as I bent down to pick the thing up Stewart pulled it towards himself, stood it on its end, spun it around and layed it back down. B******, he was on to my game and I knew then that I was taking the head.

Once we had carried out the necessary business it was now a case of getting down to finding out what we could about the deceased. Stewart decided to take on the scullery while I settled to searching the main room. I opened a long thin filing drawer no wider than an envelope and found it to be jammed with paperwork. Surely I would discover something relevant here. I did find some minimal information along with £3,500 in cash which had been stuffed in numerous envelopes throughout the drawer. I was continuing with the search when I was stopped abruptly by what I can only describe as a blood curdling scream. It sounded like a girl falling from a cliff but I knew that it was Stewart. The scream was quickly followed by Stewart's appearance in the main room. He was unable to speak and stood shaking from head to toe mumbling unintelligibly.

I could only imagine that he had seen a ghost or something equally scary but it was clearly going to be some time before I was going to get any sense out of him. I was quite used to being unable to get any sense out of Stewart so I wasn't that concerned. "What's wrong?" I asked. "Mm, mm, mm,mm,mm." "What happened?" "Mm, mm, mm, mm, mm." he responded. I couldn't help but notice that even in the darkness he had gone quite pale and I was hopeful that he might be suffering from a serious illness as that would be suitable revenge for his lack of concern when the van door had almost broken my leg. "For god sake Stewart, tell me what happened?" Eventually he calmed down enough to mumble the words "A Rat!" "A Rat, what about a Rat?" Stewart had been searching the scullery and had opened a full length wooden cabinet with shelves stacked from top to bottom. He had been working by the light of our infamously useless car torches and in its feeble beam he had spotted a cash box at the rear of the cupboard. What he hadn't spotted was the Rat sitting perched on top of it. As Stewart reached in to remove the box, instead of his hand closing around the handle of the box it closed around a very unhappy Rat. A frantic wriggle and a squeal registered on Stewart's brain and hence the scream and his appearance in the sitting room suffering a near heart attack. Oh well that would teach him for laughing at my misfortune. I felt totally vindicated.

Once Stewart had sufficiently recovered we both went into the scullery, by which time it seemed that the offending Rat had made good his escape which was both lucky for it and for us. We had both armed ourselves with our police issue batons and were prepared to put up a stout defence in event of both of us being scared shitless. The cash box was recovered and on opening it we discovered that it contained a £750 win from Littlewoods pools from the mid 1950s. The cash was still wrapped and unopened and was as it would have been when delivered.

We had not had much success in finding enough information to complete a formal sudden death report and we knew that the deceased had no living relatives that we were aware of on the island which left us with only one option. We had to take the bull by the horns and visit the fabled wife, or maybe not wife. This particular report was my responsibility so it was down to me to make the initial approach and I hadn't got a clue how I was going to be received. How do you deal with a situation as apparently sensitive as this one! It was definitely another first for me. I suppose subtlety is an obvious answer but I was never renowned for that particular attribute. Bull in a China shop is probably the best description of my interview technique but

I knew that I had to make a special effort on this occasion

We called at the single storey stone built Croft House and I had by now steeled myself for an uncomfortable reception. I wasn't relishing this interview but it had to be done. I knocked on the door and after a fairly lengthy wait an elderly man, certainly in his eighties if not early nineties eventually answered. He was fully dressed which would not be unusual but he was still wearing a jacket and a flat cap. May I say that this mode of dress while in your home is not particularly unusual for people of a certain era and most commonly within the farming community? "Yes Officer." "Hello Mr Smith, I am terribly sorry to bother you." The name Smith is, I hope, an obvious alias for the purpose of the story. "I am investigating a sudden death at a croft further up the road and I need to speak to your sister." A look of concern followed by a defensive, "Why would you need to speak to her?" indicated to me that I was at the right place and that I had been correct in my assumption that this was likely to be a difficult interview. "We don't have anything to do with him, so I don't know why you think my sister will be able to help you."

It was time to play the trump card. "I am led to believe that your sister and the deceased were once married." The look of concern was now replaced with one of shock and with bowed head he indicated that we should enter. Going into this house was once again like stepping back in time and what we encountered would not have been out of place in a Heritage museum with the exception of the always intruding television set. An old grey haired lady sat wrapped in shawls in front of a roaring open fire and only acknowledged our presence when her brother said, "The police are here to see you." I don't know how old she was but she was certainly no spring chicken that much was certain. I introduced myself and went on as sensitively as possible to explain my reasons for calling. As I was outlining the facts I found myself being constantly interrupted by the brother who was bemoaning the fact that we had called at their house and pretty much disturbed their peaceful existence. It was almost impossible to have any form of conversation with the sister and I was obliged to take a somewhat firm approach with the brother and warned him that he was obstructing a police enquiry. The last thing I wanted to do was get anyone's back up but I realised that I wasn't about to get anywhere unless I silenced the brother.

I had managed to quieten the brother and now I began the interview. "Mr Smith has passed away and I need to complete a report. I believe that you were once married to Mr Smith, is that correct?" "Yes." Well at least that much was true and maybe I would get the information I needed to complete my report. "Could you tell me his full name?" "John Smith." "Any middle names?" "I don't know!" "Could you tell me his date of birth?" "I don't know!" "Can you tell me where he was born?" "I don't know!" I wasn't getting anywhere fast here. "What was his occupation?" "A Farmer." I had already worked that one out but at least it was an answer other than "I don't know!" Maybe I was going to get somewhere after all.

"Could you tell me his parents names?" "I don't know!" "Did he have any brothers or sisters?" "I think he may have had a brother in Canada." "Can you give me a name and address?" "I don't know!"

Without going through a complete sudden death report I expect by now that you can guess exactly how this interview went throughout. It was time to go for the sixty four thousand dollar question. "How long were you married?" "Not very long!" "I need to know for how long?" "Not very long!" She obviously wasn't about to put a figure on it so I tried to simplify the situation. "Were you married for a few years?" I enquired. "No, not that long!" "Were you married for a few months?" was met with a negative shake of her head and a mumbled "No,no!" "Were you married for a few weeks?" Once again she was performing that negative head shake and mumbling "No,no." I just didn't have the heart to pursue this line of enquiry any further as it was blatantly obvious that the local legend was indeed true and she had fled from her new husband on their wedding day, never to speak again. Local records would have to provide the missing information as she clearly couldn't.

Since they had never bothered to divorce she was the obvious next of kin and I was obliged to ask if they were willing to take on the arrangements to arrange for burial of the remains. This final request was obviously the straw that broke the brothers back as he immediately became even more vocal than previously and began shouting that they wanted no more to do with the situation. He would not be dealing with funeral arrangements and that was the end of the matter. I have to say, I did not like the brother and he was obviously the controlling influence in this household. As we were being ushered out of the door and subjected to a degree of abuse I felt obliged to have the last word. "You know, it's a shame that you aren't going to deal with the funeral. I took over £4000 out of the house and then off course there is the house and the land and more than forty sheep to be disposed of. The Sheriff will take care of that." The brother was stopped in his tracks and immediately tried to grill me for more information. This was an amazing change in attitude but I wasn't about to comply. I was quite literally being thrown out of the house and now that I had dropped the bomb shell I was eager to leave. The brother was inviting us back into the house but I told him that I still had plenty of work to do and on top of that I would have to arrange a funeral. Stewart and I left and headed for Kirkwall. As I walked in the front door of Kirkwall police station the secretary shouted," Robbie, there's a phone call for you." Stewart and I had been taking bets on how long it was going to take for this particular phone call to be made. He must have timed our arrival to the second but here was the brother explaining that he had discussed the situation with his sister and that he now intended to make all necessary arrangements for a funeral and disposal of property.

Call me a cynic, but it must have had something to do with the poor sheep.

The Old Man of Hoy is a world famous stack of rock which rises out of the Pentland Firth some five hundred or more feet. I am sure that I could quite easily get the exact height of the stack but for my purposes it is enough to know that it is pretty tall. This stack is a magnet for climbers from all over the world and is visited on an almost daily basis by those relishing its particular challenges. I remember watching the first televised climb of the rock some time around 1967 and it was off course then in Black and White. One of the climbers on that occasion was Joe Brown and he was to return in the mid eighties to repeat his climb, but this time accompanied by his 16 year old Children's television presenter daughter Zoe.

The B.B.C. were filming this event in partnership with a Japanese company who sponsored a French climber and I am led to believe that the total cost of this project was somewhere around £500,000. That is a lot of money today and bought even more back then. The main island was awash with B.B.C. outside broadcast trucks which had set up a satellite repeater station just outside of Stromness. The logistics of getting this mountain of equipment and vehicles from mainland Scotland to the main island was far outweighed by transporting the same again and more to Rackwick on the island of Hoy. From Rackwick the crew then had to manhandle and helicopter equipment to the top of the cliff opposite to the stack. The whole operation must have taken a couple of weeks not to mention the planning stages for one day of filming. On the day of filming the police presence on Hoy was doubled to include Jimmy Williamson and me.

I was on a Rest Day and once again made my way across to Hoy on Stevie Mowat's ferry which had been chartered by the company. I was met at Hoy Pier by Jimmy Williamson and together we drove the few miles to Rackwick where I was amazed to see an incredible set up of trucks and other equipment watched over by two B.B.C. employees. This was where the fun started as we were ushered into a container which had been set up as an airport arrival and departure lounge. Here we were able to read the long list of destinations we could fly to from this point which with the exception of the Old Man of Hoy were entirely fictional.

Destinations such as Hawaii and Tahiti were undoubtedly inviting but less so the made up figments of these two bored employees imagination. We were also obliged to pass through customs and read a very long list of what could and could not be carried on the aircraft and items which would be liable to taxation such as livestock and sex toys. Our handcuffs and batons apparently fell into this category but we were given a special dispensation to carry them. After being subjected to a pat down search which stopped short of a full body cavity search we were then seated to await the arrival of the helicopter. This, although the only lounge, now became a V.I.P. lounge with our presence and we were consequently offered refreshments consisting of cold coffee and stale sandwiches which we politely refused. These guys had had a couple of weeks to build up their line of patter and we were certainly entertained.

I don't know if everybody was subjected to this routine but if they weren't then they missed a great laugh. As the helicopter arrived we had to remain seated until one of the pair announced departure and we were run through safety instructions narrated by one while mimed by the second. "If you believe that the aircraft is about to crash scream for your mum and prepare to kiss your arse goodbye," did little for my confidence. If you did happen to have a slight fear of flying then you were likely to be terrified by the time this pair had finished. I don't know if the B.B.C. knew the real talent they had working for them but as a double act this pair took some beating. Thanks guys, whoever you were.

It was a beautiful day and a beautiful two or three minute flight to the top of the cliff opposite to the stack where, as we came into land we could see the full extent of the set up required for filming this event. It looked a bit like a small village had sprung up out of nowhere. Everybody was wearing nylon stockings over their faces and I couldn't help getting the feeling that I was about to get mugged. The nylon stockings, the crew had discovered was their best defence against the relentless Scottish Midge and was far more effective than any of the insect repellents that they had been obliged to purchase. The place was a hive of activity and I took a moment to take in the scene. A commentators hut had been built right on the edge of the cliff and locked in place by chains and ropes.

This hut was positioned directly opposite to the stack and the full glass front from where the commentators observed the climb was precariously perched protruding over the cliff edge. A herd of charging elephants couldn't have convinced me to step inside that structure. All along the facing cliff edge I could see B.B.C. camera men perched on and locked into position on various ledges. The same scenario was repeated on the stack itself. A large barbecue had been set up and stacks of supplies were being constantly ferried in by helicopter. The crew had decided that they could best cater for themselves rather than try and set up a catering unit at this location. I wont even try to describe the array of food and drinks that were available other than to say that it was quite outrageous and not only were the crew fed that day but pretty much every onlooker that had gathered to watch. People had come from all over Hoy and the main island to witness this event.

The day was going well as was the climbing. Joe Brown and his daughter were climbing the same route as he had in the 1967 televised climb while two other climbers were attempting a previously untried route. I don't remember exactly but I believe that live broadcasts were going out every half hour and I later learned that the audience had numbered in its millions. The French climber, for reasons unknown to me had pulled out of the climb. There wasn't much for me and Jimmy to do other than marshal some of the crowd away from the edge of the cliffs and constantly to remind parents to keep an eye on their children. My heart seemed to be permanently in my mouth as some parents seemed quite oblivious to the obvious dangers of allowing their children to play so near to a cliffs edge. I avoided the cliff edge with a passion as, as I have already said, I have a morbid fear of heights. Everything was going reasonably swimmingly when an incident occurred that was destined to put me in a state of extreme terror.

It was the era of Margaret Thatcher's government and the Miners strike. A group of supporters had seen this live broadcast as an opportunity to highlight the miner's plight and had canoed out from Stromness to the base of the stack where they racked up and unfurled a large banner which read, "Miners don't climb down." The directing staff relayed an immediate instruction to all camera men to the effect that they were not, under any circumstances, to train their cameras on this group. Once again, I don't exactly recall how, had some part of this instruction been relayed by Tannoy or what but the protestors became somewhat annoyed. They canoed into the bottom of the stack and began to throw large rocks onto the rock surface which boomed and echoed all the way up to the top of the cliff. The effect of this behaviour was to distract the climbers and their was clear obvious dangers associated with that. Jimmy and I were being approached by one of the gaffers and I was pretty much anticipating the reason for his visit. "That lot are managing to distract the climbers and we have to do something about it."

Although I would have loved to have been able to help I couldn't see how other than climbing some 500 feet or so down the cliff and surely he wasn't about to ask me to do that. "Wrong!" That is exactly what he wanted the two of us to do. I think he must have registered the look of horror on my face as he immediately followed his request up with, "It will be okay we've rigged a scramble up all the way and all you have to do is follow that." If Jimmy was having the same problem with this request it certainly wasn't apparent. What the Hell was a scramble, I didn't have a clue but I was about to find out. As much as I wanted to refuse I just couldn't bring myself to admit that I was terrified by the prospect of this climb. "Its no bother, our guys are going up and down it all the time carrying equipment on their back, it's a walk in the park." That last statement translated to me as: "You're a big calf if you don't do it." What option had I got, it was either a case of dying horribly as a consequence of a fall from a great height or admitting that I was scared shitless.

I have already said that it was a beautiful day, but was it a beautiful day to die, I didn't think so. A widowed wife and orphaned children kept springing into my mind along with the thought that I couldn't trust Stewart Irvine as far as I could throw him. The gaffer stepped over the edge first followed by Jimmy Williamson with yours truly taking up the rear. If I thought I was going to fall I could always grab hold of Jimmy and drag him to his death with me. At least I would have some company on the way down and after all, he was Stewart Irvine's brother in law. Small consolation. The first stretch wasn't too bad as we stepped onto a fairly large wide ledge and at this point I couldn't see down.

Now I came across the scramble which amounted to no more than a rope fixed to the face of the cliff which snaked up and down the cliff face following the safest route. As safe as it may have been, which in my opinion it wasn't, I clung to that rope for dear life. Every so often I would find myself looking down a sheer drop of several hundred feet to the rocks below and I wasn't coping with this scenario particularly well. It was almost inevitable that these would be the very points that I would meet somebody making their way up the scramble carrying large quantities of equipment on their back as if they were out for a Sunday stroll. "Its no bother, our guys are going up and down it all the time carrying equipment on their back, it's a walk in the park," kept springing to mind. What he didn't say was that our guys were all professional climbers properly equipped for the job. As they passed me I refused to go out around them and they had to go around me as I held on as tight as I could with my eyes closed.

The journey down that cliff was an absolute nightmare that seemed to last forever and I learned the true meaning of your legs turning to jelly. As I reached the bottom of the cliff it became apparent that the reason for our presence there had long since left and I had been forced to endure this terror for absolutely no purpose. I swear, I had no control of my limbs and threw myself down in a heap among a group of large and small boulders where I lay attempting to recover some dignity. As uncomfortable as I was I had to stay where I was for some time to stop shaking.

The gaffer now suggested that we should begin the climb back up and that was the point at which I broke. "There is no way that I am climbing back up that f****** cliff, you can send the helicopter down for me." "But the helicopter can't come down while they are still filming," he protested. "Fine, I'll just wait until they stop filming." He made only one more attempt at convincing me to climb the cliff and following my response must have decided that it would be wise to wait for the helicopter. A short time later the helicopter which couldn't land where we were hovered above us as we climbed aboard and were whisked back to the top of the cliff.

The remainder of the day remained somewhat uneventful and the crowds were beginning to wander away until eventually only Jimmy Williamson and I and maybe half a dozen or so B.B.C. employees were left watching the culmination of the climb. As Joe Brown and Zoe were about to reach the top the commentator came out of his hut and instructed us to make as much noise as possible when they stepped onto the top. I saw the repeated programme some time later and listened to the commentary as the commentator said, "As they reach the top a tremendous cheer erupts from the large crowd on the opposite headland." We were making as much noise as we possibly could but the large crowd did only consist of about eight of us. As well as the two groups of climbers going up the rock there was also an attempt at the longest travois in history.

The veteran Scottish climber Hamish Macinnes entered the Guinness book of records with this one. The helicopter dropped a cable on top of the Old Man of Hoy and then flew the other end to the cliff top where we were where it was anchored in position. I believe the distance covered was near to 600 feet and a world record should it be achieved. I watched with bated breath as Macinnes pulled himself out onto the cable and began to pull himself hand over hand to the opposite side, dangling hundreds of feet over the rocks below. This from where I was standing was a real feat of bravery and not nearly as straight forward an exercise as he initially made it seem. Once he had passed the midway point and was on the uphill pull we very quickly realised that the cable had not been sufficiently tensioned requiring a Herculean effort on the climber's part to make any progress at all.

Further tensioning of the cable at this stage served very little point and it was down to Macinnes himself to find some way to overcome the problem. He was past the point of no return and going back would only have presented the same problem. He was being hampered by his safety rope which was preventing him from getting a good purchase on the main cable so he just disposed of the safety rope. If anything happened now he had no safety back up and he would plunge to his death. I was far from comfortable with what I was witnessing but you couldn't help but admire the man. A tension filled 15 minutes or so eventually saw Macinnes haul himself onto the headland to well deserved back slapping and applause. It was another one of those days that were so different and never to be forgotten.

John Ratter and Jimmy Scott, both of whom I have previously mentioned had been transferred to Orkney. John was to be the new Chief Inspector and Sub Divisional Officer while Jimmy was filling the post of Inspector and his deputy. This combination of two particularly good friends in the two senior police posts on the island was never going to do me any harm and opportunities were about to arise for which they had me earmarked. We were expected to attend at local primary and secondary schools where firstly we would build up a rapport with the teaching staff and secondly, but most importantly, deliver appropriate road safety and personal safety messages to the pupils.

I was always more than happy to carry out this function and drew a deal of satisfaction from seeing the youngster's enthusiasm as they took part in whatever the message of that particular day may be. Not every police officer was suited to this function and some saw it as a particular bind being appointed as a liaison officer to a specific school. From a convenience point of view I frequently covered all of the schools on the West Mainland which meant that my colleagues had no concerns about monthly returns as I pretty much had it covered. The full time post of Community Involvement Officer, based at Kirkwall had become vacant and some fairly urgent annual events were about to arise.

Jimmy Scott called me up and asked if I would be willing to deliver the National "Stranger Danger" campaign to all schools on the island which would mean that I would be off shift for two weeks. I agreed and before I had finished the job I was now approached to take up the Cycling Proficiency scheme which would take a further 3 to 4 months. The Duke of Edinburgh Award, local island initiatives and countless other requirements were soon piling up and I was unofficially in the job full time. I kept asking John when he was going to advertise the post so that I could get back to Stromness and he kept on telling me that he was about to get round to it but wouldn't I consider the permanent post myself. I was to find myself fulfilling this role for the remainder of my time on the islands, although never officially.

That time had arrived when I was due to take part in the Orkney Folk Festival. I hadn't been looking forward to this moment but I really felt that I couldn't let the organisers down even though I was of the opinion that I had pretty much been railroaded into taking part. David Inglis was over in Orkney on a fishing holiday and had decided to accompany me to the event for which I was extremely grateful as here at least was some moral support. I attended at Holm Community hall armed with my script which I had slaved over for some time and hoped that I had the aplomb to pull it off. Once again I was shitting myself and my state of panic was in no way even slightly alleviated when I peered through the curtain and saw the hall teeming over with festival goers. An event like this was a walk in the park for the artistic line up but for me it was a nightmare.

I just knew I was going to walk on to that stage and die a slow agonising death. I would have given anything to be anywhere but there at that time. My concern wasn't helped by actually recognising some of the artists in the line up. I know I have said that I knew nothing of the folk scene but even I knew who Artie Trezise and Cilla Fisher of Singing Kettle fame were and if that wasn't enough here also was the soon to become world famous recording artists, Capercailie.

My body language accompanied by mad eyes and streams of sweat pouring down my face must have transmitted my fears to the waiting artists and I found myself being approached by Artie Trezise, Cilla Fisher and the lead female singer from Capercailie, all of whom went out of their way to offer me reassurance that everything would be just fine. I wished that I was as confident as they were about the outcome but I just couldn't get rid of this feeling of tragedy. All too soon it was time for me to make my first appearance on stage and open the concert. I had taken the precaution of writing enough material to either simply make the introductions or in the event that the audience were with me, do a few minutes between acts.

I was introduced by one of the festival organisers as the compere for the evening and it was then time for me to take my first steps onto the stage. Even though this audience hadn't a clue who I was my entrance was greeted with an enthusiastic round of applause which lifted my spirits no end. It could only go down hill from here. I had been practicing my opening lines and working on some local observational humour which I hoped might set the tone for the evening and this was the moment of truth. My opening lines drew gales of laughter from the audience and set what I can only describe as a mild electric shock coursing through my body. It felt a little bit like static and I imagined that my hair must have been standing on end and that must have been the catalyst for the laughter.

All I knew was that I liked it and I wanted more. I had experienced a similar feeling when performing in the Stromness Hotel and all I can say is that the laughter and applause was turning me into some sort of monster. I decided that a couple of minutes warm up was called for and the more the audience responded the lesser inclined I was becoming to leave the stage. I introduced the first act and walked behind the curtain with my whole body tingling. Artie Trezise and company wasted no time in boosting my confidence with further words of encouragement and congratulations on my opening slot. I was delighted but I was also aware that I had a whole evening in front of me and things could very easily go down hill fast.

I was growing in confidence and every time I stepped onto the stage I was becoming loath to leave it I was enjoying myself so much. The acts were great and the audience were clearly intent on enjoying themselves. I had worked out relevant jokes and lines of patter which I hoped allowed me to slide gently and seamlessly into the introduction of each artist and it appeared to be working well. I now found myself introducing a professional poet who along with the other professional artists had travelled to the island to take part in the festival. Everything up until now had gone without a hitch and I had no reason other than to believe that this contribution would be any different. I am reliably informed that at some time or another every artist experiences the feeling of not being appreciated by the audience or to put it another way, dies on stage.

This guy looked every inch of what he purported to be and undoubtedly was, a passionate poet with something to say. He was a fairly big guy with a very noticeable receding hairline which he compensated for by growing his remaining hair to a considerable length which worked well with his booming voice and dramatic gestures. He introduced himself very slowly and took considerable time in outlining the content of his poem and his reasons for writing it while his audience listened intently. After a lengthy descriptive presentation he then launched into his poem with extreme gusto and delivered the whole epic in Gaelic. I would care to bet that about the only people who may have understood the language present in the hall that night, would have been the poet himself and some if not all of the members of Capercaillie. This figure may have represented about 1% of everybody present. It seemed to me that this poem was going on forever and where the audience had initially been listening politely they now began to grow restless. I was becoming aware of low conversations amongst the watching crowd which was accompanied by the scraping of seats and people moving back and forth to the toilets.

I was becoming embarrassed and once again I began to sweat. The performer appeared to be oblivious to the audience reaction and just as dramatically as he had started he brought the epic to a close. The audience were caught unaware that the performance had ended and very slowly a smattering of polite applause emanated from the group.

It is a terrible thing to say but I was relieved that the poem had ended and I was preparing to enter stage right when he began to narrate the content of a humorous poem which he had written and his reasons for writing it. "Oh no, he's going to do another one!" I heard myself say as I cradled my head in my hands. I was whispering to myself, "Come off, come off," but as much as I may have been willing it, it didn't look very likely to happen. All of us to the rear of the curtain were suffering for him and without exception we were all of the same opinion, it was time to come off. As humorous as this poem no doubt was, I didn't hear a single titter of laughter as once again the whole thing was delivered in Gaelic.

Things were getting worse, the audience were by now having group conversations and a considerable buzz was almost drowning out the performer. I wanted to roll up in a ball and die. Occasional peals of laughter I could only put down to someone in the audience telling jokes and the movement out of and back into the hall was almost becoming a constant stream. Still the performer appeared totally oblivious to what was going on around him and if he was dying on stage he wasn't showing any signs of distress. The poem came to a close and once again the audience were caught unaware and it was some time before a smattering of polite applause could just be heard above the ongoing conversations. "Thank God, he's finished!" I thought. Thank God he's finished, everybody thought including the audience and his fellow performers.

I had written a poem for the occasion and was hopeful that I may recover some of the audience attention by delivering an amusing poem with a local slant. I was waiting for the performer to come off when I realised that he obviously hadn't had enough and was going for third time lucky. If he was going down he was intent on going down fighting. Those of us to the rear of the curtain were by now almost involved in group hugs, offering each other moral support whilst preparing a wake for the passing of a fellow performer. I don't know what I may have been muttering but I couldn't help overhearing mumbled "Oh No's," and "Don't do It's." Once again we suffered the lengthy narration and the by now clearly displayed lack of interest on the part of the audience.

Eventually he finished, bowed his head and offered thanks to the audience who responded with a less than enthusiastic odd clap of hands. Behind the curtain we were in silent celebration and really quite jubilant about his decision to stop when somebody offered me a gloomy, "You've got your work cut out when you go out there." As if I needed to be told. I stepped onto the stage to witness an audience still involved in entertaining themselves and wondered if this was a case of me being thrown to the Wolves. A few coughs and calls of "Ladies and gentlemen," saw the restoration of some semblance of order before I called on the audience to put their hands together for the previous performer which drew a reasonable response.

I was taking a chance but I decided to deliver my own piece of poetry especially written for the occasion. I had managed to hit the spot again and the audience were very quickly howling with laughter at my projected take on a version of the Orcadian newspaper with outrageous claims surrounding the future of the island and its economy. The rest of the night went like a dream and I found myself being invited to participate in the following year's event. I explained to the organisers that I could never project where I might be in six weeks time never mind twelve months. With the same determination as was employed to get me there in the first place I was being put under considerable pressure to agree to return the following year. "We will pay all your transport and accommodation costs." "You can bring your wife and family and make a holiday of it." I wasn't about to be forced into any agreement and as it was that was to be my last public performance as on the opening day of the festival in 1987 I was aboard the ferry en route to my new posting at the single man station in Halkirk.

Orkney was a great period in our life which we will never forget.

CHAPTER 16

HALKIRK

Saying farewell to the Orkney Islands wasn't very easy for several reasons. John Ratter was extremely keen that I should take the Community Involvement job on full time and was offering me every conceivable carrot to do so. We had grown to love the island and would have been happy to stay but Joyce's dad had died the previous year which meant that her mother was on her own in Caithness. The family commitment far outweighed our desire to stay. We had made some wonderful friends in the form of Marie Seatter and her family and Freddy and Honey Breck, the proprietors of the Blue Star Garage. The photographs that I keep of Joyce crying her eyes out when we first left Caithness to go to Orkney was easily balanced with a similar set of photographs where she can be seen in an equal state of despair because we were leaving.

I have said it before and I will say it again, I will never understand the female mind. I will always carry a scene in my minds eye of Joyce wrapping herself around a fully uniformed Stewart Irvine as he was about to step of the ferry having wished us a final farewell.

We had very quickly established our new home at the Police Station in the village of Halkirk about seven miles outside of Thurso. I had a very romantic notion about policing a village community and decided that I would try to make considerably more use of my discressionary powers than I possibly may have in the past. It didn't take me very long to realise that I wasn't really going to be allowed to be a policeman in my own beat. The very first day that I was due to start duty for my first shift in Halkirk I received a telephone call from Thurso. "Robert." It was the duty sergeant from Thurso informing me that the Wick station was short staffed and I would be required to carry out my shift there. Wick wasn't even in my section but when the order arrives you have no option but to comply and I duly set off for my first day of duty in Halkirk, in Wick.

Wick, off course is my home town and I didn't require any direction from the duty sergeant or the other officer on duty that day to find my way about the office or the town. It was early June and the most glorious day so the town was busy with locals and tourists alike making the most of the weather. We received a call reporting a drunk lying unconscious down at the riverside who was being guarded by a wild dog. You already know my feelings about wild dogs and although I didn't have any problems dealing with a drunk I certainly did have a problem with dogs. At that point I couldn't begin to imagine how much of a problem I was going to have with this particular dog. My colleague and I made our way in a police vehicle down to the car park which serves a local supermarket and there at the end of the car park in the middle of a grassed picnic area I spotted the reason for my attendance. In the middle of the green, lying spread eagled on his back on a raised concrete plinth I spotted a character who had been well known to me for years. He was more frequently drunk than sober and regularly so much under the influence of drink as to be incapable.

All the while that he was lying there he was being circled by a rather large, very unfriendly Alsatian dog who snarled and bared it's fangs at anyone who attempted to come close. A crowd of onlookers had already gathered which was growing steadily larger as they undoubtedly sensed a drama about to unfold. Any approach that I attempted to make was very quickly repelled by the dog and as much as I called out to the unconscious drunk I failed to arouse him. It was beginning to look like I was going to have to go in. I remained on site while I dispatched my young colleague to the police station to pick up padded gloves and an extending noose which I hoped would offer me at least a little protection when I attempted to control this dog. What I didn't know was that some public spirited citizen had phoned the local rag and informed them of the unfolding situation and only became aware of the presence of the press when I later saw the photographs.

A short while later my colleague returned with the limited protection available to me and I began to garb up. The by now large crowd were treating this situation as unexpected outdoor entertainment and were beginning to look to me a bit like a Roman mob waiting for the Christian to be thrown to the Lion. I don't know if they were taking bets but I certainly wasn't sure if they would give me a thumbs up or a thumbs down if I ended up lying on my back having my throat torn out. They looked like an ugly crowd to me.

I couldn't really put the evil moment off any longer and as I was preparing to move on the dog I spotted some movement from the prone figure. I decided that I would give one more try at arousing him and after several goes I saw the drunk struggle up to a seated position. "John, it's the police," I called out to him. "Bugger off, leave me alone." Not an entirely unexpected response but neither was it one that I was willing to accept. "John, I want you to get a hold of your dog." "Why, what has the dog done?" "Never mind what the dog has done just get a hold of it." "Why?" "John, I am not going to argue with you just do as I say and get a grip of that bloody dog." This last instruction delivered much more forcefully convinced the drunk that he should comply and with a commanding "Here boy," the Alsatian gambolled up to his master and began playfully licking his face. The on looking crowd were beginning to sense that their entertainment was beginning to draw to a close and they were unlikely to witness a policeman being savaged by a large dog. "John I want you to take the dog over to the police car." "Why?" "Never mind why just do as I tell you."

After several attempts John managed to rise into an extremely unsteady standing position and then made his way towards the police vehicle where I was waiting to get a noose around the dog's neck. The spectators at least had enough sense to move further back as the operation moved into its final phase. Before I could stop him, John opened the door of the police car and the dog jumped in to what was to become his territory. Any approach to the police vehicle was now greeted with savage snarls and bared fangs and to make matters worse, the effort of walking to the police car was enough to cause John to fall back into his drunken stupor. The crowd were loving it. What was I going to do now, how did I rectify this situation? The whole thing was beginning to become extremely embarrassing. Here we were, two policemen who were unable to get into their police car because a dog had taken up residence in it. It was time to call for a Vet.

A ten minute wait or so saw the arrival of a young Vet who on approaching the car was greeted in the same fashion as we had been. He was clearly unwilling to enter the police car and I couldn't blame him. It was time to work out a strategy. I had the extending noose and the Vet had the means to render the animal unconscious. After several attempts I managed to noose the dog through the slightly opened window of the police vehicle which caused the animal to move into an absolute frenzy.

As I held on for dear life the Vet very quickly leaned in through the opposite door and stabbed the dog with a tranquiliser before getting back out again faster than he got in. A short wait saw the dog gently drift into an unconscious state and we were able to load the police car up with his equally unconscious master and drive them both to the police station. Both dog and master were carried into the police station where they were both allowed to sleep it off.

Bad enough an appearance in the local rag but this one managed to make the Sunday nationals. The Sunday Mail carried a large photograph of me struggling to hold the dog in position while the Vet administered the tranquiliser and I didn't even know that the photograph had been taken. I was otherwise engaged.

It was the 27th of June 1987 and it was Joyce's birthday. We had arranged to meet up with my nephew Garry and his wife that evening for a celebratory meal. Garry was at that time the police officer in the neighbouring beat of Reay. It was early afternoon and I was just returning from having carried out a minor enquiry and as I was bringing my car to a halt outside of the police station I was passed by an Ambulance with blue lights flashing and sirens sounding travelling at a considerable speed. My personal car had not as yet been fitted with a police radio and the only way that I could find out what was going on was to take off in pursuit of the ambulance. I followed the ambulance at considerable speed to a railway level crossing on the outskirts of the village. As I pulled in to a stop I could see from the broken fencing and considerable amount of debris laying about that an accident had obviously occurred but as yet I was unaware of the nature of the accident.

Two of my Thurso colleagues were already in attendance having just arrived ahead of me. I approached Sgt Rory Mackenzie who informed me that he had ascertained that a car negotiating the crossing and the East bound train had been in collision. As we looked along the length of the track we could see debris following the line for a considerable distance and approx two thirds of a mile further along the track we could see the rear of the train where it had come to a halt. Constable Gayle Farquhar remained at the level crossing dealing with the traffic situation there while

Rory and I began to walk the track.

As we walked along the track we began to build a picture of what had occurred. We were discovering pieces of a motor vehicle which appeared to have been ripped apart. A car bonnet was followed by a wing and then headlamps and a door and as we walked here was a complete engine block lying at the side of the track. Our view was totally unobstructed and as far as we were seeing we couldn't discern anything larger than a single panel and both of us knew that we were looking for a body or possibly bodies. Nothing could have survived this impact. I noticed in the distance that the train driver and guard had now stepped down from the train and were beginning to make their way towards us. We continued to walk along the track picking our way past the debris and eventually we spotted the body of a woman who was clearly dead.

There was nothing to be done for the deceased and we continued on in the event that the vehicle had more than one occupant. We met up with the train driver and guard and told them what had occurred. It was no surprise that either of them, or indeed as I was later to find out, any of the sixty or so passengers were aware of the nature of the incident. A large diesel locomotive pulling six carriages and travelling at a line speed of 50 mph is not going to register any degree of noticeable impact when colliding with a small Ford Fiesta motor car. The train couldn't move, it was evidence and had to be examined and all of the passengers had to be interviewed.

This all had to be done as quickly as possible and the site had to be secured in order that tests could be carried out on the visible and audible warning systems located at the level crossing. My immediate priority, having assured myself that this was a single victim incident was to identify the deceased. From paper work recovered from the wreckage I was able to ascertain that the deceased was a British woman who had become a naturalised American when she had married in to a very high profile American family.

Enquiries established that the victim had been on a fishing holiday in the neighbouring County of Sutherland and had travelled to Thurso that day to arrange rail travel to London in order for her to attend the opening days of the Wimbledon Tennis tournament. Other than carrying out the enquiry into this incident I also had to have contact with her family in America and over the telephone, as much as you may try, it is difficult to convey your sorrow for their tragedy. I was obliged to outline our procedures to the husband and the necessity for a post mortem examination, following which, assuming no complications; they would be able to make arrangements for burial or cremation. This was clearly going to be a complex report but first of all I had to complete a sudden death report and transport the remains the following day to Inverness. Needless to say we didn't manage to celebrate Joyce's birthday as we had planned. The following day I travelled to Raigmore hospital at Inverness where I spoke with the pathologist and identified the remains. Arrangements had already been made for the body to be left there and later uplifted by a local undertaker who had been contracted to fulfil the arrangements for transportation of the remains back to America.

I had done all that was necessary to allow immediate arrangements to be carried out and had completed summary reports outlining the circumstances of the incident. Now I had to begin the mind numbing task of preparing a completely comprehensive report covering every aspect of something which I didn't completely understand. The completion of this report was to take me a full three months in which time I had to educate myself about matters that any train spotting geek would consider basic stuff. Line speeds, the operation of permanent magnets, train weights and line slows, to name just a few of the terms I had to become familiar with and am not about to explain in the event you may be inclined to take your own life, just about drove me crazy. Meetings with the Procurator Fiscal, British Transport Police, Railway Engineers and hours of scanning differing scale size drawings of the area while continuing with my everyday duties didn't leave me with a lot of free time. I really was glad to see that report completed and submitted and was fairly confident that should a fatal accident enquiry be required I had pretty much covered all of the bases.

I did however reach a personal conclusion in respect of the cause of this accident which may or may not have been the case. This particular crossing, as is the case with all non barrier crossings shows no form of audible or visual signal unless a train is actually approaching. Once a train is approaching the crossing it trips a thing called a permanent magnet which in turn activates alternating lights and sounds an audible alarm for a full twenty seven seconds prior to the train passing through. In America, I am led to believe, a level crossing is permanently indicated by flashing lights and once a train is approaching barriers are brought down into position. I believe, but I could be wrong, that the victim in this case saw what she believed to be a level crossing indicated as she would expect it to be but didn't realise that here it meant that the train was coming.

The Halkirk station covered what we refer to as a country beat and given that there are only two towns of any significant size in Caithness the rest of the County is made up of numerous small villages and pretty much hunting, shooting and fishing estates. Rivers running with Salmon and hill ground populated with herds of deer and all kinds of ground and flying game presents its own kind's of problem.

There were always rumours about the kind of thing that went on in the dead of night and it inevitably surrounded poaching. I was upstairs in the toilet getting washed and shaved about to start my tour of duty when Joyce shouted to me, "Robert, come and pick this fish up off the door step." Did she say pick a fish up off the door step, surely not, I must have misheard. A more urgent and annoyed summons emanated from the bottom of the stairs, "Robert, will you please come and pick this fish up from the door step." I had obviously heard correctly and went downstairs to investigate. There, lying at the front door of the police station lay a huge Salmon. All the stories I had heard about country stations came flooding back. Obviously some poachers had netted the river the night before and this was my pay off for letting things lie. A bribe, if you like. I began to panic. How long had this fish been lying here? How many people had seen it lying there? What was I going to do with it? I had a quick look around and seriously considered throwing the thing into the unoccupied and overgrown garden belonging to the District nurse next door.

Even in the midst of my panic I decided to carry out at least minimal enquiry with Joyce. "What am I going to do with it?" "Eat it I should think, but I don't know how to cook it," she replied. "But we don't know who may have seen it lying here." "What has that got to do with anything?" "It has everything to do with it if it has been poached from the river," I tried to explain. Here was someone who had been a police officer for nigh on thirteen years and she wasn't grasping the significance of this doorstep find, at a police station of all places. "Don't be stupid it hasn't been poached from the river." "How do you know it hasn't been poached from the river?" "I know because the man McCarthy handed it to me at the gate."

Eddie McCarthy was then and still is the River Superintendent and had handed the Salmon to Joyce with a suggestion that it would make a lovely Sunday dinner. Joyce although having been brought up a fisherman's daughter had a natural aversion to handling raw fish or shell fish but had no problem eating it. Having taken the fish from Eddie, contained in a fish sleeve, she had gingerly made her way towards the door at which point the Salmon had slid out of the sleeve and landed perfectly on the doorstep as if placed there. She was not about to pick it up and hence the demand that I attend and remove the offending item. I have to say the explanation was quite a relief.

For those of you who are Salmon fishers you will know the name Eddie McCarthy as one of the most knowledgeable fly fishers in the country and most probably a considerable number of you want to be him, except maybe, a little taller. Eddie is dedicated to the art and spends most of his waking hours on ways not only to improve the fishing on the river Thurso but all other types of Salmon fishing throughout the county. His river and I do mean, "His River," is fished by celebrities from all over the world including Royalty and it is not a case of Eddie McCarthy knowing celebrities it is a case of Celebrities making claim to knowing Eddie McCarthy.

Living in an area such as the Halkirk beat a major part of the local policeman's duty involves the regulation of firearms. Everybody and his brother own at least one or possibly several firearms and have been brought up with them as a way of life. This familiarity with the use of weapons sometimes breeds a degree of contempt for just how lethal they can be and frequently I would find these things lying about in farm steadings with no thought given to any form of security. On one occasion I found a rifle with a round up the spout in an area to which children had frequent access. Inevitably such instances led to me having to lay down the law in no uncertain terms and leave the offender in no doubt what was likely to happen should I witness a recurrence. Occasionally I would be obliged to submit a report surrounding the unsuitability of an individual to hold a firearms licence.

The biggest problem most country bobbies have with firearms is the holders failure to renew their certificate timeously and in some instances these could be known to be months out of date. Headquarters always sent out reminders to the certificate holders and to the local policeman to chase the individuals up. It would not be unusual to receive as many as three or four reminders before I would eventually get a hold of the offender and brow beat them into completing their renewal forms on the spot and paying their renewal fee. I have already said that most of my duty time was spent out with my beat area and the only way to chase a lot of these people up was on my rest days. You had to do it for the love of the job and to stop from landing yourself in the shit because as much as you may have had valid excuses, bosses didn't tend to listen.

I had already had three or four shots at getting this particular farmer to renew his firearm or shotgun certificate and decided that it was time to take the most direct approach. I was on rest day and called at his home on a Saturday afternoon only to find that he wasn't in. The farmer's wife didn't know me from Adam and given that I wasn't in uniform, why should she?

I had gone armed with a blank renewal form and a number of reminder notices just to highlight how many opportunities he had been given to put his house in order. Before I had an opportunity to explain who I was and my purpose for being there I was ushered into the house and through to the kitchen where the woman pointed at her washing machine and said, "There it is." It was definitely a washing machine but her reason for pointing that fact out was lost on me. "I have been waiting for you for days, I can't get any washing done, and it's just terrible." I had obviously called on this woman in the midst of a major domestic disaster and she had mistaken me for her saviour in the form of a washing machine repair man. I explained that I was the local policeman and I was there to see that her husband's certificate, which was long overdue, should be renewed. As much as I tried to make my point and explain the urgency of the situation she wasn't about to listen until I was aware of how important it was to have her washing machine fixed.

Each new attempt by me to explain the situation was countered by the urgent nature of having an in operative washing machine repaired. It didn't take me to long to realise that I was wasting my time and accepted that the conversation was now going to be all about her washing machine and how long it was going to take the repair man to call. Having given in to the inevitable I enquired as to the model of the item and what was wrong with it. "It won't drain and the washing has been stuck in it for three days," she told me. "How long have you had it," I asked. "Five years." "And how often do you clean the filter," I enquired.

This last question was met with the response, "What filter?" I now suspected that I had some idea of what may be wrong with this washing machine. Five years and the filter had never been cleaned. Oh well, I wasn't getting anywhere as a police officer so just maybe I could achieve something as an impromptu washing machine repair man. Two hours later I left a very delighted farmer's wife who now had an operational washing machine and thought I was wonderful.

The following day I was pretty much as usual on duty in Thurso and on my return home I was met by a fairly delighted Joyce. The elusive farmer had turned up at the police station with a duly completed renewal form and fee, two large bags of turnips, bag of potatoes and two dozen fresh eggs. It seems his wife had commanded him on pain of death to take immediate steps to renew his certificate and sent along a reward for the nice policeman for fixing her washing machine.

For a considerable period I found myself being the only rural police officer in the area as the other single man stations were unoccupied. This scenario caused me considerable inconvenience as more calls were being made on me to work night shifts and back shifts in Thurso. Little consideration was given to any personal life you may have had or indeed any prior arrangements I may have made, all of which would need to be cancelled and where possible re scheduled. Donald Mackay was always the single exception and allowed me four hours overtime at the beginning and end of a week tour of duty in Thurso in order to bring my own local enquiries up to date. Donald never forgot what it meant to be a single station officer and the demands this put on you and your family whilst clearly others in a supervisory rank clearly did.

It would be wrong of me to imply that this scenario was all bad as, as I have already said, "it is an ill wind that blows no good." Being the only available officer I frequently found myself landing the odd jolly. John Wares and I found ourselves being detailed to pick up a prisoner in Harrowgate in Yorkshire and were dispatched by train with all our outward and return journey pre booked and seats reserved. Our journey down to Yorkshire went without a hitch and we made all our connections absolutely as planned.

A short connecting journey from York to Harrowgate saw us picked up by a waiting police vehicle which transported us to the police station where we made the necessary arrangements to pick our prisoner up the following morning. John is a great lover of Chinese food and his first enquiry was to obtain directions to a suitable Chinese restaurant prior to being transported to our pre booked overnight accommodation. We were transported in a police prisoner van in which I chose to occupy the caged area to the rear deferring to both John's seniority and greater age thus allowing him to occupy the front passenger seat. The young police officer who had been detailed as our taxi driver was expounding the delights of our guest house accommodation which he told us was owned and run by a retired police officer and assured us that we could look forward to a warm welcome and first class breakfast in the morning. It was all sounding pretty good to me and not only that, it was looking pretty good when we pulled up outside of a large Georgian Villa set in its own grounds. It was then, that for no apparent reason to me, John exploded. "What bloody idiot booked us in here?" he demanded of the young officer.

I hadn't got a clue what could possibly be wrong it looked all right to me. John ranted on for a short period claiming unknown persons to be idiots and leaving our driver in little doubt that he was less than pleased. It wasn't the young officer's fault but he was nearest to John at the time and someone had to be aware of his displeasure. Both I, and indeed our young colleague, hadn't the slightest clue as to what had upset John and I felt obliged to enquire as no doubt the outcome would equally affect me. "What is wrong John," I asked? "Look," he said, as he pointed in the direction of the entrance door where all I could see was an obviously perturbed landlady who had clearly overheard the disturbance. "Look at what," I enquired? "It's no bloody smoking, that's what," he responded.

I have to admit that I myself am a smoker but I hadn't yet managed to accumulate the years of addiction that was then afflicting John although I fully understood his concerns. How he had managed to identify the miniscule "no smoking" sign from where we had parked I found hard to believe, he must have had the eyes of a hawk. "I don't suppose we have any bloody option, we will just have to stay here," he grumbled as we unloaded ourselves from the police vehicle. On making our way to the entrance our host greeted us with an almost apologetic "I'm sorry, it's no smoking," a statement which John deemed worthy of no more than an acknowledging grunt.

Once we had been shown to our room which we were sharing John couldn't get out of the place quick enough to have a cigarette and go and have our Chinese meal. We had a lovely meal throughout the course of which John bemoaned the difficulties this smoking issue was likely to cause him and I tried my best, although unsuccessfully, to assure him that he would manage. We then moved on to the police club which occupied the top floor of the local police station and rivalled anything similar we had in Caithness operating on a commercial basis. A few drinks and considerably more moaning saw us make our way back to our accommodation where we stood outside packing in as many nicotine fixes as possible before entering the building and going directly to bed.

John never made any secret of his morning routine which consisted of a complete pot of tea and several cigarettes before he considered himself fit to meet the world. This morning was very much destined to be different. We had awoken early and John had spent his time constructively pacing the bedroom not unlike a sentry at

Buckingham Palace in one sense, and in yet another sense, not unlike a caged lion. As John paced back and forth cradling a hand rolled cigarette while at the same time cursing his inability to smoke it I offered a way out of his predicament. "Why don't you stick your head out of the window and smoke it," I said? "No, I can't do that, I shouldn't have to." "Well that's the only way you are going to get a cigarette short of trekking all the way outside and standing in the cold," I reassuringly replied. John continued to rant and curse and I was getting rapidly fed up with his moaning. Several times I offered him the same suggestion and each time he refused until eventually he had had enough and concluded that the head out of the window scenario was his only option.

I was delighted as I had concluded that the only way that I was going to get any peace was if John got his smoke. John carefully opened the window and carried out an initial scan of the area to ensure that the coast was clear and on convincing himself that all was right with the world prepared to light up. The next thing I became aware of was John's frantic and rapid retreat from the window sill accompanied by a bellowed, "The bitch is watching me." I could not possibly repeat the remainder of John's exclamations but suffice it to say none of it was pleasant. I confirmed John's claim with a quick glance out of the window where I observed the landlady at the kitchen window maintaining observations on our bedroom window. John was raging about the bedroom and I was less than supportive as I couldn't help but see the funny side of things. I was curled up in a ball laughing which was only succeeding in making matters worse for John. He was obliged to admit defeat, accept the situation for what it was and join me in laughing about the ridiculous situation in which we had found ourselves purely because of our addiction to the evil weed.

We did have a nice breakfast and shortly thereafter we were both outside well in advance of our projected pick up time taking an extremely unhealthy joy in sucking on several unhealthy cigarettes each. John had satiated himself and was beginning to change back to the amiable Dr Jekyll I generally knew him to be and both of us were ready to begin our journey home. We picked up our prisoner as planned and were then transported to Harrowgate railway station where we joined our connection to York. A short wait at York and we now boarded a nonstop express all the way to Edinburgh, or at least it was meant to be a nonstop express. Our prisoner was a young fellow a few years younger than me and a lot of years younger than John and we found him to be extremely compliant. He wasn't about to cause us any trouble and we had agreed that while we were aboard the train we would allow him to travel uncuffed sitting at a window seat.

We had no sooner left York than the train came to a halt. Here we were five minutes out of York and the train had developed some sort of fault that took more than an hour to put right. At this point we had not been informed of the problem, neither had we been told how long we may expect to be delayed. The train started eventually and once again we began our journey which lasted another five minutes before we came to a halt. After thirty minutes or so the rail authorities decided to buy us off by announcing that they would be issuing vouchers for a free cup of coffee. Another thirty minutes and we set off again for another five minutes before coming to a stop. More free coffee and another hour of sitting about saw the train start accompanied this time with an announcement that the train would terminate at the next station where we should disembark and await the following express which had been instructed to stop for us.

John had already worked out that we had missed our connection from Edinburgh to Inverness and the way things were going we would probably miss the one after that as well. I don't know what station we got off at but the platform was mobbed and it wasn't looking good for us finding a seat on the next train. A few minutes later the next train arrived and we boarded. There wasn't a seat to be had and we found ourselves along with a prisoner and all of our luggage, standing shoulder to shoulder with everybody else. This really wasn't good enough and John was in aggressive mode by the time he spotted a guard struggling through the mob of standing passengers. Everybody was complaining and the guard was dismissing these complaints as fast as he could make space to continue his passage. John was not about to be dismissed and there was no way the guard was getting beyond us until something had been sorted out. "Excuse me," no response, "excuse me," still no response, "hey you, I'm speaking to you, don't ignore me."

The guard was just in the process of dismissing John when he was presented with a warrant card right on the tip of his nose accompanied by the words "now pay attention." John left the guard in no doubt that something would have to be done as we were two police officers escorting a prisoner and woe betide the guard if we were left in this position throughout the course of a several hour train journey. Whatever mission the guard had been on was now re prioritised and we were put right to the top of his list. "Please follow me gentlemen," he requested as he about turned and once again made his way back through the throng of standing passengers closely followed by us. After passing through two or three closely packed carriages we now emerged into a sea of tranquillity then known as "First Class." All of these people were standing shoulder to shoulder so crammed together that they couldn't have collapsed if they wanted to and here we were in a beautifully appointed carriage which held only one other passenger.

We were in exalted company as John and I both identified Sir Clive Sinclair, the inventor of the ZX Spectrum and Sinclair C5 as our only other travelling companion.

A more than pleasant journey with constant supplies of drinks and food delivered to our table by our personal waiter saw our eventual arrival in Edinburgh. We had missed all of the connections to Inverness but luckily a decision had been made to put on an additional train and we just had enough time to telephone North to advise them of our predicament. A police car was waiting for us in Inverness to drive us the remaining 110 miles to Wick and I eventually made it home at about three am that morning.

Eddie McCarthy reacted the same way to me when I told him that I had no interest in fishing as Joyce did when she discovered I wasn't interested in football. I am fairly certain that he thought I was a bit strange and made it his mission to initiate me in the way of the fisherman. At least Joyce had accepted the situation as much as she may have considered me effeminate whilst Eddie was not about to admit defeat. He supplied me with what I can only describe as long pieces of stick to which he had attached a rope with feathers on the end and instructed me to flail the river with the implement, I can only assume for some imagined misdemeanour. I was later to learn that this piece of equipment was in fact a fishing rod designed for the capture of fish, all of which evaded my feeble attempts to catch them with considerable ease.

The line attached to my fishing rod spent more time entangled on the embankment than it did in the actual water and I concluded that I was likely to be more successful in snagging a passing sheep or rabbit than hooking a Salmon. Eddie was unperturbed at my initial failure to capture one of these beasts while I had expected to return home to Joyce with at least a dozen. It was one of those "Robert got that one wrong again," moments. Eddie made several attempts to teach me the finer points of Salmon fly fishing but in the end he was forced to admit defeat.

Another benefit attached to being the only available officer saw me involved in security duties at the Castle of Mey whilst Her Majesty, the Queen Mother was in residence. This particular role had me working 13 hour night shifts patrolling the area surrounding the castle and being particularly well fed at the local hotel. The Queen Mother particularly enjoyed her privacy here and took long walks along the shoreline and throughout the Castle grounds. The instructions were clear. Her Majesty should be allowed her privacy and should she be encountered then conversation should only be initiated by her. This instruction led to some fairly funny moments as she might be met on turning a corner or strolling through the garden, her presence inevitably announced by the Corgi's preceding her.

Sighting of the Corgi's acted as a signal to throw yourself into a nearby Rhododendron bush or make a quick about turn and march quickly away in the opposite direction. I often wondered if she was ever aware of the eyes watching her progress from the bushes and the sighs of relief when she did eventually pass. It was however impossible to avoid her all the time and I frequently wondered if she may have made a game out of sneaking up on us, just to see the reaction. On the occasions that these encounters were unavoidable I never knew her not to speak and almost inevitably thank you for your presence. There was a general consensus amongst all the officers that she was in colloquial terms "A fine Wifie." A five or six week period at the castle did absolutely no harm to your bank balance and Her Majesties' presence was most welcome.

I was on my final night of duty at the castle when a major incident, in the form of a murder enquiry manifested itself in the neighbouring county of Sutherland, in a small village called Tongue on the North coast of Scotland. The village policeman at Bettyhill, Paul Eddington, following a series of circumstances had concluded that a man who had been frequenting a local hostel may be a wanted murderer. A female visitor who he had befriended had not been seen for some time and this was the point at which Paul had become involved. His initial enquiry led him to believe that this man may have been the same person who was wanted for the murder of an elderly man in Yorkshire. Paul had done his homework and now believed that the missing woman may well have been his second victim and wasted no time in communicating his concerns to the powers that be.

For the purposes of the obvious media attention this case was likely to attract we were searching for a missing person although everybody was pretty certain that we were covering the hill ground in search of a body. Police and civilian search teams were out scouring the hills while plain clothes officers were split into teams to carry out enquiries to trace the couple's movements. I had been detailed to man the incident room which had been set up in the village hall. A team of officers were located in the incident room dealing with calls, prioritising enquiries, dealing with accumulated evidence and recording every aspect of the enquiry. The incident room was a buzz of activity, but not while I was there. I had landed the overnight duty and found myself dealing with the rare telephone call and the odd fax message which I would record and pass on to the enquiry team in the morning.

My routine over this period meant leaving Halkirk at 6pm and travelling to the main station at Thurso where I would uplift any necessary documentation and then continue the 50 or so miles to Tongue where I would arrive just before 8pm. If I was lucky I would manage to return home by 10am the following morning. I wasn't always lucky and frequently found myself retained on duty for some reason or another not returning home before 2pm. Following a six week stint of 13 hour shifts at the castle and now sixteen and occasional 20 hour shifts at Tongue, although the bank balance was healthy the same couldn't be claimed of the body.

Although I wasn't exactly busy and I could have settled down in a corner and gone to sleep for a few hours, I never quite mastered that art and I do believe that my conscience wouldn't allow me to. The local and national press were no slouches either, they knew that an operation of this scale didn't swing into action for something as common place as a missing person and I frequently found myself fending off aggressive enquiries from some persistent hack or other who refused to accept my redirection of their enquiry to the force press officer. They were always looking for more than the official line and I suppose that they thought a phone call to a half asleep officer in the middle of the night may just give them the scoop they were looking for. I would never blame them for their persistence, after all they have a job to do but frequently I could have seen them far enough.

Being in the incident room I had pretty much easy access to all the accumulated information and had a fairly good idea of where we were from one day to the next. It was becoming much more obvious to me, as it was to all of the enquiry team, that we were dealing with a murder and at this stage although we could identify the victim and the murderer, we didn't have a body.

The breakthrough came when a civilian search team reported finding some items of clothing and a handbag on the hill and were instructed to discontinue the search from that point. All the indications were that it was most likely that a body may be found on this line of search and it would be necessary to protect the scene. A police search team was inserted at this point and I was instructed to control the access to the search area. Privy as I was to the up to date information through official sources the press had clearly got wind of what was going on through unofficial sources.

Everybody entering and leaving the search area passed through me and more than one member of the press tried to pass themselves off as some sort of official and once it became clear that they were going nowhere tried to pump me for any information they could get. It wasn't very long before the level of activity and the nature of the individuals passing through became a fairly clear indication of a discovery of some significance. Before I was stood down at the end of a more than 24 hour shift I knew that the body of a woman bludgeoned to death with a rock had been found.

The murderer had, we discovered, returned to Yorkshire and had by chance been arrested there. Detective Officers were sent from our area to interview him and before a case had been prepared to bring him to court for both murders he had hung himself in his prison cell. In this case the vigilance of a village bobby had played a major part in bringing a murderer to some form of justice. Paul Eddington currently holds the rank of Chief Inspector and it will be no surprise to me should he rise further through the ranks.

I now found myself on the move again but no great distance. I was destined to finish pretty much as I started, in Thurso. This time I was going to Thurso with Joyce in tow and Lynsay and Ben making up the Sutherland family.

CHAPTER 17

AND FINALLY

When I began writing this book I don't know if I really believed that I would reach this point but here I am. If I can't believe that I have made it this far then how can I expect any potential reader to have made the journey? Doesn't really bode very well for making a pound out of book royalties, does it?

We had moved into Thurso and taken up residence in Mount Pleasant Road. Lynsay and Ben had started at a new school and had to make a whole new set of pal's and it wasn't going down too well. Children do however manage to cope with these situations and it wasn't to be too long before they were quite happily settled in to their new routine. Joyce had already managed to find a job when we were still in Halkirk and was working part time for the Local Enterprise Company. I, on the other hand, found myself back in a situation that I had not been familiar with for a number of years. I was now, once again, working a fixed shift system, theoretically on a shift with three other officers, a sergeant and a shift secretary. I use the term theoretically, as the situation surrounding transfers, annual leave, training, sickness absences and a myriad of other reasons more often than not found us down to two officers and chasing our tails. I enjoyed being busy but there were times I was glad to see the end of a shift and have some rest days.

Our shift secretary was a young Irish girl called Sheelagh Patterson who would never forgive me if I didn't give her a mention. Sheelagh and I had a bit of laugh going as the rest of the shift members frequently referred to her as my personal assistant as they claimed difficulty in having their work typed as she inevitably prioritised mine. I always found that it was a good idea to make a mate of the shift secretary. Just to add to the mystique that my shift colleagues had created I would occasionally, very publicly request that Sheelagh prepare a report for me based on the very briefest details. Sheelagh would request minimal details and a brief verbal summary of the circumstances and would a few hours later present me with a complete report which required only my signature. What they never knew was that I had already given Sheelagh a handwritten script and all we were doing was f****** with their heads.

It was during our final days in Halkirk that Joyce adopted our third child. I don't know if we adopted him or he adopted us but he has been pretty much a permanent fixture in our home since. Mark Macintosh was a twenty year old painter and decorator and recently recruited Special Constable. Although I had worked with him on a couple of occasions in Halkirk I now found him frequently manning up on our shift at weekends.

We were working a night shift and Mark was working a 10pm until 2am in the morning which meant that he overlapped onto my shift and had been teamed up with me. It was one of those nights where everything was happening and we were rushing from pillar to post sorting out minor disputes and shepherding drunks home in order to keep the peace. It was during the course of this full moon that I became aware of my two other colleagues being directed to an incident in a housing estate in the town. At that stage I did not know the nature of the incident that they had been called too and had no reason to believe that I might become involved. About ten or fifteen minutes later I received a radio message requesting that I attend at the same address with the fibre glass coffin shell. This was now clearly a sudden death which had to take priority and the late night revellers had to be left to police themselves.

Mark and I returned to the station where we picked up the necessary equipment and then attended at the address. A doctor had already been in attendance and pronounced life extinct but was unwilling to issue a death certificate which meant that we had to take possession of the body. My two colleagues had been in the midst of an incident when they had been called to attend here and needed to return to complete their enquiry. Although I don't enjoy dealing with any form of sudden death, where need's must you just have to step up to the plate. Realising the urgency of their first enquiry I suggested that Mark and I would deal with the sudden death in order to release them to continue the investigation. What I didn't realise was that Mark had never dealt with or handled a death in his life. The victim, in this case was a very large man who had passed away while sitting in his armchair and the scenario was as straight forward as they came. As I set about the initial preparations for moving the body I realised that Mark was looking very pale and obviously uncomfortable with the situation. There was absolutely no possibility that I would be able to deal with this on my own so I took some time to reassure Mark that he would manage just fine. I explained the procedure that we needed to carry out and then showed him that the remains were nothing to concern himself with as the body was not about to cause him any harm. I placed my hand on the back of the victims and explained to Mark that he was cold to the touch. I then had Mark do the same. Next, I placed my hand on the victim's brow and had Mark repeat the procedure all the while reassuring him that there would be no problems. Finally, before moving the body, I explained the possibility that the remaining air in his lungs were likely to be expelled thus causing a groan, which to the uninitiated may indicate life. I wasn't about to rush the situation and only set about the job when I was reasonably happy that Mark understood the process and was ready to continue.

Getting the victim into the shell was a serious struggle owing to his size and weight and Mark and I had to take a rest before we started the next stage of removing the body from the house. The next stage of the process was equally hampered by tight doors, narrow passageways and a very small vestibule necessitating our standing the coffin on end to negotiate it out of the house. Another rest was called for before we could begin the lengthy carry to the nearest point at which we had been able to park the police van. It was about 3am in the morning and just as well as it was pitch black and there was nobody about to observe our slow progress. The coffin shell was fitted with very narrow metal handles which if you were wearing gloves you could just about cope with, but, if you weren't wearing gloves felt as if they were tearing your hands to shreds. We weren't wearing gloves and had to set the coffin down several times before we got to where we wanted to be. I was so thankful that it was dark as I couldn't begin to imagine what any passerby might be thinking seeing two policemen sweating and blowing in the company of a coffin.

The body was transported to the mortuary and I then began the process of completing the necessary records. Mark was due to go off duty at 2am but remained behind to assist. By 5am I had already made several suggestions to Mark that he should go home to bed and it was only once I had assured him that he could do no more that I dropped him off for the night. It is only in recent years that I discovered what happened after that.

Mark was twenty years of age and it had only been a few months earlier that he had moved out of the family home and occupied his own house on the opposite side of the town. He was alone, just dealt with his first sudden death and his imagination was running riot. Every shadow was hiding some unimaginable horror which was just waiting to leap out and scare him to death while every noise was just further confirmation that he wasn't imagining things. As much as he tried he just couldn't bring himself to stay in the house alone. There was only one thing for it, "phone his mum!" A less than happy George Macintosh was roused from his sleep and immediately dispatched to pick up Mhairi's boy. Mark stayed with his parents for four days before he could bring himself to return to his own house. I was twenty years old once and I think I understand how he felt.

A back shift covered 4pm until 12 midnight unless I was obliged to work overtime. The best I could hope for was to arrive in through the door at 12.20am but frequently it would be one, two or three in the morning with the worst scenario being an all night shift. If I was likely to arrive home by 3am I could pretty much guarantee that Joyce would be sitting up in bed reading and awaiting my arrival. Every back shift without fail I would purchase a large bar of chocolate to take home to Joyce and she had grown to expect it. I always played out the same process every night. I would walk into our bedroom in full uniform and sit on the side of the bed. At this point I would then say, "Hello young lady look what the nice policeman has got for you," and then extract the bar of chocolate from my top pocket which Joyce inevitably snatched and devoured with gusto. I did like to think that she was waiting up for me because she had missed my company but the truth was that she had become addicted to the chocolate. It was a long time after that she told me she didn't particularly like the brand of chocolate I always bought but as she put it, "Hey, chocolate is chocolate."

During my time in Halkirk I had become very friendly with an American Navy Chief Petty Officer by the name of Tom Stalker. Joyce and Tom's wife Elaine had met at the school nursery and as both of them were new to the area had struck up a close friendship. It was through this friendship that I found myself being invited to take part in their welcome aboard programme. The U.S. naval radio station at Forss, just outside of Thurso had a considerable turn over in staff and each time a new batch arrived they had to undergo a few days of familiarisation which included a two hour input from me. I covered a little of what they may expect to encounter in a small Scottish community and outlined the differences in the law. These events always went down very well and I found myself on nodding terms with a considerable number of American naval personnel.

Tom and I frequently got together and Eddie McCarthy and I would occasionally attend at the base when Tom was fulfilling the Officer of the Day role where we would make full use of their first class fitness facilities. Somebody, I might add not me, had decided that it would be a good idea to set up an indoor football match between the Americans and the local police and it was down to me to make the arrangements. The boys at the station were considerably more up for it than I was given my total lack of interest in the sport. I don't know if it was the challenge or the certain knowledge that the hospitality following the event would be of a standard difficult to rival but the date was set. I would happily describe myself as worse than a man short when it comes to playing football but I was certainly unrivalled at keeping the electronic score board. Everything was initially going very well other than we were down by something like ten goals in the first fifteen minutes or so and I was obliged to doctor the results in our favour.

I don't know how it happened but any onlooker would have been more than likely to have described the event as a re enactment of the American war of independence rather than a friendly football match with the local constabulary. Our casualties were mounting, ranging from minor wounds to concussion and even a broken foot. It was beginning to look like that scene from Gone With The Wind with off duty police officers fulfilling the roles of the injured soldiers lying about nursing their wounds and moaning in despair. Our numbers dwindled rapidly and our rivals sportingly decided to call it a draw which bore absolutely no resemblance to the actual score line as we had been soundly thrashed.

Brushing the injuries aside we then transported the wounded to the bar where the proceedings were brought to an excellent close with first class hospitality. It had been a long time since I had received a summons to the Inspectors office but I did. Hamish Milne was in about as much despair as our injured had been the night before. We had lost a number of officers that we could ill afford to minor injuries but to crown it all, and was obviously the straw that had broken the camel's back, Sgt Rory Mackenzie had been signed off work for 6 to 8 weeks with that broken foot. I strongly suspect that the cause of this tragedy was being placed firmly at my door and the truth was that I was in no position to offer any defence. I hate the bloody game and I had cause to hate it much more at that particular moment. I can only conclude that the Americans were unaware that football, unlike their version is not meant to be a contact sport. To be fair to Hamish he politely requested that I should refrain from arranging any further conflict with a major power and ally as we couldn't afford to lose the manpower. I was happy to oblige.

I need to finish here with just a little information about Tom Stalker. Tom became a very close friend and schooled me in the art of barbecues at which he was an absolute master, and managed to hook me on this social event to such a degree that I suffer from withdrawal symptoms if I can't manage to arrange at least one major event a year. Tom is something of a fitness fanatic and part of his then daily regime was to complete two thousand push up's and run at least ten miles. He was the American Navy European Heavy weight boxing champion and the base Racket Ball champion. He had pitched a no hitter in a junior league Baseball match and was thwarted in following a professional career in American Football following a multiple leg fracture. He now lives in Virginia Beach, Virginia and I would love to meet up with him some day.

Although there are countless other stories I could relate there comes a time when you must bring a book to a close and I suppose this is where I must do the same with just a few asides.

The title of this book, "Cop O' The North," is not a reference to my considering myself to be anything special. There are some 700 police officers in Northern Constabulary, all of whom have stories they could tell but just haven't gotten round to doing so. "Cop O' The North," is in fact recognition of the Caithness Constabulary badge, "Cock O' The North," under which the guys who trained me, served. As part of my contribution to the building of the new police headquarters at Wick I insisted on and was successful in having the badge reproduced and displayed on the station gates. This, I felt, honoured all of the retired Caithness Constabulary officers who although many of them were gone, were not forgotten. The badge was for some time referred to as Robert's Cock.

Since I began to write this book my very good friend and favourite Sergeant of all time, "Donald Mackay" has passed away. I attended his funeral service which was held in his beloved garden and saw many of the old retired guys who were young fit men when I joined. One in particular, Charlie Simpson, was sitting on a garden bench looking at Donald's coffin and I don't doubt reminiscing about some of their adventures. Charlie had been a Highland Games athlete of renown and I know he will not be offended when I say that age and the ravages of time have been chasing him down. It was all I could do to approach him, place my hand on his head and ruffle his hair. Charlie's smile when he looked up at me said it all, we didn't have to exchange words.

The police service has been very good to me, it gave me a job and best of all it provided me with the most wonderful wife who I continue to be deeply in love with. I still can't quite understand why she married me but it is enough for me that she did. If this were the 20th of September 1975 I would quite happily do it all over again.

I moved full time into a Community Safety post in 1991, but that is a whole different story. If you have indeed managed to read this far then I hope that you have enjoyed the read and maybe have formulated a different view of the police service, or at least understanding.

Thank you for reading my book.